Theorizing Post-Disaster Literature in Japan

New Studies in Modern Japan

Series Editors: Doug Slaymaker and William M. Tsutsui

New Studies in Modern Japan is a multidisciplinary series that consists primarily of original studies on a broad spectrum of topics dealing with Japan since the mid-nineteenth century. Additionally, the series aims to bring back into print classic works that shed new light on contemporary Japan. The series speaks to cultural studies (literature, translations, film), history, and social sciences audiences. We publish compelling works of scholarship, by both established and rising scholars in the field, on a broad arena of topics, in order to nuance our understandings of Japan and the Japanese.

Advisory Board
Michael Bourdaghs, University of Chicago
Rebecca Copeland, Washington University in St. Louis
Aaron Gerow, Yale University
Yoshikuni Igarashi, Vanderbilt University
Koichi Iwabuchi, Monash University
T. J. Pempel, University of California, Berkeley
Julia Adeney Thomas, University of Notre Dame
Dennis Washburn, Dartmouth College
Merry White, Boston University

Recent Titles in the Series
Theorizing Post-Disaster Literature in Japan: Revisiting the Literary and Cultural Landscape after the Triple Disasters, by Saeko Kimura
Mito and the Politics of Reform in Early Modern Japan, by Michael Alan Thornton
Wild Lines and Poetic Travels: A Keijiro Suga Reader, edited by Doug Slaymaker
A Transnational Critique of Japaneseness: Cultural Nationalism, Racism, and Multiculturalism in Japan, by Yuko Kawai
Literature among the Ruins, 1945–1955: Postwar Japanese Literary Criticism, edited by Atsuko Ueda, Michael K. Bourdaghs, Richi Sakakibara, and Hirokazu Toeda
Living Transnationally between Japan and Brazil: Routes beyond Roots, by Sarah A. LeBaron von Baeyer
Tawada Yōko: On Writing and Rewriting, edited by Doug Slaymaker
*The Unfinished Atomic Bomb: Shadows and Reflection*s, edited by David Lowe, Cassandra Atherton, and Alyson Miller

Theorizing Post-Disaster Literature in Japan

Revisiting the Literary and Cultural Landscape after the Triple Disasters

Saeko Kimura—Translated by Rachel DiNitto and Doug Slaymaker

LEXINGTON BOOKS
Lanham • Boulder • New York • London

Published by Lexington Books
An imprint of The Rowman & Littlefield Publishing Group, Inc.
4501 Forbes Boulevard, Suite 200, Lanham, Maryland 20706
www.rowman.com

86-90 Paul Street, London EC2A 4NE

Copyright © 2022 by The Rowman & Littlefield Publishing Group, Inc.

All rights reserved. No part of this book may be reproduced in any form or by any electronic or mechanical means, including information storage and retrieval systems, without written permission from the publisher, except by a reviewer who may quote passages in a review.

British Library Cataloguing in Publication Information Available

Library of Congress Cataloging-in-Publication Data Available

ISBN 978-1-7936-0536-8 (cloth)
ISBN 978-1-7936-0538-2 (paperback)
ISBN 978-1-7936-0537-5 (epub)

Contents

Translators' Foreword, *Rachel DiNitto and Doug Slaymaker*	vii
Preface to the English Translation	xv
Preface: Following My *Shinsaigo Bungakuron* (On Postdisaster Literature)	xxv
1 Postdisaster Literature and Minorities	1
2 The Problem of "Fukushima"	23
3 From Fukushima to Hiroshima and Nagasaki	45
4 From Disaster to War	67
5 The Hauntology of Postdisaster Literature	85
6 Post-Fukushima Sublime and the Anxiety of Hauntology	107
7 Radiation and Precarious Life	125
Epilogue	143
Bibliography	147
Index	155
About the Author and Translators	159

Translators' Foreword

This translation of Kimura Saeko's 2018 *Sonogo no shinsaigo bungakuron* was completed in 2021, the tenth anniversary of the triple disasters that ravaged Northeast Japan on March 11, 2011. There are a number of compelling reasons to translate Kimura's 2017 book into English. One is the encyclopedic nature of this book; it is of a piece with the comprehensive theorizing of postdisaster literature that Kimura has produced during the last decade. Few have written as widely or as provocatively on these topics as she, and the international nature of the research—extensive use of French and German sources—makes it unique. This is hinted at in the title of this work: *Sonogo*, "after," "volume 2," or a "following up on" her first reading of postdisaster literature, the 2013 *Shinsaigo bungakuron* (Postdisaster literary theory). This current volume, like the earlier one, serves as a reference for a large number of works that appeared in the years following the 2011 disasters. Kimura has provided summaries of and introductions to a wide variety of fiction, but also to art, film, and theater, and photography, manga, and essays on nonliterary topics, and thus provides something of a handbook for those looking to approach the stories in English first. We note that the same is true for the Japanese original: these discussions are useful for plot summaries and theoretical considerations of works one has not time to read in full. This is what, in part, has prompted this translation.

Another compelling reason is the sophisticated arguments being made on these pages. For example, Kimura asks whether the "post" of "postwar" is the same as the "post" of "postdisaster." At the time she was writing, many of us felt very strongly that, indeed, they were parallel and that life events and societal experience would continue to be measured as before or after the disasters in the same way that Japanese cultural memory has been divided into a before and after the war. The breaks were never that sharp, of course, but that division accurately describes a powerful felt experience for many. Ten years out from the disasters, March 11, 2011, no longer feels as unequivocally clean a break as it did even five years ago. The disasters do, however, continue to be at the forefront of a great many artists' and writers' undertakings; they continue to energize much creative activity in contemporary Japan.

Another of Kimura's powerful arguments lies in her development of how many writers used postwar tales to think through postdisaster life. This is cogent and provocative. Kimura also brings an eye to queering of gender and sexuality in these works; she pays close attention to disability in ways not seen before. As she notes, many stories contain not just humans permanently disabled by the disasters but also a range of androids and cyborgs now disabled: perfectly serviceable but with damaged limbs and no replacement parts. Kimura likewise makes a great contribution by teasing out the ways that many of these works participate in global events and flows, as for example with broader readings that include the experiences at Chernobyl.

As translators and scholars we were drawn to this fiction for a variety of reasons. Doug's relationship with these events and the fiction of the disasters begins at a personal level:

> I arrived in Japan on the evening of March 10, 2011, intent on getting some research done during my institutions' spring break week. I was thus jet-lagged and nauseous in the afternoon of March 11. I was also two stories underground in the Waseda University library. Those of us with experience in Japan usually sit tight and ride out tremors. Not this time. Books were coming off shelves. This was the first and only time I attempted to walk to a safer space *during* an earthquake. It was that long and that violent. It was also up-and-down in addition to side-by-side—a sure sign of an especially powerful and destructive earthquake. Watching monitors with the librarians upstairs, we realized we were not sitting on the epicenter, as we had assumed given the violence. We shuddered to imagine what was going on in Fukushima, the actual epicenter, 300 km to the North.

At the time of the disaster, Rachel was teaching at a university in Southeast Virginia:

> Many of my students were worried about family and friends in the US military and diplomatic corps who were living in Japan. I began offering classes on the disaster in an attempt to respond to the many questions and concerns of my students. A few years later when I moved to Oregon, the disaster took on another level of lived reality as I learned of the impact the tsunami and radiation had on the communities along the Pacific Coast of the American Northwest. My research on postdisaster fiction grew from an epilogue for a separate project into a monograph on this compelling literature.

Personal connections are not, of course, the main reason to work with post-disaster fiction. Rather, it is mainly because so much of that literature is brilliant, much is fresh and energized; some cynics even say that the disasters provided a boon to researchers struggling to find interesting topics in the Japanese literary world. Be that as it may, Kimura Saeko quickly became a go-to source for her writings—not just these two books, but numerous journal articles, as well—on postdisaster literature. Disciplinarily speaking she is a scholar of Heian era (twelfth century) literature, but she has also read nearly everything published with ties to the disasters, and followed up with trenchant analysis.

One motivation for a translator's forward is the plethora of complicated terms that need more explication for non-Japanese readers. Many have been encountered already in the paragraphs above. Among these: what are the events of March 11, 2011, and how should one refer to them? For reasons that will be described below this translation refers to the events as "disasters" in most cases. As for the events themselves, many will no doubt know the rough outlines: at 2:45 in the afternoon of March 11, 2011, the northeastern region of Japan (Tohoku) was struck by a massive earthquake which triggered a record-setting tsunami, and then the nuclear meltdowns followed when the Fukushima Daiichi Nuclear Power Plant was flooded. At 9.0-magnitude, the earthquake is the most powerful ever recorded in Japan, and the fourth most powerful in the world since such records began being kept in 1900. The earthquake shifted Japan slightly more than 71 centimeters to the east and shifted the earth on its axis by as much as 25 centimeters. The tsunami waves which followed topped 30 meters in some places; the landscape in many places was wiped clean. Many towns no longer exist. After the disasters, 18,500 people were dead or missing, the single greatest loss of life to Japan since the atomic bombings of 1945. Photographs of the cityscapes are uncannily similar: in 2011 as in 1945 we see entire cityscapes scraped clean. Two hundred thousand people were evacuated for fear of radiation from the nuclear meltdowns and at least 470,000 people were displaced; there are still huge areas uninhabitable because of it. Radiation spreads unevenly; radiation is not part of everyone's disaster experience. All of which is to say, there were three disasters: earthquake, tsunami, and nuclear meltdown. This book therefore refers throughout to the "disasters" or the "triple disasters" unless one is being singled out. Many flooded areas, for example, were not threatened by radiation; areas devastated by earth tremors did not necessarily receive threat from water or radiation. Of course, radiation and earthquake were threats in places little touched by water. Since the spread of radiation was wildly divergent, much postdisaster fiction takes up the arbitrary designations that permit access to some areas and forbid it for others. As with all boundaries, the line that demarcates one spot as dangerously high in radiation allows equally high levels a meter away to be designated a different, "safe," zone. More important in this experience, however, is the actual divergence in radiation levels that can be found in the same place. Relatively low levels of radiation at the top of a knoll may be accompanied by dangerously high levels in the depression at the bottom. Likewise, levels vary according to temperature, to wind, to time of day. Radiation has no respect for borders and boundaries. As with Chernobyl, this event has no conceivable end in sight; the once-in-a-century disaster looks to be a centuries-long mess. Also, again like Chernobyl, it will not be confined to borders—we need only to think of the debris washing up on the west coast of the USA—or to neat categories—to see how radiation is unequally distributed. The arbitrary, capricious nature of the radiation that we cannot sense is a common theme across these works. The arbitrary, capricious nature of governmental and regulatory bodies is equally prominent.

"Fukushima" also needs unpacking because it easily becomes an over-determined stand-in for the disasters. Fukushima is a large and lovely town that serves as capital for an expansive and beautiful prefecture, the third largest in Japan. It is tempting to use the shorthand "Fukushima" to refer to these disasters, as in the "Fukushima disaster" or "Fukushima meltdown." In this book you will find that Fukushima appears in quotes. This replicates Kimura's use of katakana script to write Fukushima. The same happens for Hiroshima and Nagasaki. One wants it remembered, especially if one is from any of these cities, that these place names mark an area much richer than a single nuclear disaster. In Japanese, Fukushima, Hiroshima, and Nagasaki are often written in the katakana script to express linguistic demarcations for the radiation events that we now associate with them. (As a foreign city, Chernobyl can only be written in *katakana*.) Kimura addresses this choice in her first chapter. Place names consistently rendered in *katakana* or *hiragana* script, however, are not as jarring in Japanese as is having every instance be in quotations in English. This can be cumbersome in English, but it has been adopted as the best solution to remind us that Fukushima does not equate with a nuclear meltdown and to replicate Kimura's use of *katakana*.

A word about the officially designated "zones" is in order. Kimura explains them in her writing, but not until some way into the analysis: there is no need, since Japanese readers encounter these terms almost daily in the press. For non-Japanese readers, the zones range from areas that register levels above the annual twenty millisievert level and are designated "hard to return to areas" (*kikan konnan kuiki*), to areas that are actively being decontaminated and rebuilt in hopes that the limits will drop (*kyojū seigen kuiki*), to areas that are below the annual radiation limit and are therefore preparing to repatriate residents (*hinan shiji kaijo junbi kuiki*). In note twenty-nine of chapter 2 we get an added breakdown of some of these terms. Like everything else here,

Translators' Foreword   xi

including the radiation the categories are intended to delimit, these zones are not really stable either, and often change, usually by government fiat.

The date of the disasters raises similar issues of demarcation and classification. It is tempting to refer to the disasters by the date of their occurrence: 3.11. For many, this sets up a resonance with the U.S. 9/11 terrorist "disaster." For most, however, this is not a happy resonance, since it places Japan in something of a shadow of the United States, a common phenomenon across much of the last century, as though the Japanese cannot even have their own disaster. More to the point, however, is that "3.11" suggests a disaster of a single day's duration. The aftermath of these disasters, however, especially the radiation, will stretch centuries into the future. Towns wiped off the face of the earth may be rebuilt, but they will look and feel nothing like the places known to those who grew up there. Hence we speak of "triple disasters," which allows us to incorporate all these concerns.

Another of issue here is with what is often referred to in English as the Second World War. In this volume it is most often referred to as nothing more than "the war," as is consistent with Japanese discourse; at other times it is referred to as "the Pacific war" (*taiheiyōsensō*). That distinction is important, and probably obvious once pointed out: Japan's experience of "the war" started with the 1931 invasion and occupation of Manchuria. The year 1937 marks the beginning of war with China, the second Sino-Japanese War. Japan invaded Thailand, Malaya, Singapore, and Hong Kong in 1941. They attacked Pearl Harbor in that same year. "The Pacific War" or "The Pacific Theater" is of U.S. Occupation coinage and is why we, Americans at least, think of the war as spanning only 1941–1945. There was no Europe—"world"—for Japan in this war. The landscape of most postwar Japanese fiction, in the 1940s onward, as Kimura discusses here, was China, Philippines, or Japan itself.

Some discussion of the word we take in English as "nuclear" deserves a note here as well. In English, "nuclear" is the word for both nuclear power and nuclear weapons. In Japanese, nuclear power is *genshiryoku* or *genpatsu* (itself an abbreviation for *genshiryoku hatsudensho* or "nuclear power plant" 原子力/原発), where the character *gen* signifies the nuclear. Nuclear bombs, however, are *kakuheiki* (核兵器), with *kaku* serving to denote the nuclear (actually, "nucleus") or the atomic. The reason for this distinction is long and fascinating, but it was also an intentional splitting, as when, for example, U.S. President Eisenhower sold Japan on nuclear power as "atoms for peace." Disambiguating in this way was a conscious choice precisely to prevent an easy association, in Japanese, between "nuclear power" and "nuclear weapons." The point being that for English speakers the association with "nuclear meltdown" is almost immediate to "nuclear weaponry." This would seem to explain the quick association of Fukushima with Nagasaki and Hiroshima in the Western press. In Japanese the association between these two did not come as quickly. On March 28, 2011, Japanese Nobel laureate Ōe Kenzaburō made this very connection in an essay for the *New Yorker*, but it took time for his ideas to gain traction in Japan. In his essay "History Repeats," Ōe linked the victims of these two disasters, as does Kimura, and this term, *hibakusha*, also calls for explication. The word *hibakusha* can be written in multiple ways depending on orthographic choice: one refers to victims of the atomic bombs (被爆者), a second to victims of nuclear exposure like meltdowns (被曝者), and another to victims of all forms of radiation (ヒバクシャ). Kimura adheres to the Japanese conventions, but the nuance is lost in English translation.

The more immediate association of the disasters was to the war, especially for the many elderly residents of the affected prefectures who had lived through it: once again, they found an inept and untrustworthy government bundling people off to concrete evacuation centers such as schools with no apparent plan for the future. As Kimura points out here, even the food rations were the same as seventy years earlier: curry rice and *onigiri* rice balls.

As an aside, we recount a comment made by poet Arai Takako and her work with the poetry of Ishikawa Takuboku (1886–1912), the much-loved poet from Iwate prefecture, in the Tohoku region. This region has long been ravaged by earthquakes and tsunami. Arai traveled to Iwate after the disasters to work with octogenarians to "translate" Ishikawa's poems back into the local Kesen dialect. The result is a fascinating book and film project.[1] Arai recalls asking an elderly woman, "Where were you and what were you doing during the disaster?" to which she replied, "Which one?" They had been through this before. If millennia of history are any guide, they will again.

At the conclusion of this project many thanks are in order. First, to Kimura Saeko herself for graciously and generously aiding with phrasing throughout the project of translation. In the end, she reread the entire manuscript for a book she no doubt thought she was finished with many years ago. Chris Lehrich's copy-editing saved this from many infelicities. Joe O'Neill untangled German phrases that seemed suspended between three languages. Akiko Takenaka was often called on to clarify and suggest. Lexington Books editor Eric Kuntzman again shepherded a manuscript to completion. We thank them all.

Rachel DiNitto and Doug Slaymaker

NOTE

1. Takako Arai, *Tohoku Onbayaku Ishikawa no Takuboku no uta* (Poems of Ishikawa Takuboku in the voices of Tōhoku Grandmas) (Tokyo: Miraisha, 2017). Yoi Suzuki, dir, *Tohoku Onba no Uta: Tsunami no umibe de* (Songs Still Sung: Voices from the Tsunami Shores), written and produced by Takako Arai, DVD, 2020.

Preface to the English Translation

On the occasion of the English translation of this book I want to update the reader on my thoughts in the year since this volume appeared in Japanese.[1]

Now that more than ten years have passed since the Great East Japan Triple Disasters of March 11, 2011, it is easy to think that disasters of that scale are rare on earth, but we find that the opposite is true. In Japan we were afflicted in quick succession with many more disasters in the decade following: major mudslides in Hiroshima in 2014; a powerful earthquake in Kumamoto in 2016; an earthquake in the Iburi area of Hokkaido in 2018; any number of typhoons across the years and the concomitant damage; major flooding from excessive rainfall. When, on February 13, 2021, a magnitude six earthquake struck in Fukushima and Miyazaki prefectures, it seemed an ominous ten-year anniversary memorial. Here we are, ten-plus years since the Great East Japan Disasters and still, at least for those of us who continue trying to make a home in Japan, there appears to be no end to these catastrophes. No one could have foretold that in this year of the 2020 Olympics—taking place in 2021—the entire world would be oppressed by the Covid-19 virus. Those Olympics were, many years before the decision for Tokyo to host the Olympics, devised to extol Japan's complete recovery and safety from the events of March 11, 2011, radiation in particular.

Olympics and Covid-19 aside, the events of these years take us back ten years. For example, on February 27, 2020, it was mandated that all elementary, middle, and high schools throughout Japan would go into hiatus with an early start to the Summer vacation period. On March 24, it was announced that the official opening ceremonies of the 2020 Olympics would be further postponed; at this point in the year countries across Europe had already entered a period of lockdown. It was only on April 7, much later than everyone else, that the Japanese government declared a state of emergency and requested a period of self-quarantine (*jishuku yōsei*) in which schools, businesses, and public facilities were to remain closed.

It was in the midst of these events that, in March, universities cancelled graduation ceremonies. This was followed by cancellation of school opening ceremonies in April. Then, in order to properly prepare for online instruction, the beginning of the semester was postponed until the end of May, coinciding with the "Golden Week" holidays. I am drawing attention to the fact that this entire sequence of events in response to the pandemic was exactly the same pattern of response in Tokyo following the 2011 disasters. Then, too, educational facilities and schedules were confused and in disarray, shops were shuttered, and city-centers were empty of people. It all resembled, again, our experience in the period following the triple disasters.

Now, when it comes to escaping the dangers of radioactivity, there are numerous options for getting as far from ground zero as possible. Some people evacuated overseas; others gathered up their children during the summer vacation to flee the radiation and set up residence as far away as they could in Japan. But Covid-19 has driven home the fact that no matter where in the world one might go, danger lurks. Before our eyes we found a scenario reminiscent of so many science fiction tales, in which not just a single country, but the entire world, lives in fear of an imminent nuclear accident.

It is in this situation that I realize how, when my university students read Tawada Yōko's *Kentōshi* (*The Emissary*), they read it as a description of the world they live in now, not the world we assume Tawada had in mind in the months following the disasters.[2] She describes a postdisaster world, a Japan totally closed off from the rest of the world in an Edo-style closed-border *sakoku* where free travel has been completely suspended; it resembles our world in the midst of the coronavirus pandemic. Students currently attending university were about ten years old at the time of the Great East Japan disasters. Students from the affected regions feel differently, of course, but as the years pass memories of the disasters grow faint. Among the adults for whom memories of the disasters remain fresh, Covid-19 takes them back again to those March disasters; the opposite proves true for these young students: it is from the realities of Covid-19 that they can imagine what happened on that March day in 2011. I offer this as one significance for an English translation of this book in the midst of the pandemic: it might just be that people around the world will be able to read postdisaster literature with a sense of contemporary reality.

Covid-19 is a worldwide pandemic; Covid-19 afflicts nearly everyone across the globe. It is an extremely rare situation in human history where throughout the world people read the same fiction with similar emotional responses as though in the same situation. I think here of how Albert Camus'

The Plague, for example, was a bestseller in Japan, of course, but also across the entire globe. I think of other works—Giovanni Boccaccio's *Decameron*, Daniel Defoe's *A Journal of the Plague Year*, Alessandro Manzoni's *The Betrothed*, Thomas Mann's *Death in Venice*—tales of a calamity in one corner of the world that have felt relevant across the globe.

In 2020 the National Book Award for translation was awarded to Morgan Giles' translation of Yu Miri's *JR Ueno Kōenguchi (Tokyo Ueno Station)*. This might provide readers in the English-speaking world a pathway to understand the experience of Covid-19 via the Great East Japan Disasters. Yu Miri herself moved to Minami Sōma, a town greatly damaged by the tsunami, and began hosting a radio show, then opened a bookstore, then started a public theater. That is, *Tokyo Ueno Station* was written by someone who can be said to have experienced the disasters and was giving her all toward bringing the area back to prosperity, even though they were not there on that day. I have more to say on this point below.

Now, as the entire world faces the calamity of widespread infectious disease and we can compare how individual countries have responded to it, we see again how the outcomes of a calamity grow out of political choices and government policies. With that in mind, it is harder to say that poor helmsmanship of the government in the days following the Great East Japan Disasters was an exception; rather, we find that Covid-19 has made all the more clear the foundational problems latent within governments. Such hopelessness also brings to mind the mood in the days immediately following the disasters. The Covid-19 pandemic may be a calamity entirely different from the disasters, but, in this crisis situation, it may offer us another opportunity to read anew the postdisaster literature I cover in this volume.

POSITIONALITY (*TŌJISHASEI*): WHO CAN WRITE OF THE DISASTER?

One constant result that has emerged in literary criticism in these ten years since the disasters, at least in the world of fiction and fiction writing, is the position of the author (*tōjishasei*)[3] relative to the disasters themselves. Criticism has been exceedingly severe, perhaps overly sensitive, to charges of appropriating, perhaps misappropriating (*ōdatsu*), the voices of the dead of these disasters if one was not there (*tōjisha*) at the time, if the author was not a victim themselves. In the face of severe criticism that one therefore has no qualification to narrate such events if not directly affected by them, many writers have chosen to keep their distance from anything that might be called "postdisaster" literature. For example, Hōjō Yūko, who in 2018 was awarded the Gunzō New Writer's Award and was a finalist for the Akutagawa Prize, became the subject of much controversy for her *Utsukushii Kao* (Beautiful Face)[4] because she had not fully disclosed the secondary sources that she had consulted and because of how she had quoted from other sources. The fact that she had unequivocally stated that "I have never visited"[5] the disaster-stricken areas cannot be unrelated, in my view. Had the author herself suffered as a victim of the tsunami to the same degree as the protagonist, I doubt that these accusations about improper citations would have grown to the scale of problem that they did.

Utsukushii kao is not written in the style of a journalist who has come up from Tokyo to gather materials in the evacuation centers of the disaster region. Rather, it is written in the voice of a high school girl and in a prose style that makes clear that this narrator has performed for the journalists just as they expected; she displayed for them youthful vitality from the time she learned of her mother's death until she finally gets through her grief. One of the characteristic features of this story is in the point of view that suggests journalism and their account of events are not to be trusted. People are likely to give the journalists what they want, hoping they will go away. I find it unfortunate that the controversies accompanying this work have overshadowed the freshness of this writer's attempt to bring an entirely new perspective to the portrayal of events and experiences following the disasters. The newness of this approach has been lost.

At the same time, some works have been able to nimbly overcome the issue of positionality by creating an entirely new form of literature. I am thinking here of the writings of Seo Natsumi. She moved to tsunami-ravaged Rikuzentakada shortly after the disasters and started writing about the things she heard. We have, for example, *Awaiyukukoro: Rikuzentakada, shinsaigo wo ikiru* (The Period of Waning Light: Living in Postdisaster Rikuzentakada) and *Nijū no machi/Kōtaichi no uta* (Double layered town/Making a song to replace our positions).[6] Seo, together with filmmaker Komori Haruka, headed north from Tokyo to volunteer immediately after the disasters and settled in Rikuzentakada. While living there they were attentive to the disappearance and reappearance of buildings via the reconstruction (*fukkyō*)[7] taking place in the town. Rikuzentakada was completely washed away by the tsunami waves. In the process of rebuilding, a nearby mountain was razed and the earth used to raise the level of the town. But "rebuilding" cannot mean a return to exactly the sort of life that came before, particularly in this case, where construction energies have gone into elevating the ground on which the town stands. For the disaster victims this amounted to nothing less than the experience of the town being destroyed one more time. Not only were the houses in which many had been born and raised no longer standing, but now even the ground on which those houses stood was being buried. When Seo speaks of a "double-layered town" this is what she is referring to: the original town now buried under a mountain's worth of earth as well as the new town that exists on top. In a situation such as this, it is hard even for an outsider to feel that this is some kind of "rebuilding." Working together, Komori and Seo make films to document this double-layered tragedy: *Nami no shita, tsuchi no ue* ("Under the Wave, On the Ground" 2014) and *Nijū no machi/Kōtaichi no uta wo amu* ("Editing Double layered town/Making a song to replace our positions 2019").[8] In addition to this there have been art installations featuring paintings and text by Seo[9] as well as an internet radio program hosted by Seo, *Jyūnennme no shuki* (Notes at the Ten Year Memorial), which included nonspecialists and gathered recollections of the disaster experience from those who were quite clearly not from that area nor there at the time (*tōjisha*).

In general, one is inclined to think that anyone who was in the disaster area is a *tōjisha*: a concerned party. But the farther one travels from the epicenter into the affected regions one finds that distinctions of disaster are less precisely delineated. One result is that even those directly affected by the disasters begin to question whether they can actually refer to themselves as *tōjisha* because of the way the severity of individual suffering and loss is measured by the relative damage in the area in which they reside. One's house may have been destroyed but no family members were lost, for example, or family members were lost but not the house, or some members of the family may have perished but not all: the sorting of who is or is not a "true" *tōjisha* is based on such a range of postdisaster conditions and bureaucratic categories. Not surprisingly, we find that many people in the midst of this cannot narrate their own disaster experience. Seo seems to be someone who understood this situation, this lack of voice, at a very early stage. She charged off from Tokyo immediately after the disasters and became a narrator (*kataribe*) for Rikuzentakada in a way that makes the entire *tōjisha* debate moot. She was not there, but she narrates with the authority of one who was. She was able to accomplish this because she had complete confidence that, precisely because she is a traveler (*tabibito*) from a faraway place, she could understand and relate the narratives of the place, even if she was not actually there at the time.

REPORTAGE (*KIKIKAKI*) AS A NEW LITERARY METHOD

Seo Natsumi's *Awaiyukukoro* was also awarded the Seventh Tekken Heterotopia Literary Prize. The same prize was also awarded to Ono Kazuko's *Aitakute kikitakute tabinideru* (Wanting to meet them, wanting to ask them, I set off on a journey)[10] that year. Ono serves as organizer for the "Miyagi minwa no kai" (The Miyagi Prefecture Folktale Society) and is well known for her work gathering folktales from the Tohoku region. *Aitakute kikitakute tabinideru*, however, while recounting the ancient tales and folktales she has collected, records her real-time interactions with those telling the stories, meaning that here she is not an objective, absent interlocutor. The reportage practice of writing down what one hears (*kikikaki*) is usually understood to mean that what is recorded precisely matches the original narration; as part of this practice, the folklorist usually excises the particulars of the narrator and the situation in which the tales were narrated. Ono gives us a new form of reportage that includes her own travels to record these stories. Seo's *Aiwakukoro* brings the *kikikaki* approach to Twitter posts. These new approaches lead me to think that contemporary literature is searching for this new style of *kikikaki*, one that mixes the objective and the involved, a style of reportage not from a journalist but from a novelist.

For example, Itō Seikō, the author of *Sōzō Rajio* (Imagination Radio),[11] also took up the practice of *kikikaki* in his postdisaster fiction projects. He has told how, following the publication of *Sōzō Rajio* in 2013 and while he was visiting bookstores in the Tohoku region, "I realized that this is not the time for me to be talking. No, it is now places all across Tohoku that are talking, and it is my role to listen." The time had come, he says, for him to travel to Tohoku not to write but to listen.[12]

From January 2018 to April 2019 the *Tokyo Shinbun* ran Itō's monthly column *Hanashi wo kiki ni Fukushima e* (Going to Fukushima to listen to tales). The series continued with five more installments in the journal *Bungei*, from the Summer 2019 through the Summer 2020 issue, and appeared in its entirety in book form as *Fukushima monolōgu* (Fukushima Monologue).[13] One installment comes from the town of Ōkuma, where a woman works at a place they have called "Moo Moo Farm" because they care for cattle that were slated to be disposed of because of radiation levels; many installments report stories from women who have left husbands behind and evacuated with a daughter; one story is of a woman who has started an FM radio station for the residents of a Tomioka evacuation center; one is of a woman who lost her father in the tsunami; another is of a woman from Kawauchimura, a town rendered uninhabitable because of radiation. These are all stories told by women. In all of them, we get nothing of the questions or comments from the interviewer, Itō: they are presented as monologues. In the afterword Itō writes that this writing style follows the "close listening" mode employed by psychiatrists.[14] Because they are presented in monologue form, the reader finds themselves in a position of being able to listen directly to tales from the Fukushima narrators. That is, Itō has given access to stories from the *tōjisha* even though he is not one himself.

In the fourth installment there is a passage, out of character for this book, in which it is clear that Itō is the interlocutor. The narrator is a woman who lost her father to the tsunami and who reports that, "When I start speaking about [my father] I start to cry and cannot keep on talking." She then embarks on a story about how, before her father's body was discovered, she found a white flower peeking out from one of her boots, almost as though her now dead father had come back to say "hello" and find out how she was doing. This is a story she also wrote about, "writing through flowing tears, writing while crying," in a tale entitled "Shiroi hanabira" (White flower petals) that she sent off to the *Michinoku kaidan purojekuto* (The Deep North Scary Tales Project) in 2011, and was awarded a prize for it. She seems to have been thinking of Itō Seikō's fiction while writing, apparently invoking his *Sōzō Rajio*:

> I agonized while writing this tale, I worried I might be writing too objectively, or that people would think of me, the *tōjisha* writing as a *tōjisha*, as a victim: "Isn't this much too sad?" I think [I worried] the same as a non-*tōjisha* might [when writing fiction]. At any rate, those who have no means to write, those who have no position from which to speak publicly, they are waiting for someone to come and put their stories into words for them, which seems like, I don't know, how this tale came to take on this form. That's when I thought of your novel *Kore, kore, kore!* (This, This, This!). I read it. The idea that the living and the dead might occupy the same space provided a kind of a salvation for me, a way out (*sukui*). I had the sense that this might finally provide some relief (*yurusareta*) for those whose family members had perished.[15]

It is through writing that this *tōjisha* becomes able to talk about her father, and yet it is also clear that this writing is accompanied by a certain amount of hesitation and doubt (*mayoi*). Even more importantly, on the flip side of her experience of death and the white flower communicating a sort of sign, she is able to find a place of calm and stability via the "non-*tōjisha*" Itō Seikō's novel *Sōzō Rajio*. The relationship between narrator and interlocutor is in this way sometimes reversed; in this moment the new *kikikaki* reportage style is formed.

Since 2016 Itō has traveled the world visiting disaster areas and evacuation camps, accompanying the Médecins Sans Frontières.[16] He wrote about entering areas like Gaza and Palestine, saying of this experience that "for someone like me who has lived my life without even once having the barrel of a gun pointed at me from a long distance away, propelled me, in a mere instant, towards a future of war journalism" with a feeling of "Wait a minute, this is going too fast."[17]

Itō Seikō is a multifaceted artist also known as a singer and a TV personality. He went on to note that when he started following the Médecins Sans Frontières, it was not as a journalist but as a literary writer. He has pointed out that while undertaking this project he thought often of writers who went before him to war zones and disaster areas, such as Kaikō Takeshi and Hino Keizō who wrote from wartime Vietnam, or even Natsume Sōseki who wrote from Japanese-occupied Manchuria and Korea.[18] Given this, we can certainly categorize Itō's reportage of his time with Médecins Sans Frontières as literature written by a novelist (*bungakusha ni yoru bungaku*).

The examples above are of a new style of literature, a *kikikaki* style that has emerged after the disasters. Another development, now that a full decade has passed since the Great Eastern Japan Disasters, and while still embracing the full force of the disasters, is that it has become possible for the disasters to be narrated in fiction as though it is a tale of a minor event, the sort of event that, for those who did not lose homes and families, can be treated as an insignificant disaster. Kudō Rein, for example, who was born in Morioka in Iwate prefecture, has given us *Tsurara no koe* (Voices from Icicles), which was a finalist for the 165th Akutagawa Prize in 2021. In the afterword Kudō tells us that the characters in the work were constructed from "interviews" (*shuzai*) she conducted with seven different people. She asked them to "Please tell me about your relationship to the disasters, all the 'things you could not say,' or 'things you didn't think worth saying.' I might work them into story, perhaps not though."[19] She writes that the "information" she received from these "interviews" (*shuzai*) was by and large gathered from ideas that developed from random conversations. This novel, together with this intriguing method of character construction, also forms a space where all those who "thought they 'had no position from which to speak'"[20] come together in mutual echoes. Again, this new approach allows one to narrate experience of the disaster as a *tōjisha* even if they were not there at the time of the disasters.

As we found with 1995 Nobel Laureate Svetlana Alexievich [writing of Chernobyl], the *kikikaki* reportage style is nothing if not literary. Likewise, following the disasters we have new ways to read Ishimure Michiko's writings about Minamata and mercury poisoning. She too employed what seems like a simplistic interview style and yet the result is something much more literary than a mere interview. This method of *kikikaki* reportage does not get encumbered by the issues associated with *tōjisha* positionality and does not get hung up on whether or not one was present at the time of the disasters. Indeed, postdisaster literature, as it appears in the examples above, seems to have discovered a new method of writing, one that is able to overcome the *tōjisha* issues. These are all examples of how the Great East Japan Disasters have greatly changed trends in contemporary literature.

In the summer of 2021 I visited Matsushima, Ishimaki, Onagawa, Minami Sanriku, Kisennuma, and Rikuzantakada, small towns that few had heard of previously but are now iconic because of the disaster damage. Rather than take the old Route 45 that followed the Tohoku coastline, now ravaged and disaster-beaten, I drove on the pristine, immaculate E 45 that had been built upon the recently constructed elevated roadbed. It was all brand new. There were also signposts along the side of the road that pointed out areas that had been ravaged by the tsunami and that showed which places had been danger areas. The former damage is thus readily understood even by a first-time visitor to the region. At the same time, looking down at the expanse from atop the bridge, one sees an undulating plain of verdant grass stretching from the nearby riverbank out to the distant seashore, and it is hard now to imagine that this plain was once filled with row upon row of houses.

One finds at the sites of damage close to the seashore, cenotaphs, damaged buildings preserved to display the damage, and memorials along with shops and other business facilities. These have arisen in the ten years that have now passed, springing up together with and in response to the calls for both memorialization and revival (*fukkyō*) of the area. In the region along the sea, now raised with infill and sea walls to a height presumed to be safe, one sees some new business enterprises, but there is no hint of people returning to the homes. The construction of levees, embankments, and the high sea wall continues apace; all this activity means that no one can forget the disasters even now.

In postdisaster literature the voices of the dead have been a main theme. The dead themselves have been unable to tell of the days that have passed. But now, ten years from the disasters, I feel that we are slowly becoming able to draw out those voices.

NOTES

1. Kimura has written an update every year since the disasters discussing events and fiction of the past year. For this preface Kimura excerpted from the 2021 version, "Shinsaigo bungakuron 2021—atarashii bungaku no hō he." *Subaru* 43, no. 4 (April, 2021): 153–67.

2. In Margaret Mitsutani's translation *The Emissary* received the National Book Award for translation in 2018. This prize too is surely related to the fact that it called U.S. readers to look the crisis of democracy straight in the face following the election of Donald Trump and the various methods he and his supporters employed to fan the flames of hatred and division.

3. While this word is relatively unproblematic in Japanese, it presents the translator with some challenges. "Tōjisha" is almost as pedestrian as is "the concerned party" or "the affected party" in English. It is not, however, as clunky as the English would be had we dropped such a phrase into each instance. *Tōjisha* refers to someone who has physically, bodily, temporally experienced the event in question. This wording also carries with it a long debate in the Japanese context traceable to the Atomic bomb literature of Hiroshima and Nagasaki. Then too, there was much debate as to whether one who was not radiated under the atomic cloud could write about the event. The bias was decidedly on the side of "no." Perhaps most famous is the trajectory of Nobel Prize Laureate Ōe Kenzaburō who travelled to Hiroshima years after the bombings and wrote about the experience of it; he was roundly criticized on the grounds that he was not there so has no authority from which to write about it.—Trans.

4. Hōjō Yūko, *Utsukushii Kao* (Tokyo: Kodansha, 2019), n.p.

5. Hōjō Yūko, *Utsukushii Kao*.

6. Seo Natsumi, *Awaiyukukoro: Rikuzentakada, shinsaigo wo ikiru* (Tokyo: Shobunsha, 2019), and *Nijū no machi/Kōtaichi no uta* (Tokyo: Shoshikankanbō, 2021).

7. As we will see, this term *"fukkyo,"* wielded by bureaucrats to mean "reconstruction" and "revitalization," strike many of the residents as hollow and misguided, bringing buildings and facilities they neither want nor need.—Trans.

8. Seo Natsumi and Komori Haruka, dir. *Nijū no machi/Kōtaichi no uta wo amu* (Tokyo, 2019). Note: I have been unable to determine further production information about these materials—Trans.

9. *3.11 to Ātisto: Jyuunennme no sōzō* (3.11 and the Artists: Imagination at the tenth year), Mito Museum of Art, February 20–May 9, 2021.

10. Ono Kazuko, *Aitakute kikitakute tabinideru* (Sendai: Pumpquakes, 2019). There were actually three recipients of the prize that year: the third was Kobayashi Erika's *Torinti, Toriniti, Toriniti (Trinity, Trinity, Trinity)* (Tokyo: Sūeisha, 2019), a novel that combines issues of radiation with the 2020 Olympics.

11. Itō Seikō, "Sōzō rajio." *Bungei* 52, no. 2 (Spring 2013): 17–94. Reprinted as *Sōzō rajio* (Tokyo: Kawade bunko, 2015).

12. Itō Seikō, *Nihon bungaku wo 3.11 go no shiza de yomu—Sakka Itō Seikō to tomo ni* (Reading Japanese Literature after 3.11, together with author Itō Seikō) (Presentation, *3.11go bungaku wo konnichiteki ni kangaeru* (Thinking about post 3.11 literature in the present moment) Paris, INALCO 2 February 2019.

13. Itō Seikō, *Fukushima monolōgu* (Tokyo: Kawade Shobo, 2021).

14. Itō Seikō, *Fukushima monolōgu*, 392–93.

15. Itō Seikō, *Fukushima monolōgu* "4. a flower" (sic), *Bungei* 59, no.1 (2020), 428–29.

16. His reportage on these travels appeared as *"Kokkyō naki ishidan" wo mi ni iku* (Traveling to observe the Médecins Sans Frontières (Tokyo: Kodansha, 2017). In *"Kokkyō naki ishidan" ni narō* (Let's become Médecins Sans Frontières) (Tokyo: Kodansha, 2019) he reports from Haiti, Greece, the Philippines, Uganda, and Southern Sudan.

17. This comment is found in the preface to the reprinted book version. Itō Seikō, "Maegaki," in *"Kokkyō naki ishidan" wo mi ni iku* (Tokyo: Kodansha bunko, 2020): ii.

18. See *"Longu intabyū, Itō Seikō toraerarenai saiyaku, shōsetsu ha kakerunoka"* (Long Interview with Itō Seikō: Can one even write as fiction the calamity we cannot grasp?), *Bungei* Summer 2020: 391.

19. Kudō Rein, *Tsurara no koe* (Voices from icicles) (Tokyo: Kodansha, 2021), 117.

20. Kudō Rein, *Tsurara no koe*, 119.

Preface: Following My *Shinsaigo Bungakuron* (On Postdisaster Literature)

ON FORGETTING

At the end of 2013, my *Shinsaigo bungakuron: Atarashii nihonbungakuron no tame ni* (Theories of Postdisaster Literature: Toward a new theory of Japanese literature) appeared from Seidosha. "Theory" is there in name only, since the book is primarily an introduction to the novels and films that deal with the Great Eastern Japan Triple Disasters of March 11, 2011 (earthquake, tsunami, nuclear meltdown). Before I had time to carefully think through something like a "theory of literature," I hurriedly rushed it into print because I could see, before my very eyes, how quickly the reality of the disasters was fading from memory.

Right before my book appeared, Michaël Ferrier's *Fukushima: Récit d'un désastre* came out in Japanese with the title *Fukushima nōto: Wasurenai saika no monogatari* (Fukushima notes: The tale of an unforgettable catastrophe). In the preface added to the Japanese edition Ferrier argues:

> Not even three years have passed and yet "Fukushima" has already been forgotten. That, at least, is my impression. "Fukushima" remains, to be sure, a topic of conversation. In the TV news and the well-intentioned speeches of politicians it appears, but like a mere *shadow*. Its influence is rumored of in the newspapers. But in reality, we have forgotten "Fukushima."
>
> We have the fear, anger, and despair that plagues the hundreds of thousands of people separated from their homes. It is the largest displacement in Japan since World War II. The victims, who have not yet gotten compensation payments, spend their days with forms and litigation, not knowing when it will end. We have forgotten them.[1]

The "we" of this passage refers to those in Tokyo who felt some effects from the disaster, who thought that things must change, or that we ourselves must change, yet clung to the thought that they could return to their predisaster lives as soon as the signal permitting it came. There have been numerous opportunities—in elections, for example—to signal their intentions. But judging from the results of those actions we can see just how surely "Fukushima" has been forgotten. The meltdown at the Fukushima Daiichi Nuclear Power Plant was reported internationally as "Fukushima." And while some countries decided to abandon nuclear power in response and, given that "Fukushima" has now become a global nuclear issue, not even within Japan is there agreement about how to deal with "Fukushima." It is instead dismissed as a calamity of a remote part of the country. But "Fukushima" refers to an issue that needs to be discussed at the global scale; it is not simply a one-time accident.

The path whereby we could avoid even thinking about this was skillfully created early on. Slogans touting "the bonds that unite us" (*kizuna*) were spread widely, but this came from the desire for a single-minded solidarity leading to reconstruction of the affected areas (*fukkyō*); it never advanced in the direction of joining with victims in support of their attempts to appeal for claims of responsibility at the national level or that of the Tokyo Electric Power Company (TEPCO), the company that owned and operated the plant. The term "damaging rumors" (*fuhyō higai*) was widely circulated, such that even suggestions that there might be radiation damage were fiercely criticized as impediments to the reconstruction of Fukushima prefecture, of course, but also the entire Tohoku region. As a result it was possible to pretend that such a thing as radioactive damage may never have existed. With the term "decontamination" (*josen*) came the illusion that radiation could be completely cleaned up, while the reality was the opposite: a landscape of black vinyl bags filled with contaminated soil piled high, one bag atop the other, right in front of people's houses and along roadsides. Further still, the electric companies had long and aggressively put it about that nuclear-generated power could never explode and was, therefore, entirely "safe" (*anzen*). So, whenever criticism arose that nuclear power might be anything other than safe, the electricity companies, having once reassured us that nuclear power plants would never explode, swapped their safety measures and implemented evacuation measures. They pushed this further with the logic that since escape routes already existed there was no danger even should explosions occur. They then began to push for restarts of the idle plants. This method of forgetting: have we not in fact seen it repeated any number of times since the end of the Asia Pacific war?

One of the earliest novels to question this forgetting was Nagashima Yū's *Toi no nai kotae* (Answers to unasked questions).[2] Nagashima's work progresses with more than thirty characters at times being replaced one for the other, at times having one standing in for the other, and with the topics abruptly changing as well. It is a Twitter-like novel. The characters form loose connections via Twitter after the disaster; the fractured nature of Twitter functions as a technical aspect of the novel. I very much want to remind us that this was a period in time when Twitter could be used to best advantage. It was a moment when, even though regular phone and mail service were out of service, one could communicate via Twitter. It was the medium that could be relied on in crisis, proving to be the device by which announcements about what was happening in the disaster zone could be conveyed. This was the environment in which Wago Ryoichi, who was living in Fukushima at the time, began tweeting *Shi no tsubute* (Pebbles of Poetry)[3] and quickly gained many followers. But Wago's words were not mere reports for bystanders. Rather, he gave words to the desperation, was able to layer and interweave the feelings of those still engulfed in the disasters, and provided words they were looking for and wanted. In this sense, it resembles the ways that people were participating on Twitter in Nagashima's *Toi no nai kotae*.

In *Toi no nai kotae*, three days after the disasters, novelist Nemuo uses Twitter to invite those needing a diversion to join in word games. Nemuo finds himself unable to write fiction after the disasters. Those who respond are, like him, unable to get back into their work or they find themselves depressed. The game begins with the question of invitation: "Suppose you have received a three meter rod; with it, 'what would you like to do'?"[4] But at first the "what would you like to do?" alone is posted, and only after everyone has provided their own answers is the entire question published. The responses all come in haphazardly and the various possible meanings are, equally haphazardly, determined by those in the group. It works a bit like "Mad Libs."[5] The novel's characters join with an enthusiasm bordering on addiction. While participants join from all over Japan they are, by and large, residents in the vicinity of Tokyo (*Kantō*).

Character Nanami (meaning "seven seas") posts that, "Carried by the blackest of waves a huge fishing boat rests in a farm field. In this situation where words themselves have become strange, she is totally absorbed in this diversion—if that is what it is—that makes a mess of words."[6] The earthquake split the glass of her computer desktop and she has been working on the floor with her monitor ever since. Yet this is in Tokyo, and not in the so-called disaster area. We read that Nanami "cannot explain why she has become so lethargic," unable to drag herself to work, burning through her savings while staring at her computer screen.

In the Twitter world people interact warmly, everyone seems very kind. It reminds one of the 2004 sensation *Densha otoko* (*Train Man*)[7] that got its start on 2channel.[8] In that work, the main character, a self-described "Akihabara otaku," is supported by others in his 2Chan group who guide him to successfully find a girlfriend. In contrast to this, in 2008, a twenty-five-year-old man posts a frightening number of grumblings and complaints (*tsubuyaki*) online, and when no replies appear, turns into the perpetrator of the "Akihabara massacre of 2008," a random murder spree at midday. The different outcomes of these two 2Chan stories that begin similarly are profound. We should also be thinking about these outcomes in the case of a novel about characters supporting each other in the wake of the disaster with words on Twitter.

Another strand in the book follows novelist Saki, a teacher of creative writing at a vocational school. We read that she is analyzing the posts of the Akihabara Massacre killer Katō Tomohiro in class. Even though she doesn't really understand the questions she is answering, she is quite obsessed with Nemuo's word game. In the process she comes to a sudden understanding of Katō. She comes to realize that his actions were an "answer to an unasked question" and that "By wielding his knife Katō was not posing a question to society, what he did was to, out of the blue, provide an answer to a question that was never asked."[9]

This conclusion differentiates between the wordplay of Twitter and Katō's posts to online bulletin boards. Although no more than half of the questions were clarified, someone was putting the questions out there and other people were answering. These were answers to an appeal. We cannot simply consider these to be "answers to unasked questions."

At first glance, given the degree to which *Toi no nai kotae* is based on actual incidents, it would appear to have no connection to a post-2011-disaster novel. But there's more to it. When high school student Fukiyama Fukiko enters the novel, we encounter the historical events of the March 2007 murder of Lindsay Ann Hawker by Ichihashi Tatsuya, and then the murder of popular singer Amuro Namie's mother in March 1999. These two events would appear to be brought together through mere coincidence, but given that both occurred in March we are to understand that they are thus connected to the March 11 disasters. Likewise, these events were all able to get the television talk shows abuzz at the time of their occurrence, but they seem now to have been completely forgotten. Which is to say, these are all linked by the issue of forgetting. The novel continues,

> People wouldn't be able to live if they were to remember all the sad and painful things. Being able to forget is an important function for humans. That's what they say anyway. It is not a question of who but of all of us.
>
> Sounds about right to me.
>
> On the other hand, there are many things in this world we are implored not to forget. We hear "No More! No more."[10] Stone monuments are erected and the words are carved into the sturdy stone.

The TV no longer shows images of the tsunami. This is not because they want to act as though it didn't happen, but because they take for granted that it will never be forgotten. They restrain for fear that if it is overemphasized, everyone will drown in waves of fear.

But we will forget. So thank god for YouTube.[11]

Seemingly unrelated events serve as analogies to the "incident" that is the Great East Japan Disasters. Just as we have forgotten those other events, I imagine we will completely forget this disaster too. The "No More, No More" of Hiroshima and Nagasaki will not be forgotten as a slogan, and while one can say we continue to remember its original sense, nevertheless in any essential way, we seem to have forgotten. As if to prove the point, the radiation of "Fukushima" calls forth yet again the issues associated with "Hiroshima" and "Nagasaki."[12]

When the meltdown of the nuclear power plant appears in the last part of the novel, the characters begin to review the relationships between the questions and answers. In the second half of the novel, Saki, aware of the participation, in the Twitter wordplay game, of high school student Hifumi from the disaster area, heads to Ishinomaki to interview her. We read of Saki as she is headed to the tsunami-stricken areas, that "whenever she had been invited to an anti-nuclear demonstration, she never knew whether or not to go," and she now vacillates on the nuclear power issue:

> Nuclear power is necessary, some people insist. We do not need nuclear power, other people insist. Who is right? She didn't feel that clear of a divide. Even though they were expressing opposing views, both carry the same whiff of the unpleasant.
> This is not something that can be easily answered. It is a problem we must continuously confront and mull over, other people say.
> She is inclined to think that continuing to mull over things without coming up with an answer is the wisest course. But is it? Who knows.[13]

This question of "Who knows?" verbalizes a distrust of one's "own good sense that that is how it is."[14] Nemuo responds to Saki's doubts and continues and draws out the story: "Ever since images of the nuclear power plant with its roof blown off were broadcast the other day, [my friend] Nonohara just disappeared, just left with his tasks unfinished."[15] Nonohara fled with no plan, heading west, and ended up at his family home, exactly the same distance from the center of the evacuation zone as where he started, no further from the epicenter. Nemuo smirks at what he calls his "trajectory as a run-of-the-mill failure-of-a-man,"[16] but then wonders, "But is it?" He continues, "Maybe ditching work and fleeing back then was the right thing to do. But why did so many go back to their offices? Why did they start working again? I mean, after a thing like that."¹⁷

Toi no nai kotae portrays a situation where all of the answers have already been laid out before one's eyes. It is a story of people searching for their own "questions." It is only by setting up the "questions" that, for the first time, one begins thinking. The novel progresses through the year following the disasters. It portrays characters who, at the moment when, stuck in malaise, become engrossed in wordplay on Twitter, make the first step toward their questions. The novel's method of having the characters appear one after the other, like Twitter posts, looks not unlike a string of episodes lacking narrative conclusions. While the novel, on the one hand, provides lively descriptions of portions of one boring day following the next, the language of the novel draws ever closer to incidents that occurred with the disasters.

The fact is that, after the disasters, people were waiting for answers. Is radiation dangerous or not? Should we flee west, leave Japan entirely, or should we stay put? Is this food safe to eat, or should we reject it? But straightforward answers were not forthcoming. In fact, the exact opposite message was delivered over and over. Those who decided for themselves went in completely opposite directions. Are these not also "answers to unasked questions"? The "answer to an unasked question" of the title is not something simply decided by some person in possession of correct answers. It is a game, one of examining the process of thinking through all of these things. The game suggests that the act of thinking is more important than coming up with an answer.

THINGS TAKEN UP BY DISASTER LITERATURE

On February 19, 2017, Hayashi Kyōko, an author who wrote throughout her life about her own experience as an atomic-bomb victim in Nagasaki, died. Seirai Yūichi, whose parents were also exposed to the bomb in Nagasaki, followed in Hayashi's wake as a writer of "atomic-bomb fiction." In Seirai's novel Hayashi appears as "H-san." Shortly after, in the January 2017 issue of *Bungakukai*, this "H-san" appears in Seirai's story *Koyubi ga moeru* ("The Burning Pinky Finger"). Even though Hayashi was still alive, reading it gave one the strange sensation that Hayashi had already departed and was a ghost in the realm of the dead.

At the outset of *Koyubi ga moeru* the narrator, an author of novels that do not sell, is visited by an "established author" who was "formally a politician." We read that this Ishihara Shintarō-like older author,[18] "realizing that they were still writing many things about the last radiation explosions, and clearly exhausted by the topic, said, 'you still goin' on about that'?" He urges the narrator to write novels that will sell and to set their eyes on writing a bestseller. This "you still goin' on about that?" is, without a doubt, exactly the sort of criticism that Hayashi Kyōko herself, who never stopped writing "atomic literature," faced. The nuclear accident at the Fukushima plant led to new *hibakusha*[19] and Hayashi's writing garnered renewed attention. In particular her 2013 essay, "To Rui, Once Again," demanded serious consideration.[20] With this the memories of atomic victims were revived. Nakagami Kenji once criticized Hayashi's work as "atomic fascism." Nakagami's use of "atomic fascism" and "atomic fascist" in 1982 was clearly aimed at Hayashi's works that centered on her experience as a Nagasaki *hibakusha*.[21] Nakagami had earlier claimed that "nothing has poisoned Japanese novel fiction to such a degree as atomic bomb fiction," and went on to consistently criticize this literature.[22] Seirai, while being Hayashi's successor, is also able to deploy this question of "are you still at it?" which suggests some sense of a guilty hesitation and some doubt about these tendencies in atomic-bomb literature.

To be precise, what needs to be kept in mind here is that what Nakagami was so stridently criticizing as "the activity of organizing *ressentiment*" was that he finds "in atomic literature . . . there is nowhere a point of view questioning the process of why it should have developed as it did." One of Nakagami's particular arguments was on the question of why is it that the form of Japanese literature has, from its very beginnings, been subject to certain restraints. According to Nakagami, Japanese literature, going back to its earliest origins, has been written "always from a child's point of view . . . not a single thing has been written from a father's point of view."[23] Which is to say, everything is narrated by the victims. Not a single thing is narrated by those who carried out the wars, the invaders—those who were the aggressors. This is precisely why Nakagami aimed for a new literature. He intended to smash the forms of narration (*monogatari*) and write from the perspective of the father-as-aggressor.

Seirai writes in *Koyubi ga moeru*, "[Hayashi's] novels were often lumped together as 'atomic literature,' but if you read carefully and trace that single character's life, you will find it can be understood as taking up experiences of many people at various stages in their lives, it can serve as a map for reading many people's lives."[24] Even though Seirai continues to defend Hayashi's work in this way, the fact that *Koyubi ga moeru* also digs up the memories that remain buried in Nagasaki's soil, brings up the war in the South Seas, and writes of the most gruesome experiences of cannibalism and aggression, would seem to also affirm Nakagami's criticism.

Literature since Fukushima cannot but take up the issues that Nakagami identified when writing about catastrophes. This concern for *ressentiment* and sentimentalism also runs through the fiction of Furukawa Hideo, who carries a deep respect and love for Nakagami Kenji. Furukawa's play *Tōmin suru kuma ni soineshite goran* ("Go lie down with the hibernating bears") echoes the facts of Fukushima, to be sure, but it also contains a history of the Japan Sea coast and of Niigata's oil fields.[25] Circuitous though the play is, one finds that, at the endpoint of the energy wars which began back in the Meiji period, there is the present.

Furukawa Hideo seems to me to be one of the authors who have responded most strongly to the disasters. This is not simply because he is a Fukushima prefecture native. Indeed, despite his being so deeply agitated by the shock of the disasters, Furukawa's descriptions, from the perspective of an interested party, are exceedingly ascetic. This may come from his hatred of those enraptured with "sentimentality." But what forced him to recoil was something in the ways that the words he continued to write in his own novels came back to attack him, almost like a curse.

In January 2011, he started serializing a theory of creativity in the magazine *SWITCH*. He began by writing about the novel he had long been wrapped up in, called *Kuroi Ajia tachi* (Black Asians). This "novel that develops through the history of pigs, cats, and oil extraction [which] is also a novel about Asians"[26] was at a standstill and seemed unlikely to be completed. The reason, he wrote, was that the part he had completed writing right before the disaster, entitled "Oka wa bidōdani shinai wake dewa nai" ("Not as if the land will even escape the small tremors"), was "set in a post-earthquake Asia, (here the Kalimantan region of Borneo) a place ravaged by a colossal earthquake." What he had conceived, almost prophetically, then appeared in reality right before his eyes in March. At that juncture, he wrote, following the unprecedented earthquake that struck eastern Japan, there was no way that he could publish such a novel. In a mere moment, everything had collapsed.[27]

Then in March 2012, at the Salon de Livre Paris, Furukawa was asked if *Beruka, hoenainoka? (Belka, Why Don't You Bark?)* was a prophecy. Was not the scene in *Belka* where four dogs are abandoned in an uninhabited area reminiscent of images of animals abandoned in the restricted zone after the 2011 disasters? If what is written can be prophetic, then one wishes that if the writing is to be prescient blessings and not curses for the future could be written and come true. At the opening of a collaboration with traditional painter (*nihonga*) Kondō Keisuke, "E tōhō kyōfu tan" ("Picture scrolls of Eastern fears"), Furukawa wrote the following:

> I have thought about many things
>   Why is it that the eastern part of the country is so full of dread and fear?
>   And then me, a bit too prophetically, have all these scary stories that have been put inside me, then sealed over, over here in the eastern part of the country, this "made-up area." Why is that?
>   Because there is within me fault and sin? Is that why?[28]

Preparation for the exhibit had been completed before the disasters, although the exhibit itself opened only after. Then a year following, it was held again. This time it was entitled "Fuku tōhō kyōfu tan" ("Picture scrolls of eastern fears, in disguise"). He wrote "I have premonitions of things to be constructed. In the same way that 'I construct words' I have the strong sense that I am constructing mansions."[29] To those who were in fact rebuilding their homes and their lives, these words rang like benedictions.

Furukawa's *Tōmin suru kuma ni soineshite goran* was written to be directed by Ninagawa Yukio and performed from January 9 to February 1, 2014, as part of the twenty-fifth anniversary celebration of the Bunkamura Theater in Tokyo. The play moves between the present day and the Meiji-Taisho eras, oscillating across time periods and the experiences of two characters who overlap: the elder of the Kawashita brothers, Hajime, who is an Olympic shooter; and a bear hunter who lived four generations back. It is set in Niigata. Shortly after the curtains open the bear hunter and his dog face off against a mother bear and her cubs on a snowy mountain. With gun pointed at the bear the hunter says, "I ain't gonna shoot your cubs." Given that he makes his living exchanging bear liver and pelts for cash, he explains, "I don't wanna reduce the number of bears."[30] To speak of overhunting connects him directly to the traditional *matagi* hunters of the past. With that, we come to understand that this tale is a variation on Miyazawa Kenji's short story "Nametokoyama no kuma" ("The Bears of Nametokoyama").

Kojūrō, the hunter in Miyazawa's "Nametokoyama no kuma," traipses up and down mountains. He understands the language of bears. One summer, just as he is about to shoot, the bear asks,

"What are you after? Why do you have to kill me"?

He answers: "For nothing but your fur and your liver. Not that I'll get anything much for them when I take them to town. I'm sorry for you, but it can't be helped. Though when I hear you say that kind of thing, I almost feel I'd rather subsist on chestnuts and ferns and the like until I die."

The bear responds: "Can't you wait just two more years? There are still things I've got to do. When two years are up, you'll find me dead in front of your house. I promise. I will then give you my fur and my insides too."[31]

When two years have passed, the bear fulfills its promise.

Miyazawa Kenji's description of a promise between a bear and a bear hunter, and the ability to understand bear language, is all there in Furukawa's *Tōmin suru kuma ni soineshite goran*, but the proof of understanding the words (of the other) is in the desire to eat honey together. The ritual of trying to connect with the gods by eating something that the gods have provided is here revisualized through the licking of honey. The bear is lapping up honey. Borrowing the voices of a large number of human mothers who have now come bustling onto the scene, bear says to the hunter, "How about we make an agreement, you and I?"[32] This exchange plays off of the meaning of *chigiru*, the first character of the words for "agreement" (*keiyaku*), which is an invitation to engage in sex; thus, "make an agreement" can be understood as "have sex together," and indeed, the hunter then engages in sex with the mother bear.

With that the scene then switches to present day and the Olympic shooter Kawashita Hajime appears. His younger brother, Tanehiko, works for a top retail firm and is set to marry his lover Hibari. One-quarter of Hibari's hair is golden like a dog's, because she is the granddaughter of a woman who had sex with a dog. Outwitting both his younger brother and her lover Tanehiko, Hajime, descended from a bear—the result of the sex described above—and Hibari, the descendant of a dog, have sex with each other. The elopement of Hajime and Hibaru seems like an allegory where Miyazawa Kenji's bear and the dog, which have become so prominent in Furukawa's works, meet up.

With twenty-four-year-old Tanehiko having his fiancé taken away from him, the family prophecy—"My son, you shall produce a child in your twenty-fifth year. Be not early, be not late"—is now not to be fulfilled. The elder brother is already thirty years of age. This marks the beginning of an inauspicious future.

Past generations of the family had welcomed the oil drilling rush in Niigata back in the Meiji and Taisho eras. The history of oil drilling that did not come to fruition in Furukawa's *Kuroi Ajia tachi* is given life here in *Tōmin suru kuma ni soineshite goran*. It plays out in Meiji 38 (1905), when the bear hunters, caught up in schemes over drilling rights, are prodded with: "If you do not want to see the mountains that you hunt on disappear, then you should kill the oil company boss." Then in Taisho 7 (1918) the hunter is praised for his skill and deployed to Siberia with a special marksman unit. But this is part of yet another scheme, the real purpose of which is to search for large oil fields in Siberia. For his part, the bear hunter joins the oil survey on the condition that he will be able to obtain liver from brown bears.

In a past life, during the Nikolayevsk Massacre of Taisho 9 (1920), one of Hibari's female ancestors is raped by a dog. Also in a past life, the bear was king of nature, as the polar opposite of development. The bear and the dog represent the development process played out on national land, a process that sees roads and railways built, the form of those roads and railways being slashed and gouged mountains. As the mountains grow smaller, the number of bears decreases. In the current generation it is a dog that is the mountain king. Why do the dogs become feral in the mountains? Are we not getting here a portrayal of those animals abandoned to forge lives on their own in the Fukushima exclusion zones? In the final scene, Hajime is invited into a bear's hibernation cave. With the act of sleeping together perhaps once again an agreement (perhaps once again the act of sex) is consummated. I read this as a sign indicating the path by which we might live together with nature.

All of the wars fought since the Meiji period have been energy wars fought over oil. That history was repeated with nuclear energy after the Second World War. In the final stages of the play, in a scene where the bear hunter and Kawashima Hajime, now precisely superimposed, one upon the other, shoot someone down, we also find a precise overlapping of a previous generation's era of oil and the current one's era of nuclear energy. The bear hunter's assassination of the oil company president in Meiji 38 (1905) and Kawashita Hajime's assassination of a terrorist from an "imaginary enemy country" hidden inside the nuclear power plant occur on stage at the same time. Caught up in the middle of an energy war, the tribe who entered contracts (perhaps having sex) with the bears pulls the trigger to protect the mountains. The first in the family line does it for the bears' mountain, the fifth in the family for the dogs' mountain, and for the woman with whom he has agreed to a contract (or sex) with the dog.

Tanehiko, who by preventing terrorism saves Japan and who came up with the plan to destroy his brother, speaks of the issues of nuclear power in this way:

> The Japan of today and with it our nation's landscape looks as it does because of these energy wars. Who knows why, but it sure appears that the coastline of the Japan Sea makes the optimal place for siting atomic energy power plants and for nuclear reactions. They are built everywhere. This is the newest form of an energy war. There is none of "them" that wouldn't make for an object of a terrorist attack. Or an object of attack by other countries. Or for that of imagined foreign enemies even.[33]

When taken into police custody Hajime has this line: "Humans who cannot imagine one hundred years into the future will be unable to live for even twenty."[34] With this, Furukawa lobs a powerful critique straight into the issues surrounding nuclear power plants after the nuclear disaster. Fukushima-born Furukawa could easily have described "Fukushima" from the perspective of those directly affected by the disasters. But he didn't. One wonders why. It's because, as Furukawa has declared, "this makes all varieties of sentimentalism null and void. It seems to me that it will only be in the future that writers (*hyōgensha*) will feel that 'it is OK to write about this' (*hyōgen shitemoii*),"[35] all of which aligns with one of the consistent issues in Furukawa's writings, that is, a sense of pride and dignity together with an eschewing of sentimentalism.

Of great interest at this point are words of Seirai Yūichi describing how while writing *Koyubi ga moeru* the dialogue of soldiers on the South Asia front in WWII, all sentimentality had to be abolished. Furukawa had also taken a strong stance against sentimentality, as we saw above. Seirai wrote:

> I was reminded of Jewish writer Aaron Appelfeld's *The Immortal Bartfuss*, a book based on his holocaust memories. I cannot shake from my mind Appelfeld's comments in the interview included in the translator's afterword that "what must be avoided is not feeling (*kanjō*) but sentiment (*kanshō*). For example, there is something about sentimental (*senchimentaru*) music that induces human savagery. The Nazis, in the thrall of sentimental music, murdered people." Sweet lies are mixed up in sentiment; it closes your eyes to inconvenience; it leads to the feeling that one is being deceived somewhere. That's why. But me, even though I understand all this, grow weak in the face of sentiment, me, a simple run-of-the-mill writer. It may just be a hard-to-forgive decadence.[36]

Concerning the "sentiment" that rears its head when writing about catastrophe, it seems related to Nakagami Kenji's "organizing *ressentiment*," mentioned above. But that has already been taken up again by writers. Furthermore, the essential issue for postdisaster literature is not to be found in the writer's "variety of sentiment" (à la Furukawa), but in the direction that literary theory after "Fukushima" will take, which is to say, in our methods of reading.

THE RENEWAL OF READING AND CRITICISM

The literary works I introduced in my previous book, *Shisaigobungakuron*, have become widely researched, particularly by non-Japanese researchers of Japanese literature, whether as post-Fukushima literature, or as post-3.11 literature, or something similar. Edited volumes have appeared and graduate students are taking this up as subjects for theses and dissertations. As a genre, it is now established.[37] As Lisette Gebhardt states, "Fukushima" is something Japanese cultural studies scholars cannot avoid discussing.[38] Even if it seems that on an everyday level, as in news coverage, the triple disasters of March 11, 2011—the earthquake, tsunami, and nuclear accident—are being forgotten, both literary and filmic works that can be called "postdisaster" continue to appear, one after the other.

It is not just that works of film and fiction are produced taking the East Japan disasters as material, but that the existence of this postdisaster literature shakes up the convenient structures of reading and pushes for a transformation of the methods of criticism. Postdisaster literature does not simply point to works that are written after the disasters, or about the disasters, but to the entire situation of literature since the disasters. For example, if we include the many war novels set in the Second World War that flourished after the disasters, then works that urge us to reconsider past history might be the situation of literature after the disasters. If one takes up war novels written before the disasters and reads them after, as a sort of postdisaster novel layered atop the disasters, one finds that the conditions of reading have also changed. Memories of the disasters, not forgotten, become part of the reading.

Contemporary artist Sugimoto Hiroshi's exhibit "Today the world died. Or maybe yesterday"[39] was on display at the Palais de Tokyo in Paris (April 25–September 9, 2014).[40] The concept behind the display was explained as follows:

> My imagination as an artist is impeded by contemporary knowledge.
>
> In this restricted present, the only field in which my dreams can still unfold is the future, its form not yet being fixed. Imagining the worst conceivable tomorrows gives me tremendous pleasure at the artistic level. The darkness of the future lights up my present, and foreknowledge of a coming end guarantees my happiness in living today. In this exhibition you will find the worst scenarios created by my imagination regarding the future of mankind. It is up to the younger generations to take every possible step to prevent them from becoming a reality. Where I am concerned, I choose to give completely free reign to my intuitions as an artist. That does not mean that we should not continue to hope for the future. I leave it to the last survivor to record the actual course of the end of the world, and to preserve the genetic information of the human species, either by metamorphosing into a mummy, by preserving their genes in a test tube, or by safeguarding a DNA map of their genome.[41]

The list of exhibited items and Sugimoto's text appeared in the February 2014 issue of the journal *Shinchō*; a description of the exhibit appeared in the July 2014 issue of *Bijutsu techō*.[42] It is interesting to discover that the number of the exhibition pieces was actually different than what was listed, and the order of the thirty-three narratives accompanying the objects was different as well. Beginning with number four "Paleontologist" and number eight "Art Historian," the following introduction shows the tight connection with the reorganization:

> Our earth, the third planet from the sun, had plenty of water 550 million years ago when organic compounds started an explosive chain reaction that culminated in the phenomenon of human life, which in turn gave rise to civilization over the last 20,000-year glacial period. But there were many problems and civilization went into decline, until all that remained was an empty shell of humanity.[43]

After number two, "Comparative Religions Scholar," and squeezed between number eighteen, "Contemporary Artist," and number fifteen, "Aesthete," is number eleven, "Meteorite Collectors." Following this organization one imagines that the gallery-goers are beginning to imagine a map of the future somehow connected to Fukushima. What was exhibited as the "Comparative Religions Scholar" was Sugimoto's photograph of the Last Supper taken in Madame Tussauds' Wax Museum. This 1999 photo had been in Sugimoto's New York City basement warehouse, where it was damaged by the flooding after Hurricane Sandy ravaged North America in October 2012. The damaged photo seems half melted. The accompanying text, which explains how the photo was damaged by being submerged following the Hurricane, calls forth memories of the tsunami and brings back memories of the 2011 disasters. Further, the exhibit continues with the "Meteorite Collectors" exhibit in a space where the glass ceiling of the exhibit space had in fact been damaged by a meteor. The meteor's trajectory was marked with red string. The meteor struck, broke through the ceiling, smashed into the ground, and traveled through to the basement where it smashed a western-style toilet. A "beware of falling rocks" sign had been posted at that spot for a quite funny, even delightful exhibit. Nonetheless, in the text we read the following:

> Today the world died. Or maybe yesterday. An unforeseen, one-hundred-ton meteor—not so big for a meteor—broke into two pieces before smashing onto the earth's surface, one in the Pacific Ocean, the other in the Atlantic. Thirty-meter-plus tsunami waves crashed into coastal cities throughout the world, engulfing more than fifty nuclear power plants, knocking them out of commission and causing reactor meltdowns. Radiation rode the westerly winds and within one week the region was uninhabitable to humans. I took steps to preserve my genes before sleep comes on, but I hold no expectations for the future, nor do I blame people here and now for this sorry state of affairs. We humans miscalculated: Just because something has never happened before doesn't mean it won't happen in the future. Who were we kidding? As if we know even more than a few thousand years of the past. A fragment of the big meteor also fell here. Just what I always wanted for my meteorite collection![44]

Again, one becomes aware that the thirty-three stories accompanying the objects portray the ruins that follow the collapse of humanity. Curator Miki Akiko quoted the following from Sugimoto in her essay on the exhibit:

> Men have a blind belief in the capitalist myth that endless growth is the guarantee of their happiness and in order to bring about that growth the destruction of the planet continues day after day. When I think about the future of human civilization, I feel an overwhelming need to explain to myself how it began and how it has come to the appalling state it is in now.[45]

She went on to write, "In the twenty-first century, people have already had to face up to major catastrophes like 9/11 and 3.11 without finding any ideal to hang on to, without a philosophy or any kind of science that promises hope for the future."⁴⁶ Even without these explanations, I expect that most of us would associate the meteorite collector's text with 3.11 and "Fukushima." It also reminds us, with this description of the future, that this will not be the last nuclear meltdown. The text does not explicitly instruct us to read it in this way but museum goers will surely see it so. This is how we read after March 11, 2011. Thus, if that is the case, it seems we had better ask and figure out how to follow our current situation which can no longer support the previously existing perspective of criticism and of reading.

A concrete example of this is Tawada Yōko's story "Idaten dokomademo" ("How far will the Skanda deity go") published in *Gunzō* in 2014.⁴⁷ The story follows two women who have evacuated to a school gym after a massive earthquake. The scenes of individuals arranging their belongings in spaces marked out by cardboard bring to mind the same scenes we saw at post-3.11 evacuation shelters. And yet, perhaps, what is being described is not that earthquake. This conclusion is hinted at because the narrator Higashida Kazuko and her husband, before his death from stomach cancer, pay a visit to his hometown and the area appears already to have been contaminated with radiation.

The reader's eye is drawn to the wordplay that disassembles the radicals for the Sino-Japanese characters (*kanji*) used in the story. For example, we read that the husband "was a dignified man . . . who liked mountains and had never known sickness." If the first character in "dignified" (*hin* 品) and the character for "mountain" (*yama* 山) are brought together as radicals under the character for sickness (*yamai* 病), we find the word for "cancer" (*gan* 癌). The description above is completed: "he suddenly came down with stomach cancer (*igan* 胃癌)."⁴⁸ Tawada proceeds by interrogating not just the meaning of entire characters but of the radicals themselves. She develops the story via this interplay of characters, using multiple characters with the radical for horse, for example, for extensive wordplay that is nonetheless entirely meaningful.

Her manipulation of characters is not simply for the purpose of wordplay. The characters come to hold supernatural powers. For example, Kazuko's husband, as we saw above, in the encounter with *hin* and *yama* can be said to be inviting cancer (*gan*). That is why when another person, Deguchi, says "be confident (*jishin*) today" in an ikebana classroom on the anniversary day of the Buddha's death, she actually calls forth the massive earthquake (*jishin*) of the novel.

Likewise, Kazuko wed her husband in an arranged marriage after graduating from a junior college, then set up lodging in Ibaraki prefecture to support her husband's work. After his death, she stays in Ibaraki since the house is now paid off. Before her husband received radiation therapy for cancer, he wanted to go visit the home where he was raised, a place he had not visited for a very long time, so they "headed north on the local trains."[49] His wish to go home is expressed as follows:

> Kazuko's husband said he wanted to see his family home before beginning radiation therapy, so Kazuko bought a new travel bag and they headed north on the local trains. But his parents had moved far away and were no longer living in the house. Other residents of the village had also gradually disappeared. Yet, even though everything pointed to no one living there any longer it nonetheless appeared that someone traveled there to look after the rice, since the fields were all healthy and green. It was rice that no one was eating, there was only the panorama of rice fields. . . . How much longer would the tenacity to grow rice that was not being eaten continue? But even in this contaminated environment where herbicides had been prohibited, the weeds (zassō 雑草) grew quickly (hayai 早). The sharp fang-shaped (kiba 牙) weeds (me 芽) caught up to the young rice plants, and overtook and swallowed them.[50]

The fact that to the north of Ibaraki is Fukushima prefecture, together with discussions of "rice that could not be eaten" and "in a contaminated environment," could only have readers imagine a world after the Fukushima nuclear power plant accident. The "contaminated environment" is the most likely explanation for why nobody lives there anymore. We read that, while there is no sign of human life, there is a panorama of healthy rice fields. Although there is no mention of the "pollution" of the area being radioactive contamination, the earlier mention of the husband's "radiation therapy" reverberates through the paragraphs that follow and leads us to imagine, by association, that his family home was in the Fukushima exclusion zone.

That the major earthquake of the story occurs after the 3.11 disasters is made apparent in passages like the following, describing the supplies distributed as soon as the evacuees arrive at the evacuation center: "those supplies had arrived during the last earthquake, but since there had not been time to distribute them at that time, they remained in storage."[51] Were the earthquake that occurs in the story just one of the many to affect the region—that is, not unusual—why then would people have to ride such a long distance (overnight by bus) to reach the evacuation center? On their way to the center they have ridden through the night and into the next morning. The fact that they traveled such distances certainly suggests that there has been, yet again, a major nuclear accident. In any case, the reader cannot help but imagine this to be the case.

Both Higashida Kazuko and Tsukada Tōko had gotten on the bus for the ride to the shelter. On the bus their bodies greedily come together. It could be mistaken for close wrestling, as it becomes impossible to distinguish which arms and legs belonged to which body, in the same way that *kanji* characters switch around radicals among themselves. There in one corner of the gymnasium-turned-evacuation center they spend a honeymoon period, the description of which calls to mind the dreamlike atmosphere of Fukazawa Shichirō's "Furyū mutan" ("The Story of a Dream of Courtly Elegance," 1960). While on the one hand her travels with her husband are described realistically, this idea that somewhere in Eastern Japan there exists a polluted land is brought home not in the style of a science fiction or futuristic novel, but in the descriptions and style of realistic fiction. Behind the characters in their delightful wordplay dance lurks an oppressive reality that suddenly breaks through at different points.

However, when critic Karube Tadashi and novelists Fujino Kaori and Inaba Mayumi discussed Tawada's story in the critical reviews column for the literary journal *Gunzō*, in March 2014, they concentrated throughout on the skillful rhetorical play with *kanji* characters but completely avoided any mention of the nuclear disaster. More to the point, in his summary of the work, Karube leaves completely untouched the potential of reading it in the context of the nuclear disasters:

> The protagonist Higashida Kazuko starts taking ikebana lessons after her husband dies. There she is struck by a beautiful woman named Tsukada Tōko and we sense a strong curiosity towards Higashida's potent sexuality. She invites Tōko to tea, and the disaster strikes while they are at the café. As they run to safety their breathing comes together in the same rhythm. Aboard the bus, their bodies become as intertwined as the kanji characters of their names: Higashida's 東 with Tsukuda's 束, Kazuko's 一 with Tōko's 十 [because the characters in the two pairs differ by a single stroke]. Arriving at the gymnasium-turned-evacuation-center, they begin life as a married couple. One day, however, Tōko's older sister comes and takes her away. Kazuko is torn: should she wait for Tōko's return or just forget about her? One night under the full moon, a distressed Kazuko runs frantic circles in the schoolyard trying to make herself believe that Tōko will return.[52]

This reading revolves around a literary-critical axis that mobilizes all the usual things that are always said about Tawada Yōko: she is an author known for wordplay who breaks apart the usual meanings of words only to regroup them, an author who employs a method that overturns the usual meanings that native speakers give to words, one who crosses borders, one with a translator's point of view, and so on. But here, this run-of-the-mill critical stance toward Tawada's work, especially in the way it seems to skip over all passages pointing to the nuclear disasters, yields a decidedly impoverished reading. Given what has dropped out here—the point of view of its having been written as "Postdisaster literature"—only goes to show again the importance of providing a theory of postdisaster literature that includes a method for actually reading the disasters in this literature.

Furthermore, on this issue of how to read postdisaster literature, we cannot limit ourselves to literature written after the disasters. It might be a mistake to insist on reading into predisaster novels an event still-future at the time of their writing; nonetheless, it is incontrovertible that after the disasters our readings changed.

Take for example Shiriagari Kotobuki's manga *Gerogero pūsuka* (Gerogero pūsuka).[53] Originally published in 2006 in *Comic Beam* with Chernobyl as catalyst, a new edition came out in June of 2012. His images—such as a single child wandering through an unpopulated landscape in a world occupied by the elderly where children are extremely rare—match exactly what was still to come in the future: a postdisaster Fukushima as depicted in postdisaster fiction. How is one to think of this if reading it as a newly written work in 2012?

The same issues apply to the way we see art. In his *Afutāmasu—Shinsaigo no shashin* (Aftermath: Photos since the disaster), critic Iizawa Kōtarō writes how landscape photos of harbors along the Sanriku coast taken in 2008, or even 1991, come to have very different meanings after the disasters. He writes:

> It goes without saying that the harbor towns in those pictures disappeared without a trace with the tsunami. Neither Onaka Kōji nor Motoyama Shūhei took these pictures with that possibility in mind. They captured the tranquil scenes of these seaside towns; their photos were taken with the usual detachment and objective distance of a passerby, without sentimentality. But looking at these images after the disasters, the meanings that they held have changed, definitively. Pictures that were taken as carefree snapshots now document vanished places. When looking at them now, with the images of that terrifying wall of water that engulfed those towns in mind, we can only superimpose that image atop those photos.[54]

In the same way, Hatakeyama Naoya's photographs of his hometown near the Kesen river changed meaning after the disasters, as he says in his afterword to *Kesengawa*:

> Whenever I felt desolate and miserable I tried to avoid such "absolute photographs" because they too have changed. I say "absolute" but *a priori* these images did not contain anything important. Even if they now seem to possess some special quality, that is in no way due to any competence of mine but only to the event that took place. This may seem irresponsible, but trying to understand these images in the context of modern art, trying to evaluate their importance "as photographic images," is no longer of any importance to me. In a moment such as this one, photographs seem to act of their own accord without us being able to control them, and we are no more than observers of this phenomenon.[55]

Preface: Following My Shinsaigo Bungakuron *(On Postdisaster Literature)*   xliii

Takahashi Gen'ichirō used this double exposure technic on Kawakami Hiromi's "Kamisama 2011" ("God Bless You, 2011"). He analyzed Kawakami's story in the "Shinsai bungakuron" (Theory of Disaster Literature) section of his own postdisaster novel *Koisuru genpatsu* (Nuclear reactors in love). Kawakami rewrote her 1993 short story "Kamisama" ("God Bless You") shortly after absorbing the impact of the nuclear disasters, publishing it as "Kamisama 2011."[56] This publication included the original story, the 2011 version, and an "afterword." Since then it has appeared in an anthology, in English translation, and as a separate volume, always with all three parts appearing together. Takahashi intentionally reads the two texts in an overlapping fashion. He points out that the children of the 1993 story have disappeared from the 2011 version and goes on to read them in the later story only as ghosts. Below is the opening to the 2011 story with the additions to the 1993 version underlined:

The bear invited me to go for a walk to the river. I had taken that road once before in the early spring to see the snipes, but then I had worn protective clothing; now it was hot, and for the first time since the "incident" I would be clad in normal clothes that exposed the skin, and carrying a box lunch to boot. It would be a bit of a trek, somewhere between a hike and a stroll.[57]

The inclusion of "protective clothing" is likely to alert most readers to associate the story's "incident" with the Fukushima Daiichi nuclear accident. But since Kawakami refers to it simply as "the incident," its meaning need not be limited to that meltdown. One can read it as referring to some past nuclear accident or even some future nuclear accident: there is that degree of universality in this story.

"Kamisama 2011" was most likely written without any connection to Takahashi's "Sayonara Kurisutofā Robin" ("Goodbye, Christopher Robin"). But read as postdisaster literature, one quickly comes to feel that we are to read it in a relationship with Kawakami's "Kamisama 2011." In "Sayonara Kurisutofā Robin," if the characters do not keep writing stories they will disappear from the world. A "nothingness" (*kyomu*) is closing in on them. Takahashi writes the following as the impetus for this story:

And that's how, quietly, but definitively, time was marching on. Surely there were people driven by an ominous "foreboding" (*yokan*). Even so, what could they do? Stand there, hands clasped, wait for the moment to arrive, nothing else.
   And then, "the incident."
   It occurred in a mere moment, that's what was said. In the midst of it, a loud noise, and in addition, a frightening light-like something. Even so, later on, everyone came away feeling like it might have all been a made-up story.

Some said it made a "whoosh" like the sound of a match being struck. Even though, for many years now, no one had seen a match, or anything like one.

Other people said they heard a screech, like when you close an old wooden door. But, in these newest of buildings, there were no wooden doors, nor anything similar. As long, that is, as the sound from one of the doors from the old western-style building that was torn down a half century ago to make way for this one only now reached us.

Others thought it a sound like a cup hitting the floor, one from which a child, who made a mistake, was drinking milk. They went on to say that in that moment they heard, very softly, a child murmur "I'm sorry." But, in that house, the mere presence of a child, had been gone for centuries.

Someone else said that from the garden it seemed that someone had set off a firecracker. But thinking, "That's odd, it being winter and all, much less that someone would have climbed into the garden; doesn't seem likely." But then, going out to the garden in that moment, there remained a sense that someone had been out there. But of course, out in the garden, any evidence of someone being there, didn't exist, not even a scrap.

. . . .

It is just possible that one or more of those events had actually occurred in the moment of "the incident." It is also possible that the great majority of them were, in the effort to make sense of things that make no sense, ideas that arose in order to match with actual events, no more than stories.[58]

The "that incident" that appears here is set off in quotation marks as in Kawakami's story; the stories seem to be talking to each other. It is not clear if Kawakami was quoting Takahashi. What is certain is that for stories written before the 2011 disasters, there are readers after the disasters who will read them as postdisaster literature.

The same thing occurs in Tawada Yōko's *Kumo wo tsukamu hanashi* (Tales of grasping for clouds). The writings of this collection span the disaster. Even though some sections were written before the disasters, they too will be read into the disasters. If we accept that literary works change meaning in the same manner as photographs, then surely it becomes necessary to analyze literature based on those changes in meaning. This via the issue of how the world appears in photographs as a double exposure of the past and the disaster; or via the absolute (*zettaisei*) of the event. Just as it proves empty to ask, "What are they *qua* photos?" to ask, "how literary are these literary works *qua* literature?" will lead to a situation where the *existing* critical discourse will no longer hold.

Just as one can use a gender-based analysis on works that predate even the invention of the word "gender," or, similarly, bring queer analyses to works from a time period when the word "gay" or "lesbian" did not yet exist, so too, surely, we can employ the viewpoint of postdisaster literature as a method for explicating works. When ways of reading change our methods of criticism must change as well. Thus, whether or not there is any meaning in continuing to assign value with an ossified literary eye is a topic that surely will be taken up by future research into postdisaster literature.

In my previous book I wrote, "It is precisely those works written in a period when writing is difficult: that is postdisaster literature."[59] This has been quoted as a sort of definition for "postdisaster literature." But I do not think this has much meaning when it comes to categorizing fiction. Rather, it is reading and analyzing *as* postdisaster literature that provides the more important axis for our reading. In going back to revisit a theory of postdisaster literature, the issue now is how to theorize the lineage of postdisaster issues.

In that previous book, I was eager to enumerate developments following the disasters and I ended up only listing works. At this point in time we are past the stage of looking closely at these postdisaster literary developments. A number of theories of reading and analysis have since appeared. Given that, my own approach to writing has changed. Even though I still feel the need for a comprehensive approach to important works, in this volume, I intend to pose the theoretical questions of how we read this postdisaster literature. I intend to look exhaustively, and from various angles, at just what it means to make postdisaster literature the issue.

In chapter 1, I intend to do this by taking up currently issues important to us now within contemporary literary study, namely theories of gender and sexuality, and treat them in these works as an issue of minorities. While family bonds (*kizuna*) are strengthened in times of emergency, at the same time, I do not want to overlook the many ways that heteronormativity and sexism also appear, and in force. I will proceed by reading works that pull out issues of women who are struggling and that describe sexual minorities. In chapter 2 I examine literary works that ask what this nuclear disaster known as "Fukushima" has brought about, and what radiation damage really is. In chapter 3 I explore the ties between the memory of the atomic bombings of Hiroshima and Nagasaki and the radiation exposure in Fukushima via representations of Hiroshima in works like Alain Resnais' film *Hiroshima Mon Amour* (1959). In chapter 4 I consider the postdisaster appearance of war imagery with a focus on the war novels written by authors now three generations from the end of the war. In chapter 5 I draw attention to the voices of the dead and of ghosts who are often narrated in postdisaster fiction and oral tales. In chapter 6 I look at how the uncanny that has haunted us since the disaster is represented. In chapter 7 I think about how radiation has brought to Japanese society a sense of "precarious life" as discussed by Judith Butler.

Lastly, I want to say something about terminology. I follow the practice I employed in my previous book of referring to radiation as *hōshanō*. This word has been consistent through fiction and literature, in contrast to the possible "radioactive material" (*hōshasei busshitsu*). Since these works talk about the disasters, the term "disaster literature" would seem appropriate, but in this book I address this body of work as "postdisaster literature." This is a choice based on the tendencies that have plagued the naming of "atomic bomb literature," namely, the genre limitations that allow only for descriptions that continue to make central that day when the bomb was dropped. Likewise, rather than "war literature," "postwar literature" contains the possibilities for a variety of expressions. Further, given that there is no resolution in sight for the Great East Japan Disasters, especially for the radioactive damage that resulted from the explosions at the Fukushima Daiichi Nuclear Electric Plant, and that conditions change hour by hour, and that we continue to live with it as it continues, we know that there will be varieties of literature to come—some that take up the long period following the disasters and some that forces us to rethink the disasters—and that such literature will continue to be written and continue to change, as will the themes concerning the disasters, well into the future. Therefore I want to be able to include in this field all the literature that is sure to come.

NOTES

1. Michaël Ferrier, *Fukushima: Récit d'un désastre* (Paris: Gallimard, 2012). Translated by Yoshie Makiko as *Fukushima nōto: Wasurenai saika no monogatari* (Tokyo: Shinhyōron, 2013), 1-2.
2. Nagashima Yū, "Toi no nai kotae," *Bungakkai* 66 no. 10 (October 2012): 58–77. Reprinted as *Toi no nai kotae* (Tokyo: Bungei shunjū, 2013). Citations are from this version.
3. This appeared in book form in 2011 from Tokuma shoten.
4. Nagashima, *Toi no nai kotae*, 51.
5. Nagashima, *Toi no nai kotae*, 10.
6. Nagashima, *Toi no nai kotae*, 42.
7. Nakano Hitori, *Densha otoko* (Tokyo: Shinchōsha, 2004). Translated by Bonnie Elliott as *Train Man the Novel* (New York: Del Rey/ Ballantine, 2006). There is also a long series of Manga published by Kodansha with English translations available. A film directed by Murakami Shosuke appeared in 2005 from Toho Studios and Fuji Television.—Trans.
8. "2channel" or "2chan" refers to an online community that corresponds roughly to, because is the precursor to, the English "4chan," which is to say, it tends to be a right-wing community.—Trans.
9. Nagashima, *Toi no nai kotae*, 93.
10. Japanese readers would associate this with the "No more Hiroshimas, no more Nagasakis."—Trans.
11. Nagashima, *Toi no nai kotae*, 11.

12. The quotation marks around "Fukushima," "Nagasaki," and "Hiroshima" signal that Kimura uses all these words in katakana, seemingly as a way to highlight that these place names have come to stand for nuclear events rather than the cities themselves.—Trans.

13. Nagashima, *Toi no nai kotae*, 177.
14. Nagashima, *Toi no nai kotae*, 178.
15. Nagashima, *Toi no nai kotae*, 241.
16. Nagashima, *Toi no nai kotae*, 244.
17. Nagashima, *Toi no nai kotae*, 245.
18. Ishihara Shintarō was Governor of Tokyo from 1999 to 2012. He was infamous for extreme right-wing proclamations and ties. He was also one of the most provocative novelists of the 1950s.—Trans.
19. *Hibakusha*, meaning "irradiated person," is generally understood to refer to the atomic radiation victims of Hiroshima and Nagasaki.—Trans.
20. First published in *Gunzō*, April 2013, and later included in book form in Hayashi Kyōko, *Tanima; Futatabi rui e* (Tokyo: Kōdansha bungei bunko, 2016). Translated with an introduction by Margaret Mitsutani and an afterword by Eiko Otake as "To Rui, once again," *The Asia-Pacific Journal* 15 no. 3 (April 2017), n.p.
21. See his comments in the "Sōsaku gappyō" column in the February 1982 issue of *Gunzō*.
22. See Nakagami's comments in the round-table discussion, "Our Literary Stance" in the October 1978 issue of *Bungakukai*.
23. Nakagami Kenji, Tsushima Yuko, et al., "Zadankai: Warera no bungaku no tachiba—sedairon wo koete," *Bungakkai* (October 1978): 109.
24. Seirai Yūichi, "Koyubi ga moeru," *Bungei Shunjū* (August 2017): 91.
25. The work was originally published in *Shinchō* in February 2014.
26. Furukawa Hideo, *Shōsetsu no dēmontachi* (Tokyo: Suicchi puburisshingu, 2013), 27.
27. Furukawa, *Shōsetsu no dēmontachi*, 36–37.
28. Furukawa, *Shōsetsu no dēmontachi*, 183.
29. Furukawa Hideo, in collaboration with Kondo Keisuke, "Sono yashiki wo oou, kutsugaesu, oou," *Bijutsu techō* (April, 2012): 177.
30. Furukawa Hideo, *Tōmin suru kuma ni soineshite goran* (Tokyo: Shinchōsha 2014), 10.
31. Miyazawa Kenji, "Nametokoyama no kuma," in *Kōhon Miyazawa Kenji Zenshū*, vol. 9 (Tokyo: Chikuma Shobō, 1973), 237. Translated by John Bestor as "The Bears of Nametoko," in Ted Goossen, ed., *The Oxford book of Japanese short stories* (Oxford: Oxford University Press, 1997), 109. Translation modified.—Trans.
32. Furukawa, *Tōmin suru kuma*, 11.
33. Furukawa, *Tōmin suru kuma*, 203.
34. Furukawa, *Tōmin suru kuma*, 216.
35. Furukawa, *Shōsetsu no dēmontachi*, 52.
36. Seirai, "Koyubi ga moeru," 143.
37. In English, see the following sources: Lisette Gebhardt and Masami Yūki, eds., *Literature and Art after "Fukushima": Four Approaches* (Berlin: EB Verlag, 2014);

Thomas M. Bohn, Thomas Feldhoff, Lisette Gebhardt, and Arndt Graf, eds., *The Impact of Disaster: Social and Cultural Approaches to Fukushima and Chernobyl* (Berlin: EB-Publishers, 2015); Barbara Geilhorn and Kristina Iwata-Weickgenannt, *Fukushima and the Arts: Negotiating Nuclear Disaster* (London and New York: Routledge, 2017); Christophe Thouny and Mitsuhiro Yoshimoto. *Planetary Atmospheres and Urban Society after Fukushima* (Singapore: Palgrave Macmillan, 2017). In French, see Christian Doumet and Michaël Ferrier, *Penser avec Fukushima* (Nantes: Editions nouvelles Cécile Defaut, 2016). In Japanese, see Genkaiken, eds., *Higashinihon daishinsaigo bungakuron* (Tokyo: Nan'undo, 2017).

38. Lisette Gebhardt, "Various Shades of Fury: Criticism of 'System' and Society in Japanese Post-Fukushima Literature" (presentation, Tanaka Symposium in Japanese Studies: "Literature after 3.11," Pembroke College, Oxford University, June 1, 2017). Gebhardt argued that "post-Fukushima literature" is related to issues like the so-called "nuclear village," the self-restraint exercised by the Japanese media, the Abe government's Secrecy Law, and the activity of advertising companies. Furthermore, she pointed out, even if it does not appear to be linked to political issues, given current conditions something called "post-Fukushima literature" is a "political literature."

39. The phrasing of this title is intended to bring to mind the first line of Camus' *L'étranger*, which reads, "Maman died today. Or yesterday maybe, I don't know." *The Stranger*, trans. Matthew Ward (New York: Vintage International, 1989), 3.

40. The same exhibit was on display at the Tokyo Photographic Art Museum as "Sugimoto Hiroshi: Lost Human" from September 3 to November 13, 2016.

41. Kimura quotes from Sugimoto Hiroshi, "Kyō sekaiwa shinda moshikasuruto asu kamosirenai" *Shinchō* 111, no. 2 (February 2014): 256. The English here is found in *Hiroshi Sugimoto, Cahiers d'Art Revue*, no. 1 (2014), 17.

42. The photos and text described below can also be found in *Hiroshi Sugimoto, Cahiers d'Art Revue*, no. 1 (2014).—Trans.

43. Sugimoto, "Kyō sekaiwa shinda," 257. English translation is from *Hiroshi Sugimoto, Cahiers d'Art Revue*, no. 1 (2014), 48.

44. Sugimoto, "Kyō sekaiwa shinda," 262. The text of the exhibit was displayed in English and French. Further, it was handwritten and often hard to read. Thus, there is a good chance that observers did not connect these words to the exhibit.—Kimura.

English is from *Hiroshi Sugimoto, Cahiers d'Art Revue*, no. 1 (2014), 66. Translation modified—Trans.

45. Sugimoto Hiroshi, *Āto no kigen* Tokyo: Shinchōsha, 221.

46. Akiko Miki, "The exhibition is a machine for stopping time," *Cahiers d'Art* 1 (2014): 173. The English translation here and in the previous paragraph are from *Cahiers d'Art*. —Trans.

47. The story was originally published in *Gunzō*'s February special issue on "Hen'ai shosetsu" and later included in Tawada Yōko, *Kentōshi* [*The Emissary*] (Tokyo: Kōdansha, 2014).

48. Tawada Yōko, "Idaten dokomademo," in *Kentōshi*, 31.

49. Tawada, "Idaten dokomademo," 167.

50. Tawada, "Idaten dokomademo," 167. Tawada bolds the following characters: "grass" (*kusa*) in "weeds" and a similar looking character in "quickly" (*hayaku*), as well as "fang" (*kiba*) and the similar looking "bud" (*me*).—Trans.

51. Tawada, "Idaten dokomademo," 182.

52. Karube Tadashi, Fujino Kaori, and Inaba Mayumi, "Sōsaku gappyō," *Gunzō* (March 2014): 327.

53. Kotobuki Shiriagari, *Gerogero pūsuka* (Tokyo: Entāburein, 2007).

54. Iizawa Kōtarō and Hishida Yusuke, *Afutāmasu: Shinsaigo no shashin* (Tokyo: NTT Shuppan, 2011): 14–15. Iizawa raised an alarm concerning the mood of self-restraint after the disasters: "One more thing that we need pay special attention to is the manner of speaking when we say things such as 'One more thing we need to think about is the feelings of the victims' or 'We need to refrain from anything that would cause them emotional harm.' Regarding the troubles and hardships the victims are experiencing, those of us living comfortably in safe areas can only hang our heads in shame. But if we go to extremes thinking about their existence, we come to feel 'There is nothing we can say' or 'There is nothing we can do.' Artists, writers, and performers (*hyōgensha*) all have a moral and ethical commitment in this. But if we overdo it, then free expression and practice stagnates. I am not talking about intentionally hurting or showing contempt for the victims. But isn't it OK if sometimes offensive or strong language is used? Taboos can be breached on a small scale. As I have written in this work, those things that remain will continue to remain and those which disappeared will go on being disappeared. It is like the Kobe-Awaji earthquake disaster: now that more than ten years have passed we can see how this is true. To phrase it from the other perspective, unless we think in terms of these longer temporal spans, 'postdisaster photography' will not be fully realized" (151–52).

55. Hatakeyama Naoya, *Kesengawa*, trans. Marc Feustel (Paris: Editions Light Motiv, 2013), n.p.

56. It appeared in the June 2011 edition of *Gunzō*.

57. Kawakami Hiromi, *Kamisama* (Tokyo: Kōdansha, 2011): 23. Translated by Ted Goossen and Shibata Motoyuki as "God Bless You, 2011," in *March was Made of Yarn*, ed. Elmer Luke and David James Karashima (New York: Vintage Books, 2012), 36.

58. Takahashi Gen'ichirō, "Sayonara Kurisutofā Robin," *Shinchō* (January 2010): 85–86. Later collected in *Sayonara Kurisutofa Robin* (Tokyo: Shinchōsha, 2012).

59. Kimura Saeko, *Shinsaigo bungakuron* (Tokyo: Seidosha, 2013), 59.

Chapter 1

Postdisaster Literature and Minorities

POSTDISASTER LITERATURE AS QUEER FICTION: NUMATA SHINSUKE'S *EIRI* (BEHIND THE SHADOWS)

Early in 2017 Numata Shinsuke's *Eiri* was awarded the 157th Akutagawa Prize.[1] The prize was awarded to this work as a postdisaster novel but also as a work as queer fiction.[2] When we meet the protagonist of *Eiri*, Kon'no Shūichi, he has transferred from his job in the capital two years earlier to a subsidiary firm in Morioka, Iwate Prefecture, far north on the main Japanese island of Honshū. New to the area, Kon'no makes friends with Hiasa Norihiro, who spent his college years in Tokyo; he spends that first-year in Tohoku drinking and fishing with Hiasa. Hiasa, however, simply disappears one day after unexpectedly quitting his job and without saying goodbye. Kon'no had always communicated with Hiasa via his work phone, so he has no other contact for him. Hiasa is now gone, but Kon'no continues to think of him. From the description of the very first time that Kon'no took Hiasa to his favorite fishing hole, it becomes increasingly clear that Hiasa was more than a mere friend. We read of a hot day in August when Kon'no hands his water bottle back to Hiasa, walking a half-step behind, without looking at him; even so, the narrator Kon'no then stops and turns around to watch Hiasa take a drink. He continues to observe as Hiasa "tilts his head and drinks with relish." The narrative continues:

> Scrunching up the area between his sleepy-looking eyelids, Hiasa wiped his lips with the back of his hand. Catching the sweat that had pooled on his eyelids with his fingertips, he flicked it off to the side. Maybe the saké they had drunk the night before remained pooled just below his skin, for the base of his neck had an oily sheen, much like a well-polished gun barrel.[3]

Kon'no's line of sight takes in these wet lips and the nape of a neck glistening with sweat; the gaze is sensual. The narrator goes on to describe how Hiasa "straddled the fallen tree as though it were a horse"; how he embraced the trunk of the tree while measuring its girth with a tape measure; the way he "caressed the skin of the tree"; the way that he "methodically pressed his ear against the tree's trunk, moving from top to bottom"; and, further, that he was secretly taking pictures of these scenes on "his camera phone." The narrative continues, "When he reviewed the photos later, Hiasa appeared not so much as a doctor but as a hunter checking for a heartbeat in the beast he had brought down." Kon'no then realized that what he had recorded was something like the image of a hunter straddling bagged game. The narrator Kon'no, now feeling that he had been unaware of his own desire in recording these images in his photographs, was clearly smitten with Hiasa. He further realizes that Hiasa's disappearing without a word of farewell was not because of "standoffishness" (*mizukusai*).[4] After Hiasa left, Kon'no spent days wandering around the office looking for a sign of him:

> not simply because I was lost in recollections of our time together. Rather, I was searching, in this case, for the Hiasa who was a person who liked to fish; who could skillfully drive them up narrow mountain roads; another single man close in age who was easy to spend time with; someone who, once a bottle of sake was opened, proved to be the perfect drinking companion; I was, in short, looking for my friend.[5]

But we also find that all of these are words of an "unreliable narrator."[6] It is clear that Kon'no, having moved to the countryside from the capital, has found himself in an environment where he cannot talk openly about his own sexuality and is also not the type of narrator who explains all of his secrets to his reader in detail. It is simply that he enjoyed observing the unguarded Hiasa while they were fishing together.

When Hiasa, now overseeing the employee mutual benefit society of the company, suddenly shows up at Kon'no's apartment four months later, Kon'no naturally hopes that they will spend the day drinking and then go fishing the following day. But Hiasa has come solely to recruit Kon'no to join the society and to meet his work quota. When Kon'no realizes this later, he is all the more surprised when Hiasa invites him for a night of fishing. Kon'no is quite expectant as he sets out on this excursion; we assume he is expecting a romantic evening. With the "Kirsch and pickles" he has bought in anticipation, he sets out in his best clothes. But when Hiasa arrives, he is irritable and ill-tempered; worse, it turns out that one of his clients, a man named Inoue, will be joining them later. Kon'no, the narrator, has prepared table and chairs, but only for two. He stubbornly refuses to drink any sake and before long gets up and leaves. It is clear that he has now come to realize that the two of them are fundamentally mismatched. Kon'no is the type of person who has a sheepskin rug spread on the floor of his room illuminated by a floor lamp with a potted jasmine plant in the corner, and, worse, thinks Hiasa, he is a person with "snobbish" predilections. That day, for example, he arrived wearing a down vest of lambskin and spread an English tweed blanket across his knees. Later, after he has returned to his room, the narrator recalls each and every nasty thing said about him:

> Look at those titanium dinner plates: Just as you would expect a newbie outdoorsman to have bought; . . . A GSI percolator: Just the thing for a guy who doesn't have to worry about money; . . . The lambskin down vest: easy as pie for the guy getting the big city salary out here in the boondocks, just put it on the credit card without a care.[7]

All these words that Hiasa said, highlighted in the passages above, in exactly the tone in which they were said, now ring in Kon'no's ears. All of this paints a clear picture of the economic class differences between him and Hiasa and suggests how Hiasa must be disgusted that in his straightened circumstances he can only sponge off of his friend Kon'no.[8]

The narrator, feeling all of this keenly, contacts a former lover named Soejima Kazuya. Economically, they are on more equal footing. It seems that after they separated, Soejima underwent sexual reassignment surgery and now speaks "with a woman's voice." They had been talking to each other by phone about once per month.

In this story the reader comes to learn of the details of the triple disasters of March 11, 2011, via a newspaper clipping hand-delivered by a neighbor, formerly a school teacher, who is stuffing neighborhood mailboxes. The clipping is titled "Events from March 11" and written by the daughter of one of her former students. Sometime later, one of Kon'no's coworkers, a woman named Nishiyama, relates that Hiasa was likely swept out to sea by the tsunami waves near Kamaishi. It further becomes clear in this conversation that Hiasa had been asking her, even more often than he had asked Kon'no, to join the mutual aid society; moreover, she had lent him money. But it also seems that it was more than a simple story of Hiasa needing to rely on Nishiyama. Every day, Kon'no has been checking the newspaper listings of the dead and missing; three months later, in June, he goes to Hiasa's home to call on his father. There he learns that Hiasa had, for four years or more, been receiving money for college tuition but had not attended classes. Because of this, among other violations, he had been thrown out of the house. "If it's my son you're talking about, you can be sure he's not dead," the father says, continuing, "you can bet he has taken advantage of the disasters and is now one of that lot out stealing stuff."[9] But this confession that Hiasa is a swindler does not tarnish Kon'no's image all that much. After all, Kon'no had not been pestered for cash the way Nishiyama was, and he had only once been asked to join the mutual aid association.

There's more: one day Hiasa comes to visit Kon'no again, after a four-month absence and no word. When Kon'no sees him off at his front door, he discovers a number of cigarette butts scattered by the entrance. He has to wonder why Hiasa would hang around his front door in that way, as though hesitant to ring the bell. Might it be that, for Hiasa, Kon'no was the last person he wanted to get caught up with financially? He has to wonder why, on that first night when they stayed up drinking together, Hiasa called a taxi even while Kon'no was urging him to stay the night. Maybe it was actually Hiasa who was hiding his sexual orientation. Then there is that night of the invitation for night-time fishing: why was he so ill at ease? It seems entirely likely that he was actually ill at ease with himself, that it was he himself who needed to deceive Kon'no yet again, his own self that instead pricked at him for their class differences.

In the end it appears that what Kon'no felt for Hiasa was definitely not one-sided—in which case, for Kon'no, his hope is to be able to believe that Hiasa remains alive, even if, in a worst-case scenario, it is as a member of a pack of thieves.

STANDARDS FOR HETEROSEXUAL LOVE IN AN EMERGENCY (HETERONORMATIVITY): KAKIYA MIU'S *HINANJO* (EVACUATION SHELTER)

In the period of crisis following a disaster the standards for heterosexual love—i.e., heteronormativity—solidify. In normal times the existence of sexual minorities is discreetly ignored by society, which, while trying to appear inclusive, does not in fact embrace them; it is therefore no surprise that in times of emergency, the existence of those who were previously overlooked does not even enter consideration.

When they meet again some months after Hiasa has quit his job, Kon'no goes out of his way to examine the wedding venues featured in Hiasa's Mutual Aid Group materials. He cannot help but respond with a goading, "Really? Can you pay for a wedding after saving a mere two thousand yen per month?" and "These are not such great wedding venues, are they."[10] He later continues, though, "Actually, I have been thinking about this since we last talked: in fact, that's a pretty nice space for just a two thousand yen a month contribution to the Mutual Aid savings program."[11] Depending on the scene, one gets the impression that Kon'no assumes that Hiasa's reason for taking off is that he became aware that Kon'no is not heterosexual. Yet at the same time, when he and Kazuya split up, he would imagine scenarios where they would announce to everyone in his family that they were going to get married and hear people respond, "I thought those two were already married." We can see how contradictory he is in his own thinking. In the first place, sexual minorities often find that relations among family members are the most burdensome. It appears that Kazuya, in fact, has an older brother; nonetheless he is "estranged from his family, including his brother. But more than that, one got the impression that there was some deeper rift between them."[12] We find that the narrator as well has been in contact with no one in his family except for his younger sister. When he visits Hiasa's father, a tabletop lighter there brings to mind for him "the scene of the old rental house in Tokorozawa where he lived with his family as a child. It further brought back to memory the sight of his much younger parents."[13] Yet we are also to assume that the sight of Hiasa's father sitting there, saying, "I'm no longer his father" and "I've cut all ties with my second son," overlaps with memories of his own family.[14]

The family relations of sexual minorities hinted at in *Eiri* likewise suggest the loneliness felt in times of crisis. This is not only an issue for sexual minorities: traditional gender norms also harden in such times. Kakiya Miu's *Hinanjo* (Evacuation Shelter) is the tale of three women who, in the days following the damage meted out by earthquake and then tsunami, flee from the evacuation center where they have been staying.[15] That evacuation center in the immediate aftermath of the disasters is the setting for this story. In fact, most disaster victims were crammed into school gymnasiums where all ate and slept together. News outlets around the world were effusive in their depictions of evacuates meekly and calmly dividing the scarce rations among themselves. On the reverse side of that image were people pushed to the limits of endurance and patience. In *Hinanjo*, the space inside the gymnasium is a concentrated version of society at large. In the stuffy enclosed space of the shelter, all the difficulties of living as a woman get distilled and then reconstituted. There is no privacy to be found in the gymnasium, with its constant intermingling of men and women. Day in and day out one feels the gaze of others; there is no relief from the anxiety. How much worse for the young women for whom all means to protect themselves from the gaze of men has disappeared? The young women become sexualized objects; there are attempted rapes. Of course such things should not happen, nonetheless it does: the possibility of its happening is so strong that a supply of emergency contraceptive pills is kept on hand by the authorities.

One of these women, Tsubakihara Fukuko, previously worked at the Naganuma sake shop. She was returning from a run to the supermarket to buy dinner for her boss's wife at the time of the earthquake. The tsunami having engulfed her car, she barely escaped death by clambering onto the terrace of a house floating by. In this moment, her secret hope was that her husband, who didn't work and stayed at home drinking, would die in this disaster.

Urushiyama Tōno was living, with her husband and their six-month-old, at his parents' house. Her own parents died in a car accident when she was in elementary school and she grew up with her grandmother, just the two of them, and always hoped that someday she would be part of a three-generation household. But her reality now was her difficult father-in-law; she felt only cramped and constricted in that house. Her husband was studying for his civil service exam: passing meant a position in the prefectural government office and the ability to get their own house, separate from her parents-in-law. Her neighbor, at the moment of the earthquake, with her own child in tow, came and escorted them away. Rescued, they were able to flee the tsunami.

Yamano Nagisa is a single mother who divorced her abusive husband five years earlier. With her elementary school-aged son she returned to the part of the country where she grew up. She worked in her mother's shop, a coffee shop during the day which at night became, essentially, a bar. She had returned to her own house and was preparing food when the disaster struck. The entire house floated away in the muddy water; she was rescued by the fire department at the very moment she was about to be flung from the house into the water.

These three women have arrived at the same evacuation center from various places, and this is where the tale begins. Supplies too have arrived at the shelter, but it proves impossible to divide things equally among the evacuees. Nursing mothers hold their babies in their arms; even though they suffer lack of food and water, they receive no special consideration. One of the lessons learned from the Great Hanshin Earthquake of 1995 was that evacuees need cardboard to partition off private living spaces within the gymnasium. Here, the cardboard has arrived, but the self-proclaimed leader, a man we take to be in his seventies, sets a different direction when he declares: "We must get on like family here. . . . So let's deepen the bonds (*kizuna*) of familiarity among ourselves. With strengthened bonds we can overcome these adversities."[16] Since the cardboard is never distributed, Urushiyama Tōno has to cover herself with a blanket to nurse and to clean herself after. Changing clothes also takes place under the blanket. Going outside at night to use the toilet means attacks by men. In accord with the government post-mortem report following the Great Hanshin Earthquake, the "emergency contraceptive pills" now deemed necessary have also already arrived at the evacuation center; other evacuees are surprised and doubtful when they hear that such things are taking place, whereupon the leader responds by saying: "We-ell, these men have all seen their houses washed away. Their jobs are gone too. They're on edge. Guess there's not much you can do; things like that happen in times like these. You women should go easy on them, maybe let it go. Men, you know, what are you gonna do with them? They're like animals."[17]

That's all it takes to spark a change of direction. Tsubakihara Fukuko assumes leadership in the center. The cardboard is promptly distributed for partitions and a room is created for exclusive use by women. When men begin working outside the shelter, the women are put in charge of food preparation in the kitchen. But while the men receive wages for the work of debris removal, the women's cooking remained unpaid, a split that reflects traditional domestic divisions. One result is that the women have no means of earning wages in the disaster area.

The three women resolve to leave the living hell of the evacuation center after all the condolence funds and charitable contributions are distributed. These monies are restricted to legal heads of households, meaning that even in times such as these it is necessary for a woman to be somehow attached to a man. Tsubakihara Fukuko's husband is still alive but took the entire sum and purchased a BMW, after which he spends all his money on pachinko, and the car is repossessed in order to cover his debts; as a result, not only can she not receive compensation without this husband, she can only anticipate mounting debt because of him. Urushiyama Tōno has her compensation entirely taken over by her father-in-law, leaving her with no funds at hand. Yamano Nagisa, having seduced all the men from the neighborhood at her mother's snack bar, is now reviled—and then her son, on account of this, is bullied at school and stops going.

Having cut their ties with cruel male-dominated society, the three women head for Tokyo. In *Hinanjo*, even though we encounter heterosexual households, the world represented there is one where concepts such as "family" and "bonds" (*kizuna*) only ring hollow, where men dominate women, where, in a deeply traditional society, young men hold their tongues out of deference to older people. Now, while the difficulty of life in Tokyo is also depicted, the women still find it a place where they can obtain work and live independently. For the women depicted in *Hinanjo* we encounter two distinct turning points. One concern is in the handling of disaster relief funds, as we have seen above. Within the family unit, women are rarely considered to be the head of household; with the money going to the male heads of household, the women are put in a position of being supported by men yet again. It puts them in the same position as children. The second turning point, of even more importance than this and which makes possible the change of leadership to a woman, are the "emergency contraceptive pills." Even though they are called "emergency contraceptive pills," they are not actually provided as contraceptives. Rather, they are thought of as a means to stop pregnancy, a morning-after pill, in the small window of time available following a sexual assault; the assumption that sexual violence will occur is the very premise for having them. Further, the former leader goes on to say to the women, "You know, of course, that people who are in need of feminine products should not hesitate to come and ask me for some. I have quite a supply here."[18] The point being that the women's bodily needs—from menstruation to pregnancy—are being administered by men. In the end, the women are able to flee to Tokyo and attain freedom; such is the storyline of this work. But regardless of the fact that these events occur in the countryside (*chihō*), the account encapsulates events occurring all through contemporary society. For example, when the low birthrate and aging population become topics of public concern, it is always decided that it is necessary to raise the birthrate, which means control of women's bodies, and one can count on politicians saying inane things about how women cannot be permitted to not give birth to babies. Such pronouncements of the need to control women's bodies are the most basic masculine logic in a male-dominated society. Pronouncements about the "value of the family" are the same. In that sense, in times of crisis, we find that the situation of sexual minorities is quite close to that of women. Take, for example, US President Donald Trump, who, among other things, gained office on a platform of anti-foreign exclusionism, and made headlines with the misogynistic pronouncement that "If you've got money, you can do anything to women, even grab them by the pussy."[19] But women, punning on pussy's other meaning as "cat," donned pink knit caps adorned with cat ears and turned out in protest. In a time in which we are rocked by the winds of anti-foreign exclusionism, we find, in tandem with racial discrimination, discrimination against minorities and the debasement of women.

WOMEN IN A TIME OF DISPLACEMENT: KANEHARA HITOMI'S *MOTAZARU MONO* (THOSE WE CANNOT HOLD ONTO)

The reason women would throw away everything they have accumulated in their lives and flee to somewhere—anywhere that is not here—is because becoming a refugee is at the same time a bid for "freedom." If that is the case, "stories about women" can be understood as stories describing refugees. Often, in postdisaster literature, we read of women who flee from the provinces to Tokyo, or from Tokyo to overseas countries.

According to the September 10, 2015, report from Post-disaster Reconstruction Agency (*Fukkōcho*), 195,000 people were made refugees by the 2011 disasters.[20] There have been numerous natural disasters in the years since 2011: the Hiroshima landslides that followed torrential rains of August 20, 2014; the volcanic eruption on Kuchinoerabu island on May 29, 2015; the Kinugawa river levee breach due to a typhoon of September 10, 2015;

and the Kumamoto earthquakes of April 14 and 16, 2016, to name just a few. The flow of refugees continues. For people who live on the islands of Japan, the possibility of becoming a disaster refugee is not something that only happens to other people. Additionally, as nuclear power plants are brought back online, it is not baseless fabrication to imagine future explosions turning Japanese people into boat people and international refugees in the manner described in Tawada Yōko's "Higan" ("The Far Shore," 2014)[21] or Fukuda Kōji's 2015 film *Sayonara*.

The nuclear disaster at the Fukushima Daiichi nuclear power plant generated not just the obvious refugees, but also people who fled, of their own volition, across oceans to countries where they knew not a soul. Kanehara Hitomi herself moved to Paris; she also, in her *Motazaru mono* (Those we cannot hold onto, 2015),[22] described one such female refugee who settled in London.

One has to wonder from where comes the sense that one finds in Kanehara's works—it is similar to that of her 2011 *Mazaazu* (Mothers) in this regard—of the oppressive atmosphere of young Japanese housewives and mothers (*mamatomo sekai*).[23] They have married, have had children, yet the children are still small and need constant attention: this is the entire world for these women still in their early thirties. Whether one is oneself a mother or not, one knows mothers like these, comes to feel that one has had these experiences as well. This may be because this fictional world so closely resembles the world of young Japanese housewives and mothers (*mamatomo sekai*) outside of the fiction; it is a particularly *Japanese* version of female society, one that has colored the experience of society that we Japanese readers have experienced from our earliest school days.

Since the disasters we have become accustomed to the phrase "mother and child evacuation" (*boshi hinan*). In families where the children are still small and the father's job makes it impossible for him to move, the mother and children alone move as far from ground zero as possible to avoid the risk of radiation exposure. Some move overseas. Some end up divorced.

Even so, it is not as though all mothers live in fear of radiation; indeed, many mothers decided early on not to give it any concern. Whether there will even be any ill effects of radiation is unknowable; whether one should flee, or whether there will be negative effects if one stays, are questions that, even six years on (at the time of this writing; three years at the time of Kanehara's writing), have no answers. Those who are cautious and concerned about radiation over time project the appearance that they have become less cautious. They may drink only bottled water, for example, or have foodstuffs shipped from Kyushu, but they do not share this information with others. When they encounter others as concerned about radiation as they are, it is no surprise that strong bonds arise among them.

Motazaru mono takes the "mother and child evacuation" (*boshi hinan*) prompted by the nuclear meltdown as its center and narrates the discord that arises amid interpersonal relations around issues of radiation. Four loosely connected individuals—"Shu" (Yasuda Shūto), "Chi-zu" (Chizuru), "eri" (Erina, her nickname always appears in lowercase), and Akari—appear in this order as the main characters of individual sections of the work. Yasuda Shūto, who goes by Shu, is a graphic designer who has been unable to work following the disasters. He achieved fame as a young man and achieved a sense of control that he could move the world according to his own ideas. But with the radiation that descended on Tokyo, he recognized his powerlessness and that sense of control evaporated. Further, he grew desperate to protect his wife and young daughter and urged them to evacuate without him, actions that only made her angry. The result was divorce.

He relates all this to his friend Chizuru (Chi-zu), who is living overseas because of her husband's work transfer. Chi-zu is also a full-time housewife; surely this is one reason she sees Shu's self-centeredness so clearly. She berates him: Why wouldn't you evacuate together? How heartless, telling your wife to take your newborn in her arms and move to an area where she knows no one and has no support systems.[24] The one partner's over-reaction to the radiation and the other's indifference to it have nearly equal merit in the complaints; there is nothing close to a good answer to either. The process of housewives and mothers evacuating in order to protect their children constructs a system that implies that mothers who do not evacuate with their children show they are unfit to be mothers; as a result, the maternal role is reinforced and the value of a woman herself is slighted.

Regardless of how high the divorce rate climbs, marriage remains a defining event in people's lives. Even so, when a woman decides to marry, perhaps after she gets married, at some point she will dream of an alternate life. Chi-zu discovers, right before her wedding, that she is pregnant with her future husband's child. In this same period, she has an affair with Shu; for Chi-zu, Shu "symbolizes" that alternate possibility. Fully aware that she can never make it reality, she continues holding on to the thought that she can flee to Shu's side at any point; this thought helps her get through the emptiness of her life. After her son Yūto is born—a name that makes one think of Shūto—her daily life becomes more stable, but such happiness does not last long: Yūto dies unexpectedly. The novel's depictions of a child going into convulsions and of Chi-zu carrying him to the hospital in her arms bring home to the reader the lonely helplessness that accompanies raising a child overseas. Even though she becomes accustomed to living in France and can converse with stallholders at the market, for example, in this most important of moments she is unable to call an ambulance or explain her child's symptoms. As she screams, "When can I see my son?" and "When can I speak with the doctor?" we read that "She realizes that the French she is now speaking contains mistakes of one verb conjugation, two articles, and the placement of adjectives."[25] When speaking a language one does not know well, the sounds one has uttered keep coming back, reminding one each time of one's mistakes. When she asks the doctor, "What percent chance will my son die?" and hears the response—"soixante pour cent" (60 percent)—the sense of being able to understand the words, even despite the hopelessness of that answer, allows her to regain her composure.[26] We feel the contradiction here even as it rings true.

After her son's death, Chi-zu meets Shu again and comes to realize that there is no way that she can cast everything aside and start a new life with him. All the more reason that Chi-zu's younger sister Erina, who had a child and then divorced; who, fearful of the radiation, evacuated to London with her child; and who hooked up with a young dancer and took off for New York has become an object of envy and contempt for Chi-zu as well as all the other women in her circle. She seems to have too easily attained all the things that they have given up on.

In London, Erina falls in with a young mother named Chloé and a young Belgian man named Youri who live nearby and live carefree, following their own desires. Erina knows that in Japan she would be treated as an odd duck, while here no one finds anything remarkable in her lifestyle. When Shu hears from Chi-zu that Erina has evacuated with her child, he texts her: "The England Lifestyle! You have my support!" but in fact it is Erina, having evacuated of her own accord, who gives encouragement to Shu. His interactions with Erina set him back on the path to being able to get back to work.

Whether at school or at home, Erina has never felt that she belonged. One might conclude that this simply highlights the impulses toward homogeneity within Japanese culture, tendencies only strengthened when the issues of radiation are added to the mix. But the final story in the work, Akari's, smashes such simplistic configurations. While Shu, Chi-zu, and eri[27] are referred to throughout by these abbreviations that are their internet account login, that is, romanized, names, Akari is the sole character whose name is written in Sino-Japanese characters. This is entirely appropriate as she lives in a thoroughly "Japanese" environment. Akari appears fully satisfied playing the part of the wife in what she imagines to be the perfect family. However, when her husband's posting in London comes to an end and they return to Japan and to the house that they have had built in order to live together with her husband's parents, she finds that her brother-in-law and his wife have occupied the part of the house meant for Akari and her husband. Further, her sister-in-law has put up "gross" (*kimochi warui*) posters of *otaku* idols; Akari feels that her children's rooms have been defiled. She continues to uphold the standards of a good daughter-in-law, but she also works toward evicting her brother-in-law and his wife. Even as readers we are driven to exasperation by their dilly-dallying, eventually coming to feel that this is the biggest unresolved issue: rather than radiation and everything else, this piece of household management is the most weighty matter for Akari to deal with. In short, this novel is very far from insisting that evacuation is the right response to the situation.

There is no one, in the end, who, in the words of the title, "cannot hold onto others." To throw away everything, things and people we might hold, to discard all, completely and thoroughly, and then start over, is among the most difficult things to do. This may be commonsense, yet these stories bring a depth to this that we cannot look away from.

RECONSTRUCTION AND PRESSURE TO CONFORM: YOSHIMURA MAN'ICHI'S *BOLLARD SYNDROME*

According to the *Tokyo Shimbun*, in April 1, 2017, the government enacted a large-scale lifting of evacuation orders. The government discontinued the compensation payments of 100,000 yen per month to all except the 24,000 people in "hard to return to" areas where radiation levels are still too high.[28] According to the Reconstruction Agency, there were 81,866 evacuees as of October 12, meaning that almost 57,000 people had evacuated at their own expense. In other words, the government is pressuring people to return to areas of high radiation by eliminating financial support. This is the reality six years after the nuclear accident.

In Yoshimura Man'ichi's *Borādobyō* (Bollard Syndrome, 2014),[29] the town of Umizuka is in the midst of reconstruction, a place where, for unspecified reasons, "We had given up on any chance that we might live there again," and a place that people returned to eight years earlier following a long evacuation. Many residents had died in the meantime. A banner proclaiming "Umizuka: the first town to exceed the safety standards" hangs at the city hall. The town had "changed completely" in those eight years; it is now, finally, "rebuilt."[30] The main industry of the town appears to be Mitsuba Chemical: all the fathers in the town work there. The narrator of the story is Ōguri Kyōko, a fifth grader who returned to Umizuka at age three. We will only find out much later that we are reading the diary of a woman now in her thirties. The structure of the entire novel depends on this "unreliable narrator." Up until about the halfway point of the book, Ōguri Kyōko appears to be a child who does not get on well at school and who does things her own way. Furthermore, by that point the reader has come to suspect that there is something odd about her.

While the vegetables, meat, rice, and everything else for sale at the supermarket carry stickers such as "safe," "passed food inspection," and "guaranteed safe," Kyōko's mother feeds her daughter cup noodles and imported canned goods, food that is "safe," if not entirely healthy. She buys vegetables and meat, saying she will donate them to the local "facility," but in reality she throws them out. The story is constructed in ways that lead the reader to think there is something strange about the mother as well.[31]

Her classmates in the town keep dying, one after another, for unknown reasons. At school they teach the children about their "ties" to Umizuka. This word is clearly meant to echo the postdisaster catchphrase "bonds" (*kizuna*), which was used to promote solidarity. When the townspeople participate in the neighborhood cleanup day, they are provided a lunch bowl of fish atop rice. Kyōko does not like raw fish, but her mother orders her to eat it all, because the townspeople keep a close watch on everyone's activities. Avoiding contaminated food is deemed counter to the spirit of "kizuna" and strictly avoided. This kind of behavior is familiar to us from campaigns following the disasters urging us to "support [affected regions] by eating [their products]" in the name of "kizuna." "Support by eating" campaigns were built on the condition that one should not question whether those foodstuffs were safe or not.

At one point the citizens, entranced, want to sing the "Umizuka Praise Song." Even though Kyōko continually thinks "Umizuka citizens are strange," she suddenly claims to be "in tune with Umizuka."[32] Yet right after this she is removed and confined. Her claims to be like everyone else were lies in hopes to prove she was normal.

At novel's end, a defiant Kyōko has begun to interrogate all that she believed true of those who were isolated, and at this point the reader comes to understand the town's secret. Those children "born with poison in their systems" not only died young, but were born with faces and bodies not "normal."[33] There are a number of scenes of elementary school-aged Kyōko drawing portraits of her classmates. The more the portrait actually looks like a given girl, the angrier she becomes. Kyōko concludes, "As I was drawing the pictures, I began to feel a sense that I had best draw her realistically, and surely that is the reason she got so angry with me."[34] This suggests that realistic portraits made something too apparent.

Kyōko is repeatedly "strictly forbidden" by her mother to "draw pictures of your friends." In Kyōko's eyes this denies the world "as she sees it."[35] Thus, when her friend Ken draws her portrait, she realizes that "that picture is completely different from all others. . . . And of course, the world he drew was the way it should be, it is just as we see it. It was a decisive moment" for her. She is thrilled that the world she sees is shared.[36] The novel does not describe what they look like, but at the end of the novel we learn that Kyōko's pet rabbit is "missing its front legs," suggesting that all of this has to do with physical deformities:

I am grateful that there is no mirror in my room. My face and body were quite awful. Please look at this arm, this stomach. They are nearly the same as Hiroko's.[. . .] We were all born with this poison in our systems. Children throughout the entire nation must also have come to be like this. So I have to believe that the world that I see is the actual world. My pet rabbit, Uuchan, has no front legs.[37]

The narrator attributes these deformities to the fact that "We were all born with this poison in our systems." The novel does not identify what this poison or toxin is, but the source may be the "Mitsuba Chemical industrial complex" in the area near the shoreline. We read that "many of Umizika's residents work there" and it would seem to be the town's main industry.[38] The novel says nothing about the cause of the disaster, which clearly was not radiation damage, but Umizuka was once a designated disaster area, formerly contaminated. But, given that operations have not ceased at Mitsuba Chemical, we are led to think of the damage from nuclear accidents. Alternatively, if we imagine the sea being contaminated by wastewater from a factory, we are reminded of the Minamata disaster. Indeed, one can read into the "poison" of this story the entire history of public pollution—radiation included—since the industrial revolution.

What is problematized here is not that there are physical deformities caused by this "poison," but rather the unified societal pressure to act as though there are no deformities and to participate in this desperate cover-up:

> The myth that Umizuka alone was spared any effects of the disaster, that only the buildings were shattered, that vegetables and meat and fish were all safe, and that Umizuka's citizens were healthy, was a delusional myth that the town put out there as they blindly rushed forward.
> [. . .]
> No doubt not only Umizuka, but it's like the entire nation is acting as though none of it had ever happened. When you think about the scale of this, maybe the entire world was all in on it, participating in this charade.[39]

Umizuka desperately covers up the contamination and enforces "conformity."[40] It is here that the narrative world joins, in one fell swoop, with Japanese society after the nuclear accident in March 2011. The narrator's father "was involved in some kind of opposition protests" and "arrested."[41] That is why the narrator and her mother are under continuous surveillance. Further, for whatever reason, Kyōko, at the culmination of her forcible isolation, is to be disappeared. Defiant, she demands, "Are you going to incinerate me in Mitsuba Chemical's furnace?"[42] This narrative of removal and elimination of opposition forces is one also connected to a history of a society that can, as in the Holocaust, separate and exterminate people at whim.

The elementary school student narrates this story right up to the chilling twist of a plot reveal at the end. Within this skillful novelistic structure a slightly creepy present is drawn. What is also made very clear here, and what is uncomfortable for us, are the variety of physical deformities resulting from the disaster. Her questions—"I don't know why, but I have not been quite complete ever since birth. Take a look here, at this body. Who did this? All of it, is this not on account of Umizuka?"[43]—suggests how single-mindedly Umizuka has tried to conceal things. So, in the same way that Kyōko insisted on drawing realistic portraits, the deformities also appear in the faces. That is why, at the very end of the novel, Kyōko cries out, "Even with a face like this you can see me as a beautiful person, can't you? Well then, come give me a fuck, you damn cowards."[44] Everyone knows about these malformed bodies, yet they keep reinforcing the peer pressure with repeated platitudes—"so bright and beautiful you are, you all look just like dolls!" Kyōko throws her question like a curse at that peer pressure. This challenge—"then fuck me you cowards"—is aimed at those who intend to hide everything away, to those insisting, in the face of everything, that all are in normal health. We also come to understand that the premise for this story and these exchanges is that children are being born with deformities caused by the contamination.[45] More precisely, when we think at whom this "fuck me" is flung, we find that even in this narrative it is the men who manage women's bodies. Indeed, it is precisely because these births that yield deformed bodies are also managed by men that they must suppress that reality.

The result of all this is that this peer pressure polices opposing opinions as well; it puts a stop to thinking on one's own, crushes any demonstrations or other oppositional activities. If such a thing is possible, then we may have already been brought into "alignment"—and then, with such "alignment," minority voices all get drowned out. Minorities are those outside of what society deems to be our future direction; postdisaster literature is, once again, that which informs us about this.

A TALE OF EXCLUSION: TSUSHIMA YŪKO'S LAST NOVELS

Three posthumous novels appeared after Tsushima Yūko's death on November 18, 2016: *Jakka Dofunī: Umi no kioku no monogatari* (Jakka Dofunī: A Story in Remembrance of the Sea), *Hangenki o iwatte* (Commemorating Half-life), and *Kari no jidai* (The Age of Hunting). They were advertised on the book covers as "posthumous work," "last writing," and "last long novel," respectively.[46] Counting her book of essays, *Yume no uta kara* (Songs of Dreams), four books were released after her death.

Tsushima Yūko was one of the earliest and most vociferous of authors responding to the 2011 nuclear meltdowns and ensuing radioactive contamination. Beginning with her novel *Yamaneko dōmu* (Mountain Cat Dome, 2013), everything she wrote takes the nuclear accident as a historical event.[47] Into that we can read the strength of her conviction that we must not act as though the disaster never happened.

Hangenki wo iwatte is a collection of three very different stories. The title story appeared originally in *Gunzō* (March, 2016) in a special issue titled "The World Thirty Years Later: The Literary Imagination." Thirty years is the half-life of cesium 137. The term "half-life" itself is curious: sheer volume is one thing, but the fact is that we do not really understand what it means to halve. We hear about cesium this and cesium that, and there is talk of measurements in *sieverts* and *becquerels*, but at the end of the day we do not know which numerical values correspond to danger. Further, in this tale, set thirty years in the future, there is another earthquake and another meltdown, and "new radioactive substances are scattered about," meaning this half-life is nothing to celebrate.[48] In other words, we can assume that such accidents will continue to happen, and when sufficient time passes, we will reach the half-life, briefly welcome it, and stage events in commemoration.

In Tsushima's story, the older female protagonist flees her home close to the accident and lives in a high-rise apartment building for evacuees. Residents use the half-life anniversary as an occasion to go back to see their hometowns. Since radiation is invisible, no one expects any changes.

What follows in the story is that all the warning signs and dangers that have gushed forth in the last five years have now been moved and enumerated into a future world. These signs outline the unease that all of us feel in our present moment, all that we try to overlook. But this novel—well, it outlines our present, doesn't it? This novel relentlessly exposes the filthy and the ugly of society; while we may resent Tsushima for pointing out our faults, the fact is, this is reality.

In the novel, we read that about the same time as a new nuclear accident occurs, an organization of patriotic youth called ASD is formed to support the dictatorial government. Now, the name ASD is almost ridiculous, given how it calls to mind AKB, the Japanese idol girls' musical pop group; nonetheless, ASD is tasked "with the role of hounding out antisocial types."[49] When the young men and women of ASD reach the age of eighteen, they join the national defense force, even though it is unlikely that Japan would ever be at war. There would be no need, for Japan could easily be destroyed in an instant: it would only take a single missile visiting one of the nuclear power plants that Japan insists on running. Nevertheless, the government asserts that "The gods have bequeathed to us these righteous principles and we will not waver. No matter the country, we will pursue our enemies."[50] Given our present moment, where the 2015 Japanese military legislation (*Anpō Hōsei*) is being touted to promote Peace and Security when it is in fact legislation for engaging in war, there is nothing funny in this. Indeed, whether or not this is a possible scenario, it captures the mood fostered by the current [Abe] administration. Further still, we read that "the current administration was born from the lull following the Olympic frenzy"; again, whether such a thing is in fact possible is beside the point, yet we find it describes the contemporary mood of Olympics and belligerent nationalism cultivated by the "current administration."[51]

Furthermore, we are unable to laugh when we find that enlisting in the ASD is limited to pure Japanese (*Yamatojin*) alone. Not only is anyone from the Tohoku area refused membership, so is anyone with Ainu, Okinawa, or Korean lineage; indeed, they are actively "excluded" (*haijō*). In the same way that the massacre of Koreans after the 1923 Great Kantō Earthquake emerged from mass panic and mob violence, we saw history repeated after the Great Eastern Japan Earthquake Disaster, as hate speech raised its head and blatant discrimination walked the streets. This is not just a Japanese problem: we see exclusionism across the globe as people come face to face with financial crises and terrorist acts. We read further here that "The number of Tohoku people far exceeds that of the Yamatojin, meaning we will soon run out of room to 'hospitalize' them; when we arrest them, we should send them straight to special 'shower rooms'."[52] We recoil violently when Auschwitz is invoked to tell a tale of discrimination against those from Tohoku. Yet history teaches that human savagery will always burst forth, even if not to this monstrous degree. In the story, government policy allows those discriminated against to live in contaminated areas and to replace the Yamatojin as workers at the accident site. To a certain extent even now, dangerous work at the Fukushima Daiichi accident site is reliant on this very structure of inequality, because reliant on workers with few choices. In other words, even if we consider nuclear cleanup a rather mild poison, is it that different from sending them all off to the "showers"?[53]

There is here a subplot about an ill-fated love story between a Tohoku boy and Yamato girl, at the conclusion of which, after they have run away, the story line is tied together when she is given an operation to terminate her pregnancy. Tsushima had already pursued this story line in her 2011 story "Ashibune tonda" (The Reed Boat Sailed), a story set in Manchuria at the end of the Asia-Pacific war, and which traces the history of Harbin. The main character is of the same generation as the author; both were born during the war and experienced only the tail end of it, both seem to regret growing into adulthood without actual knowledge of wartime. This ties the story to the historical issue of women who were raped in the colonies (*gaichi*) and the government administered abortions they underwent upon their repatriation.

Tsushima's more recent short stories as well are linked together by this historical robust theme.[54]

Two other short stories are collected in the *Hangenki wo iwatte* collection: "Nyū yōku, Nyū yōku" (New York, New York) and "Ōtobai, arui wa yume no tezawari" (Motorcycle, or the Feel of Dreams). Both feature female protagonists who are divorced and living alone. This aspect is particularly relevant in the latter story, which consists of exhilarating episodes about a woman who buys a motorcycle and drives it all over a South Sea island in France's *outre-mer*. The intimate narrative voices of these women who embrace difficulty represent a condensed version of another side of this author.

Be that as it may, the disturbing "ASD" group which allows only "pure Japanese" youth to join described in *Hangenki wo iwatte* resembles Nazi Germany's Hitler Youth. But it also, at the same time, closely resembles the discrimination against immigrants and foreign nationals that runs through contemporary Japanese society. The Hitler Youth visited Japan in 1938 and received an enthusiastic welcome, which even included the song "Banzai Hitler Youth," with lyrics written by poet Kitahara Hakushū. Tsushima describes this event in *Kari no jidai*, where Emiko cannot forget memories of the rumors that followed her disabled brother Kōichirō: "They said that Kō-chan is 'unfit for life' (*futekikakusha*). God, I've had enough."[55] What, exactly, is so unsettling about this? Why can one feel that even one's own body is dangerous? What gradually becomes clear as the story progresses is a background history of her uncle Hajime who, while still a teenager, went off to see the Hitler Youth when they came to Yamanashi Prefecture, where he was hopelessly smitten by the blond-haired, blue-eyed youth. Uncle Eiichirō was also smitten with the scientific techniques of nuclear power. Tsushima shows that along with the postwar novels and stories featuring military deployments and battlefield deaths there are many other stories to be told. She suggests with this novel that we may still be entwined with that era's fascination with eugenics and nuclear power.

Jakka Dofunī: Umi no kioku no monogatari (2016) is also a story with persecution as its theme. Within a narrative of young Christian men and women who fled oppression and crossed over to Macao in the seventeenth century, we find connections to the Ainu, Christians, and *hibakusha*. Many people feel inferior because of their origins; Tsushima Yūko's work tracks close to these minorities and exposes the deceit of a society that turns a blind eye.

NOTES

1. Numata Shinsuke, *Eiri*, *Bungakukai* 71, no. 5 (May 2017): 9–37. Reprinted as *Eiri* (Tokyo: Bungei Shunjū, 2017). All citations come from this edition.

2. Prize committee member Takagi Nobuko explained at the award press conference that Numata's novel received the Prize because it described the 2011 triple disasters. She also noted that its merits and defects were hotly debated by the selection committee members and that "we got into heated argument" over the issue. In her own critical evaluation of the winning work, Takagi wrote: "It was as if something had come and flayed the layer covering up the thinking that was getting in the way. The novel describes a predestined outcome, at the conclusion of which human interiority collapses. In the same ways that the Tohoku disasters had, this novel's writing exposed, for both humankind and nature alike, this predestined outcome." Takahashi Nobuko, "Utsukushikumo ozomashii," *Bungei Shunjū* 95, no. 9 (September 2017): 384.

In the same vein, Anne Bayard-Sakai has pointed out that awarding the prize to this work brought the "authority" of the Akutagawa Prize to bear and confirmed that a new genre of "postdisaster literature" (or perhaps "disaster literature" more generally) does now, in fact, exist: Anne Bayard-Sakai, "Writing by Circumventing the Unrepresentable: The Case of Post March 11 Literature" (conference presentation, "Japanese Studies after 3.11," January 9–11, 2017, Leipzig University, in coordination with the International Research Center for Japanese Studies). She also pointed out that the question of whether or not this novel describes disaster has itself become a point of contention, and that determining this will be an issue decided in future critical analyses.

Critic Sasaki Atsushi positioned the novel by writing, "This is a splendid example of a 'fishing novel.' It is also a novel of an unfathomable (*fukashigi*) friendship. It is also a twisted, albeit earnest, approach to a 'postdisaster novel'" (*Nihon Keizai Shinbun*, August 19, 2017).

3. Numata, *Eiri*, 6.
4. Numata, *Eiri*, 8.
5. Numata, *Eiri*, 15.
6. Concerning the narration of this novel, Shimada Masahiko, as one of the Akutagawa Prize judges, had this to say in his remarks: "I wonder if he was also being careful about the narrow-mindedness of the countryside. The narrator is deliberate in his choice of words at the same time as he is confronting his own budding desires": Shimada Masahiko, "Shō wa kekkyoku unshidai" (In the end, the prize is a matter of luck), *Bungei shunjū* (September 2017): 388.
7. Numata, *Eiri*, 51–52.
8. Abdellatif Kechiche's film *Blue Is the Warmest Color* (2013), which describes lesbian love and reflects on the difficulties in being open, or not, about a homosexual relationship, as well as on the class differences that prompt the eventual breakup, has resonances with *Eiri*.
9. Numata, *Eiri*, 93, 91.
10. Numata, *Eiri*, 27.
11. Numata, *Eiri*, 40.
12. Numata, *Eiri*, 35.
13. Numata, *Eiri*, 79.
14. Numata, *Eiri*, 81–82.

15. Kakiya Miyū, *Hinanjo* (Shinchōsha, 2014). Reprinted as *Onnatachi no hinanjo* (Shinchō bunkō) in 2017. All citations from the 2014 version.
16. Kakiya, *Hinanjo*, 141.
17. Kakiya, *Hinanjo*, 141.
18. Kakiya, *Hinanjo*, 143.
19. He is actually quoted as saying, "When you're a star they let you do it. You can do anything.... Grab them by the pussy. You can do anything": "Trump Was Recorded in 2005 Bragging About Grabbing Women 'by the Pussy,'" Slate, accessed September 25, 2019, http://www.slate.com/blogs/the_slatest/2016/10/07/donald_trump_2005_tape_i_grab_women_by_the_pussy.html/.—Trans.
20. Currently (September 29, 2017) the number stands at 84,000.
21. See Jeffrey Angles's translation of Tawada's story at Words Without Borders, January 23, 2021, https://www.wordswithoutborders.org/article/the-far-shore.—Trans.
22. Kanehara Hitomi, "Motazaru mono," *Subaru* 37, no. 1 (January 2015): 82–189, 201–232. Reprinted as *Motazaru mono* (Tokyo: Shūesha, 2015). Citations are from this version.
23. The story first appeared in serialization in *Shinchō* (January, 2010–March, 2011 [lacking October, 2010]), later reprinted as a book (Tokyo: Shinchō bunko, 2014).
24. Kanehara, "Motazaru mono," 56.
25. Kanehara, "Motazaru mono," 101.
26. Kanehara, "Motazaru mono," 105.
27. As a login name "eri" always appears in romanized lowercase letters. As "Erina" it is written in *katakana*. Thus, in Japanese there is no confusion about capitalization.—Trans.
28. See the "Kochira tokuhōbu" section in the October 20, 2017, edition.
29. Yoshimura Man'ichi, *Borādobyō*, *Bungakkai* 68, no. 1 (January 2014): 10–79; reprints *Borādobyō* (Tokyo: Bengeishunjū, 2014; Bunshu bunko, 2017).
30. Yoshimura, *Borādobyō*, 76.
31. Yoshimura, *Borādobyō*, 39.
32. Yoshimura, *Borādobyō*, 159–60.
33. Yoshimura, *Borādobyō*, 180.
34. Yoshimura, *Borādobyō*, 108.
35. Yoshimura, *Borādobyō*, 141.
36. Yoshimura, *Borādobyō*, 115.
37. Yoshimura, *Borādobyō*, 180.
38. Yoshimura, *Borādobyō*, 50.
39. Yoshimura, *Borādobyō*, 181.
40. Yoshimura, *Borādobyō*, 160.
41. Yoshimura, *Borādobyō*, 176.
42. Yoshimura, *Borādobyō*, 182.
43. Yoshimura, *Borādobyō*, 175–76.
44. Yoshimura, *Borādobyō*, 182.
45. In Kawakami Hiromi's *Ōkina tori ni sarawarenai yō* (Tokyo: Kodansha, 2016) she describes a future of genetic abnormalities caused by the "dispersion of

radioactive particles." The work is a collection of fourteen related stories. One of the characters from story three reappears in story four, creating a loose connection that builds toward a larger overarching, interrelated story. Story one describes a future in which humans have lost their reproductive abilities and are made in a factory using genetic material from various animals. But as you read further, you realize that humanity has already become extinct. The cause for this appears in story six: "the nonstop recklessness of wars, then terrorism, and then the dispersal of toxic materials, on and on" (94). Realizing they were on the verge of extinction, the humans constructed a new system to extend the human race. Using clones for duplication and reproduction has produced a degenerated humankind able to live on for some thousands of years. This is a world where clones, equipped with artificial intelligence, are outfitted as "mothers" in order to watch over children. Those who can still have sex are prized, but this just hastens them down the road toward the destruction of humanness. Humans "give birth to things. But those things destroy far more than they birth" (258). The humans are on the path of declining numbers, and in the final story, the last human clones, Eri and Rema, are the sole survivors. Eri puts together a plan for reviving the cloned humans originally constructed from animals and creates an ideal village. That village is the world of story number one. In the end, the collection comes full-circle when the formerly independent story number one connects to the final story. Given that when nuclear accidents occur we fear genetic and reproductive damage from the radioactive contamination, this is not an impossible future. We must take Rema's words as a prayer for us from the future: "You humans, no matter when you are living in this world, I pray that you will be able, somehow or another, to figure out a way to save yourselves" (340).

46. For my thoughts on Tsushima's work, see Kimura Saeko, "Kotoba no yurikago in yurarete: *Jakka Dofunī: Umi no kioku no monogatari* o yomu," in Kawade Shōbo, *Tsushima Yūko no sekai—ochi no kioku, inochi no umi* (Tokyo: Kawade Shōbo, 2017). Reprinted in Inoue Takashi, ed., *Tsushima Yūko no sekai*, 74–99 (Tokyo: Suiseisha, 2017).

47. Tsushima Yūko, *Yamaneko dōmu*, *Gunzō* 68, no. 1 (January, 2013): 7–167. Reprinted as *Yamaneko dōmu*. Tokyo: Kodansha bungei bunko, 2017.

48. Tsushima Yūko, *Hangenki wo iwatte* (Tokyo: Kodansha, 2016), 80.

49. Tsushima, *Hangenki wo iwatte*, 92.

50. Tsushima, *Hangenki wo iwatte*, 94.

51. Tsushima, *Hangenki wo iwatte*, 104.

52. Tsushima, *Hangenki wo iwatte*, 96.

53. Tsushima, *Hangenki wo iwatte*, 68.

54. I am thinking here of works such as *Kari no jidai* [An age of Hunting] (Tokyo: Bungei shunju, 2016) and *Yamaneko Dōmu* [Mountain Cat Dome] (Tokyo: Kodansha, 2013).

55. Tsushima, *Kari no jidai*, 248.

Chapter 2

The Problem of "Fukushima"

I had the opportunity to attend the Japanese-language performance of Elfriede Jelinek's play *Kein Licht* (No Light) on October 13, 2014. Jelinek weaves a story about irradiated corpses left behind in the exclusion zone.

> The dead radiate light—beams. They cannot reach us with words. We cannot reach out in conversation to them. I lend you my sound so that you can get by, not needing to hear your own sound. That is what you desire after all. You hope that at the end, the end of the end, someone will break in and snatch your sounds away from you. Your sounds seem not to flow as you want, right? Do you think that my sounds might reach you? I am no more than second fiddle. I am travelling with you, but I do not yet see where to, so I continue, going faster and with ever greater effort.
>
> We are ourselves light—sending out beams. Please imagine it! Just as I had told you! We will not be heard at that time either, we are less than inaudible, should there such a thing be possible. But yes, we are ourselves light—sending out beams. We radiate a blueish light! Pretty amazing, don't you think? . . .
>
> The prosperous ones will poison you, contaminate you, defile you with radiation, will not steal from you. No, exactly the opposite, the prosperous have bestowed something upon you. They have bestowed you with light. But before long you will be dependent on them. Exactly! You are light—sending out beams! You yourselves will come to bestow light, just as a mother provides milk![1]

Light is often used as a metaphor for radiation in postdisaster fiction. We see this for example in Kobayashi Erika's *Madamu kyurī to chōshoku wo* (Breakfast with Madame Curie, 2014) and *Hikari no kodomo 1, 2* (Children of Light 1, 2, 2013, 2016).[2] Jelinek, however, titled her work *Kein Licht* and moves the story using the metaphor of sound for radioactive material. Given the fact that radiation is imperceptible to human eyes we have come to recognize its presence through the beeping of the Geiger counter. Jelinek brings out a violin, and the sound from squeaking strings does indeed bring to mind the sound of a Geiger counter.

In this production of *Kein Licht* by the theatrical troupe Chiten, members of the chorus are lying in the orchestra pit, only their bare feet visible on the stage, their voices alone creating sound. The stage looks like the bottom of a dark body of water with bare feet sticking out; body parts without faces also call to mind the dead. All the lines are spoken with strange pauses and intonations so that the audience is always a half-step behind in understanding the words and sentences. The resulting delay effect feels very much like listening to a foreign language. Words never coalesce into paragraphs, words do not proceed smoothly; it feels at times as though individual words are jumping out at the audience. The individual words that one manages to catch, one by one, are weighty; it becomes clear that the issues related to Fukushima since 2011 are being flung about: "scheduled power outages and information control," "radioactive particles," and, more ominously "our lives too will not reach their half-lives."[3] Then at the end of the performance, just when the audience gets used to these unnatural voices and sounds, there suddenly intrudes a group of words whose meanings are all too clear:

> Some people are sending their precious children overseas to evacuate. I ask you not to stop them. They can easily go over your heads; they will go and you can be sure that they will be aided in those overseas countries! . . . They are right! It is clear that they are doing the correct thing. They are doing the only right thing! Those who don't do the right thing at the right time will be dead. . . . [W]e are unable to smell radiation even when it contacts our skin. Sure, you can tweet all you want, but even better than that, the best possible thing in fact, is to get out of here, to evacuate to a safe place. Safety is the one and only exit available in this era. Safety first, I say. Only safety has any long-term use. Safety must continue at all costs, if you can actually find it, that is.[4]

I flinched at the directness of this work. I doubted it could be performed in Fukushima. It seared my brain. I had to wonder why. Is it because the name associated with the malfunctioning systems of the Fukushima Daiichi Nuclear Power Plant and the nuclear explosions that caused its collapse is the name of the actual place that is Fukushima? Is it because so many of the towns and villages in the vicinity of the plant have become exclusion zones, places now off limits to the residents—is that my issue here? Is my reaction motivated by concern for the feelings of those local people who are even now living in that prefecture?

The fact is, the situation of pollution from radiation and radioactive materials is not Fukushima's issue alone, for there has been serious damage outside the prefecture too. It is unquestionably not an issue reserved for "Fukushima." Which leads us to ask, what then is different between the radioactive hotspots in other prefectures and those in Fukushima prefecture? In sum, the issue comes down to this: who will be designated a victim (*hisaisha*), and where do we draw the borders of disaster (*hisai*)? From the outset, of course, there were no clear boundaries; even so, at the time of this writing—September 2017—twenty millisieverts per year of accumulated radiation exposure is used as the standard to designate the various evacuation and repatriation zones as well as to determine compensation payments.[5] Are these various boundaries and zones sufficient means for determining who is a victim?

Just as the 1986 accident at the Chernobyl nuclear power plant has come to be known as "Chernobyl," so too the accident at the Fukushima Daiichi Nuclear Power Plant has come to be known around the world as "Fukushima." Because of this, even though some areas within the prefecture were deemed evacuation zones while others were deemed safe, the entire prefecture has been saddled with the image of—and is therefore thought of as—a disaster area. So, if such close consideration is applied to the entire prefecture of Fukushima, we will soon find that the factor determining victimhood will be determined by whether one lives now or has ever lived in the prefecture; that will be the sole basis for judgment. But to say that the problem of "Fukushima" is one for "Fukushima Prefecture" alone—that is a complete mistake. In the same way that talk of "Chernobyl" cannot be absent from international conversations, discussion of "Fukushima" must also occur at international levels. In that context we see just how impressive is Jelinek's achievement: the experience was one that she had to speak about because her homeland of Austria was also a disaster area after Chernobyl.

According to translator Hayashi Tatsuki's afterword to the Japanese translation of this play, Jelinek wrote *Kein Licht* in late August 2011, right after the disaster, and it was performed on September 19 of that same year. She made it available to the public on her website on December 21, 2011. To criticize its explosive power as "indiscreet" or "unscrupulous" [*fukinshin*] is unacceptable. Kurabayashi Yasushi, for example, notes how works that plainly described these disasters came to be labeled "indiscreet" in the art world.[6] Art is not something that should be operating from within such constraints.

Following the disasters, Adorno's famous line "To write poetry after Auschwitz is barbaric" has been bandied about where silence would have been best.[7] For example, Asada Akira had the following to say in a *taidan* with Azuma Hiroki:

From the start, art—and given today's topic, thought (*shisō*) as well—is not something that has immediate efficacy. Indeed, it is only later, after the shock of the moment that, and often through quite indirect ways, the disasters can be expressed. It is best if we just wait quietly for a time and absorb the reality of the situation. Oddly, there is no need to be rushed or agitated, it seems to me. That's the reason that I felt such a strong, consistent sense of unease when all at once these artists and intellectuals (*bunkajin*) began talking about the disasters. My knowledge is not very broad, but I thought that the best response came from the Deleuzian philosopher Higaki Tatsuya, who said that, since philosophers are of no use in times like these, "We should just go take a nap."[8] Now, he said this but he also went and wrote an essay, which makes him inconsistent in the end. Be that as it may, I did in fact take a nap, and nothing more. . . . Nonetheless, Mallarmé's "I am completely dead" launched modern poetry; then Adorno told us that "to write poetry after Auschwitz is barbaric"; after which people like Celan, in order to somehow or another keep poetry alive, produced contemporary poetry. . . . This is an extreme example, but all those people, novelists and other literary types blithely going on about how the novels that had been impossible to continue writing were now writeable following the disasters—even though none needed to take a self-deprecating stance with "making a living off of other peoples' misfortune is the writer's craft" phrases—all started making pronouncements right away. I was, frankly, aghast. I have long wondered why they cannot even manage to keep their mouths shut, even for a little bit.[9]

Nonetheless, even after Auschwitz, poetry continued to be written and literature is definitely not dead—there can be no doubt that this was obvious to Jelinek in Austria, writing in German. Looking back from our present, we see that assertions like those above, that the works are slapdash and powerless, simply miss the mark: Jelinek's work remains powerful. Indeed, as the shock of those first days of the disasters grows dim, postdisaster literature has only grown weightier. The fact is that, even now, many works worthy of critical attention continue to appear.

According to Taki Kōji, Adorno revised the proclamation we encountered above: "Perennial suffering has as much right to expression as a tortured man has to scream; hence it may have been wrong to say that 'after Auschwitz you could no longer write poems'."[10] Taki goes on to say: "Of all the various ways that human existence has been considered, I am in agreement that it cannot continue as it has. But I cannot agree with Adorno's 'to write poetry after Auschwitz is barbaric.' In truth, in our situation it is only by writing poetry that we can prevail."[11] After discussing how a genocide like Auschwitz comes to be born almost by necessity out of modern society's management of human life, Taki continues:

> In fact, even now, were you to visit Auschwitz, or were you to go and see the Hiroshima Peace Memorial Museum, there is an unbridgeable gulf between

what can be observed and what actually occurred there. We can employ our imaginations, but as far as what happened in those gas chambers, as far as what it was like under that moment's flash of light and heat and raging wind, we cannot represent it. Even so, I find it hard to agree with the argument that only those who experienced war can understand it, because we can study history, we can think on its meanings. That is what it means to live in the present with history.[12]

In other words, our discussions of "Fukushima" will, and must, bring with them the history of "Fukushima." In that sense "Fukushima" is, just as "Chernobyl" was or should have been, a matter of concern shared by the entire world: it is an object of concern for world literature.[13] All the more reason that what "Fukushima" evokes links not only to "Hiroshima" and "Nagasaki" but also to the Holocaust and to Minamata.[14] Further, 3.11 establishes links to 9.11.[15]

"FUKUSHIMA" AS A NUCLEAR RADIOACTIVE DISASTER

Discussion of nuclear radiation damage has only become more difficult. Mothers who fear radioactive harm are ostracized by other mothers who have decided to not think about it. This is dramatized in films such as Sono Sion's *Kibō no kuni* (*Land of Hope*, 2012) and Uchida Nobuteru's *Odayaka na nichijō* (The Tranquil Everyday, 2012). Those who have decided to self-evacuate have been ridiculed as having "irradiated brains" (*hōshanō* 放射脳) by employing a homophone for radioactivity (*hōshanō* 放射能); they are criticized for having such excessive fear that it leads to mental breakdown. Even so, the reality is that areas not designated as evacuation regions also experience radiation damage. That fear may not be so irrational.

Two weeks after the explosion at the Fukushima Daiichi Nuclear Power Plant on March 23, radioactive particles were detected as far away as Tokyo's Kanamachi water purification plant. A warning against giving tap water to infants and children was then issued for certain areas.[16] On June 9, cesium was detected in the tea in Shizuoka, some three hundred kilometers to the south. The value registered at five times the normal amount, or over 500 becquerels per kilogram. On December 6, powdered milk baby formula intended for children nine months and older was found to have 30.8 becquerels of cesium per kilogram.[17] Even though it was below the unofficial limit of 200 becquerels per kilogram, the motivation for the producer, Meiji company, to offer free exchanges of formula is surely driven by hopes of regaining consumer trust by adhering to safety measures and as a means to address the mothers' concerns. The ingredients for powdered skim milk were all processed before the disaster and over half were imported from overseas. It would appear that the radioactive cesium in the atmosphere after the accident got mixed in during the drying process.[18] If that is the case, then it is not just the food we eat, but the air we breathe that poses danger. Further, the Meiji factory is located in Kasukabe in Saitama prefecture, significantly outside of any of the concentric circles marking official areas of danger.

Every time there are such reports, anxieties about radiation, particularly internal radiation, grow stronger. But unless one is in a government-designated evacuation area where federal funds are available, the ability to evacuate is dependent on personal resources. Safety is dependent on class. This means that we can say that the nuclear incident at Fukushima Daiichi was an event that, based on economic strength or the ability to gather information, and so on, divided those whose safety needs to be preserved and those whose doesn't. When we reflect that not everyone was in a position to evacuate, Jelinek's lines sound almost cruel: "Some people are evacuating their precious children overseas. Please don't stop them. They can easily go over your heads, you can be sure that they will be aided in those overseas countries!" Those able to "evacuate" their children overseas were, in fact, only those privileged enough to do so. Those who made the decision to evacuate even in the absence of an evacuation order are officially deemed "voluntary evacuees" (*jishuhinansha*). According to the *Nihon Keizai Shimbun* (Japan Economic Newspaper) of December 25, 2015, these voluntary evacuees were also provided temporary housing, but that support was scheduled to end late in 2016, to be replaced with rent subsidies aimed at low-income families and single mothers with children. The article also reports that voluntary evacuees from Fukushima and nearby number over 7,000 households or about 18,000 people.

The Ministry of Education, Culture, Sports, Science and Technology instituted a fact-finding survey in 2017 when it became increasingly clear that many of the children who evacuated from Fukushima were being bullied in their new schools.[19] For example, a schoolgirl who had evacuated to Niigata was called "contagion" at school. This seems likely to be because of a strong sense of aversion to radioactivity in society at large.[20]

Voluntary evacuation became a source of friction. If evacuation is, in Jelinek's words, "the sole correct thing" to do, why would voluntary evacuees get accused behind their backs of "fleeing"?[21] Might it be envy on the part of those who feel left behind, those who would have evacuated had they the means? Or perhaps it is resentment toward those with money, thinking only of themselves, somehow able to cheat the system? Or maybe it is from a sense of despair in a system where the value of life is weighed in economic terms and they are made to feel that no value is assigned to helping them. It can only be insulting, and difficult, for those householders who have chosen to stay where they are to have their holdings and way of life treated as "polluted."

This is precisely the reason that those discussing "pollution" and "safety" are always talking past each other. When people say that the radioactivity values are not that high in Fukushima, the "Fukushima" they are talking about excludes the ground zero of the Fukushima Daichi nuclear meltdown. They also exclude those areas around the plant designated "areas that are hard to return to." The only people in Fukushima who can lay claim to safety are those in areas where evacuation orders were not issued. Even so, people whose towns have completely disappeared, like Futaba and Ōkuma where the plant was sited, cannot make such claims. For them, their towns are, in particular, what is meant by "Fukushima."

The core of the problem is perhaps not the actual health effects of radioactive contamination. This argument that those who continue to live in these areas, or those who eat the food produced there, can do so because the radiation is not at levels so high that it is impossible to live, loses meaning on the single point that it is impossible for anyone to measure with any real precision the degree of radioactive harm. For both those who have decided that it is "safe" and for those who see "danger," they share the disturbing feeling that results from knowing that radiation is a fact yet a thing unseeable. It is unbearable that at every meal we must confront this foreboding and unfathomable anxiety. This sort of unfathomable anxiety then sends the pendulum in the other direction.

The issue here resides in the unfathomable anxiety. This is what "Fukushima" has bequeathed; it is at the core of what we mean by "Fukushima." And all of us, now, find we have ever since been possessed and haunted by this abstract anxiety.[22]

TAWADA YŌKO'S POSTDISASTER LITERATURE

Immediately after the disasters, France and Germany issued evacuation recommendations and arranged charter flights out of the country for their nationals in Japan. I imagine that Japanese living overseas, seeing this scene of people one after the other fleeing Japan to return to Europe, were struck with fear: I may never again be able to return, there may no longer be a place to return to. Tawada Yōko, living in Berlin, is one author who energetically published many works after the disasters, with particular focus on the nuclear damage. *Kentōshi* (*The Emissary*, 2014) is a collection of stories (and one play) that provides an overview of the early days of 2011 up to 2014.[23] In an interview accompanying its publication, Tawada described that at the time of the disasters, Germany immediately started reporting on the "meltdown" at the Fukushima Daiichi Nuclear Power Plant. This led her to wonder, "Does this mean I will never again be able to travel to Japan?"[24] It might be possible to say that this fear of never again being able to return home, the poignancy of it, was equivalent to the fear that those in "hard to return to" areas were feeling. At the same time, we have every indication that many of the people in Japan, living in their homes, carrying on their daily lives as though nothing had happened, could not even imagine this fear and anxiety. With these things in mind, it is no surprise that Japanese authors based abroad and writers with connections to Japan raised their voices in unison. One's physical distance from Fukushima, for example, or whether or not one was a direct victim of the disasters, is not necessarily equivalent to the psychological distance from Fukushima. This gap that exists between physical and psychological distance is the very paradox of radiation contamination. For almost all of the people in the world, Fukushima is somewhere far away. Even so, radiation contamination is in no way limited to the concentric circles drawn at ten-kilometer increments around the point of the meltdown. It is airborne, it rides the waves of global market systems, and it makes its way to every corner of the globe. We saw the exact same thing with the 1986 Chernobyl meltdown. At that time too in Japan we were advised not to ingest milk and spinach because they were contaminated. Indeed, the spread of radioactivity is without limit, an extraordinary thing: a portion of what flowed out to sea with the 3.11 tsunami washed up on the west coasts of the United States and Canada.

From the sense of crisis contained in Tawada's query, "Does this mean I will never again be able to travel to Japan?" comes her short story "Fushi no shima" ("The Island of Eternal Life," 2012).[25] Following a nuclear disaster in Japan, all contact with other countries evaporates: a near-future Japan returns to the isolation of sixteenth-century *sakoku*, when Japan essentially closed all of its borders. What is interesting in this story is that, even though Germany changed course on nuclear power immediately after the accident at Fukushima Daiichi, Tawada saw at the outset that Japan would never give up nuclear power, a reality reflected in her stories.

The setting for "Fushi no shima" is a massive earthquake followed by a massive nuclear event five years hence, in 2017. The entire landmass of Japan is now contaminated by radiation and relations with all other countries have been cut off. Tawada explains that the idea of a Japan that has "again reverted to *sakoku*" is based on "roots in Japanese society when voluntary evacuation was censured" and when "movement was forbidden" during the Edo period.[26] She continues by saying "this was to highlight the contrast to European society where immigration and emigration have been established."[27] Given that Tawada is based in Europe, we can say that "Fushi no shima" numbers among the ways European societies that have embraced their histories of refugees and immigrants question the developments in Japan.

After this, in 2014, Tawada published the short story "Higan" ("The Far Shore") in *Waseda Bungaku*'s fall issue.[28] This story also takes place in the near future, when an American military plane crashes into a nuclear power plant causing an explosion. The Japan of "Higan" is not closed off; rather, it provides the opposite scenario where people from Japan are made refugees and scatter to countries across the globe. That is, it imagines a scenario where Japanese have become refugees. For context we think of contemporary Japan in which even though birth rates continue to decline, the nation is known for its negative policies toward accepting immigrants.[29] In "Higan" a xenophobic politician who has unceasingly spoken ill of China ends up heading there as a refugee; the story brims with irony.

In that same year, Tawada also published *Kentōshi* (*The Emissary*) in the August issue of *Gunzō*. In a closed-off *sakoku* Japan, the old live seemingly forever while caring for their weak and sickly great-grandchildren. Japan has become a decidedly irradiated nation and is closed off. The short story "Fushi no shima," which describes a near future where the elderly are also unable to die following the effects of radiation, should probably be considered a sister-work to *Kentōshi*. Whereas in the allegorical "Fushi no shima," where the narrator has some distance on the events, *Kentōshi* is more novelistic because the narrative voice brings the reader closer to the viewpoints of the characters. Tawada has relayed how before writing *Kentōshi* she traveled to Fukushima, and how what she heard from the victims there influenced this work.[30]

Although Tawada said, "I personally experienced the tremendous loss felt by those with deep ties to the land," *Kentōshi* is less a story about the loss contained in nostalgia than an increasingly sharpened depiction of radioactive harm.[31] In the days and months following her trip to the disaster area, the ominous predictions about a postdisaster future likely came to take on a firmer sense of reality for Tawada. Even so, Tawada's postdisaster fiction is decidedly not a stern warning nor a dogmatic pronouncement meant to sound alarm bells. These are delightful works filled with jokes and spontaneous humor.

Set a half-century in the future, *Kentōshi* depicts a Japan where words familiar to us have become extinct, although not by any natural process. Japan is now an isolated country (*sakoku*) where using words that carry any whiff of foreign countries is suppressed. Citizens have self-censored all foreign loan words from their speech. The day the internet disappeared is celebrated as "Off-line Day," and the word for "dry cleaners," once written in the *katakana* phonetic script, is now written in homophonous Chinese characters that retain the sound of "Cleaning" but literally mean "chestnut-person-tool."[32] These neologisms would be humorous except for Japan's own history of blindly outlawing foreign loan words. During the Asia-Pacific War, English was deemed an "enemy language" (*tekiseigo*) and its use forbidden. The wartime Chinese character replacement terms for volleyball and handball no longer make sense in contemporary Japan, and when we think about how words like train platform (*purattohōmu*) were replaced in the war years with Sino-Japanese characters for "lobby for boarding," words in *The Emissary* like "kokusai ryokyaku taminaru," for an airport's international terminal, lose their humor.[33]

The protagonist Yoshirō is a novelist who, midway through the writing of his historical novel also called *Kentōshi*,[34] becomes aware of the "large number of foreign place names I use" and abandons the writing "for his own safety."[35] On another occasion he had considered writing a story about crossing the now-abandoned twenty-three wards of Tokyo and going to Narita airport. It seemed to him a good idea for a novel, but, even though the story was a complete fabrication, he abandons the idea for fear that he might accidentally get too close to state secrets hidden at the airport and be arrested. If one cannot use words freely, then novels cannot be freely written. If the free use of the imagination is banished, then we are in a situation where humans are suffocated. Such a dark era of literary censorship is one that in fact existed during the war. We read further, "All of Tokyo's twenty-three wards, all the best districts included, were designated as areas where 'long periods of habitation lead to exposure to multiple health hazards'."[36] The National Diet Building is a huge "cavity" and the Japanese government privatized, but the enactment of the isolation policy suggests that the Diet members are still around.[37]

> The Diet's main job was to fiddle around with the laws. Judging from how often the laws changed, someone was definitely fiddling with them. Yet the public was never told who made the changes, or for what purpose. Afraid of getting burned by laws they hadn't heard of, everyone kept their intuition honed sharp as a knife, every day practicing restraint and self-censorship.[38]

Because the laws change so often, nobody knows what constitutes a violation, so the citizens self-regulate. Here too, the suffocating proliferation of self-censorship is not just something from a futuristic novel, rather it seems like our contemporary Japan in the years after the disasters where politicians are trying to change not just laws but the constitution itself. When one does not know what is going to happen, is in a constant state of anxiety, not even knowing where the pitfalls are, people cannot speak freely.

Yoshirō is over a hundred years old and only growing healthier. He lives in temporary housing in the "Western region of Tokyo" with his sickly great-grandson Mumei,[39] whose legs are as useless as an octopus' tentacles.[40] Yoshirō takes every possible precaution in the raising of Mumei in hopes that he might extend his life even a bit. Yoshirō feels pained and helpless seeing Mumei unable to easily walk or digest food. Mumei, however, has known no other life and shows no concern about it. Mumei's innocence is a saving grace not just for Yoshirō but for the reader as well.

In another parallel to the Edo period, while the country has sealed its borders in *sakoku* some paths to the outside world remain available. There seems to be a secret organization that chooses a few children as "emissaries" (*kentōshi*) and sends them overseas. If a child is sent to the "International Medical Research Center" in Madras, India, they can "thoroughly research the state of Japanese children's health, yielding information that would prove useful if similar phenomena began to appear in other countries."[41] When Mumei turns fifteen he is chosen to be one of these "emissaries."

The elderly are unable to die, dandelion petals are so large that they can compete in chrysanthemum contests. The word "mutation" is considered discriminatory and has been replaced with "environmental adaptation."[42] The nature of that contamination remains unclear, but the grass in the fields is "contaminated" and "Mumei has not even once played in an actual expanse of grass."[43] The cause of this is never made clear in *Kentōshi*. Having read "Fushi no shima" and "Higan" the reader would be right to expect that it is radioactive contamination following a nuclear accident, but the words "radiation" and "radioactive particles" never appear in *Kentōshi*. Furthermore, although *Kentōshi* was actually written sometime after "Fushi no shima" and "Higan," it appeared first in the story collection titled *Kentōshi*, with "Fushi no shima" third and "Higan" fourth. The reader encountering them in this order cannot readily infer the radioactive damage as background for *Kentōshi*.

The reason it is necessary to send children overseas as emissaries and to research their poor health is because "it was now clear that the only choice was to think of the future as following the curved lines of our round globe."[44] What *Kentōshi* reveals is decidedly not a prediction of what radioactive damage might look like in the near future; rather, it reveals what great care is needed for people to protect themselves while living on contaminated land: it is more concerned with how suffocating it is under the coercive power that comes from places unknown and invisible. *Kentōshi* maps out in its vision of the future not the sort of physical radioactive damage that is easy to imagine in our present, rather it has opened the possible readings of the anxiety that emanates from places we cannot know.

FOOD MEMORIES AND TRADITION

Sekiguchi Ryōko is a poet and writer living in France who publishes in both French and Japanese. As a translator she has been involved in numerous projects from French into Japanese and vice versa. She is also a food specialist responsible for the food at various events and writes widely as a food critic for French epicurean magazines. Given this, she has been focusing on radiation and food safety since the disaster. In October 2011, she published *Ce n'est pas un hazard: Chronique Japonaise* (This was no accident), a work written in diary form covering the day before the disaster and ending on April 30.[45] She followed this with other publications all concerned with food: *Manger fantôme: Manuel pratique de l'alimentation vaporeuse* (Eating Phantasms); *L'astringent* (The Astringent); *Dîner Fantasma* (Phantom Dinner); and *Fade* (Fade). In August 2011 she wrote: "As I watched the disaster and evacuations on TV, I couldn't help but wonder what these people were eating. . . . What has become of the homemade pickled vegetables and miso they left behind?"[46]

At the time of the disasters, Sekiguchi was already connected to Fukushima by two chance encounters. The first was an existing request to write an article on Fukushima food for a French magazine focused on Japanese cuisine. As she thought about how the "flavors of Fukushima" had been destroyed by the tsunami and nuclear disaster, she also felt convinced that this was no time to be writing about Fukushima food. She was not familiar with Fukushima, having been born in the Kantō region of Japan and living in Paris since 1997. She had long been interested in Fukushima and assumed she could go anytime, and would someday, but now, of course, that was no longer possible.

March of 2011, for Europe, saw the war in Syria intensify, refugees scattering across the continent. This also meant she could no longer go to Syria on a whim and enjoy its food as she had previously. A friend who often traveled to various parts of the globe would frequently say to her, "If there are countries you want to visit, don't wait around, just go. The world map changes faster than you would think. Conflicts, wars, and any number of other unforeseeable things happen, and it becomes impossible to travel."[47] This led to reflection: given what her friend has said, she may indeed have totally missed her chance to visit Fukushima. But no one could have imagined that travel to Fukushima would become impossible in her lifetime.[48]

The second chance encounter was the purchase of Fukushima saké at the airport on her previous trip home to Japan. The saké was the product of a famous distiller. Fortunately, the brewery was located 60 kilometers from the nuclear power plant and had escaped tsunami damage. Cesium levels registered at an unproblematic 0.06 microsieverts. Growing the rice used to make their saké, however, was forbidden that year: she would never be able to drink that sake again. She wrote:

> It's not that I didn't trust the distiller, but the very fact that radioactive levels needed to be reported meant that, in future, whenever drinking that sake I would think about "that event." Cesium levels may not even rise, nonetheless, the flavor of that sake would change. As with so many other things, even though what might occur never does, in one's imagination it remains contaminated, stubbornly, unwaveringly.[49]

Thinking about radiation contamination and then decontamination began a train of associations that ended with Hi-Red Center's performances. The

Hi-Red Center was an avant-garde art collective formed in 1963 by Akasegawa Genpei, Takamatsu Jirō, and Nakanishi Natsuyuki. The name of the group is an English approximation of the first Chinese character in each of their surnames: *aka* (red), *taka* (high), and *naka* (center). On October 16, 1964, during that year's Tokyo Olympics, they embarked on a street performance they called the "Campaign to Promote Cleanliness and Order in the Metropolitan Area,"[50] in which members of the group donned white lab uniforms and masks and carefully wiped the streets and manhole covers with rags. This cleaning performance, replete with placards stating "Be Clean! Cleaning in Process," was a sarcastic response to the government's campaign, "Let's make the Olympic city beautiful," which had citizens turn out for a massive cleaning movement on what was deemed "Capital City Beautification Day." The Hi-Red Center's eccentric, neurotic cleaning performance was meant to show that the government campaign would not actually result in a clean city. The irony here is that the decontamination efforts of areas affected by radiation after the 2011 disaster essentially recreate the Hi-Red Center's empty performance. Sekiguchi quotes art historian Sawaragi Noi: "Art history has again been blasted by radiation (*hibaku*). Take, for example, the Hi-Red Center's 'nonsense' happenings—they are now overlain with the sort of 'decontamination.' ... Artistic expression, taste, memory, and landscape—even if they have not been contaminated in fact—have nonetheless been 'irradiated' (*hibaku*)."[51] What Sekiguchi reiterates here—the way that even though a thing may not be contaminated in fact, in our imagination it remains contaminated—seems to show the anxiety of people after the disasters, those whose anxiety is real but are nonetheless ridiculed for spreading "damaging rumors" (*fūhyō higai*).

At any rate, Sekiguchi goes on to describe being deeply engaged in the act of making of *sekihan* (sweet red beans and rice).[52] This dish is eaten in all areas of Japan and has no special connection to Fukushima. So why, one wonders, is she making, and telling us about making, *sekihan*?

The night before *sekihan* is made, the red beans are submerged in water to soak. In the midst of these preparations Sekiguchi is suddenly taken back to her grandmother's kitchen. We learn that whenever she visited her grandmother's house as a child, her grandmother would make *sekihan* for her even though it was not necessarily a special occasion. For Sekiguchi, *sekihan* is a memory of childhood; it invites a flood of memories, first of her grandmother and then her grandmother's house. Thus, she writes, in these flavors the life of her grandmother continues to exist in the world. By phrasing it this way, she reveals that home cooking and regional cuisines are not simply about one's sense of taste but are deeply linked to the memories of a living community.

In general, family cooking and the particularities of regional cuisines are passed down through word of mouth. As with all oral traditions, if the person who passed down these traditions dies, then the traditions also fade away. At the same time, if we take the example of Sekiguchi's association of the flavors of *sekihan* with memories of her grandmother, we see how such memories depend on a particular individual. When that person is gone, so are the memories. That being the case, we also see that home cooking becomes a gathering-together of all such memories. Which is to say, in short, that home cooking is coupled with human life.

The radioactive contamination from the accident at the Fukushima Dai-ichi Nuclear Power Plant inevitably separated people from their land, producing zones that are "difficult to return to," meaning people can no longer live there. It is clear that this situation destroys the rich traditions of home cooking and regional dishes. This is one of the things that Kariya Tetsu tried to express in *Oishinbo 110: Fukushima no shinjitsu* (1) (Oishinbo 110: The Truth about Fukushima (1)). In this episode of the multivolume series, a woman named Chieko, evacuated from Iitate because of radiation, was to prepare the local cuisine using foodstuffs harvested before the accident and make do with vegetables from other locales. Of the ingredients from Iitate, only those harvested before the contamination could be used. In other words, such vegetables would never again be available to be eaten. After eating the last "safe" home-cooked meal, character Kaibara Yūzan says: "Think how precious are the things we have lost. Prosperity, delight, brilliance, happiness. Things that should never disappear have now disappeared."[53]

However, it is not just a matter of contamination of the ground and any products harvested from that ground, but the loss of memory of the tastes that have been imprinted on the lives, and all that goes with it, of each and every person. This issue of *Oishinbo* is powerful in its descriptions of the people working so hard and carefully to ensure the safety of their products. Nonetheless, it also reveals how, at the same time, no matter how often radiation levels are measured and how many numerical values are displayed to ensure safety, there is no wiping away consumer aversion; in the end, these products go unsold.

Oishinbo 111: Fukushima no shinjitsu (2) (Oishinbo 111: The Truth about Fukushima (2)) contains an episode set in Kitakata's Yamato district. It focuses on fiddleheads and other wild mountain vegetables provided for a meal by "Old man Hidé" that have not been measured for radiation. The group that has traveled to Fukushima decided beforehand that "When served food that local Fukushima people eat, we will eat it. But those who are worried about it need not."[54] After eating the dishes made with mountain vegetable, Kaibara shares his feelings:

> Hidejii has received us so warmly and with such consummate hospitality here on this beautiful mountain, providing such lovely mountain vegetables. There was

not a single thing you failed to provide. It was simply amazing. Given all that, why is everyone so tense and constrained? It is because on this beautiful, prosperous expanse of land, a horrible, invisible thing has clouded over everything. This monstrous existence has deeply scarred the land of Fukushima, it has frozen people's hearts. This is the truth of Fukushima (*Fukushima no shinjitsu*).[55]

It is not only that food culture has been lost, but that the joy of eating is now etched with budding anxieties.

According to what Sekiguchi wrote in *Manger fantôme: Manuel pratique de l'alimentation vaporeuse*, with those flavors when we eat, we also eat something that cannot be further reduced. In the section "Eating the Land," she discusses how we like to buy food products which carry the name of special places, such as Guérande *fleur de sel* from France. Place names become a brand and a positive image is attached. In contrast are place names that evoke a "clear anxiety . . . [like] mushrooms harvested from areas around Chernobyl," for example.[56] In that sense "Fukushima" has likewise become a place whose name evokes anxiety. Sekiguchi writes of how at times this misses the mark while at other times it is spot on. Fukushima is an extremely common Japanese surname. Even though that surname has absolutely no connection to the "Fukushima" of the disasters, the negative image so closely tied to the word "Fukushima" means that merely uttering it also brings up the anxiety that has, at base, absolutely no direct connection.

In the section "Manger fantôme," Sekiguchi discusses how in the act of eating, at the level of flavor, there is something unknown there that we, at the same time, ingest. She offers the example of genetically modified foods which are not identifiable by taste or smell, but which we also know will at some future time affect our bodies. Although the words "radioactive contamination" are never used here, it is quite clear that we are to place genetically modified foodstuffs in parallel to irradiated food. Sekiguchi refers to this unknowability of genetically modified food as a "fantôme," that is, as incorporeal (*reiteki*). "Incorporeal" is invoked to explain something that cannot be perceived by the five senses. Ultimately, the eating of delicious food, in contrast to eating food that is simply good for us, is a pure joy, a pure pleasure. Thus, even when items are guaranteed safe by the government, the fact remains that contamination is a reality in certain areas of Fukushima, and these items therefore still give rise to anxiety. Even if that anxiety is ultimately baseless, radioactive particles are like ghosts of the dead that leave us obsessed, possessed. The radioactive disaster has given rise to a situation where the act of eating—which originally should be joyful and pleasurable—stirs up intangible anxieties. However, for Sekiguchi, the image of the "incorporeal ghost"—the *fantôme*—is to be understood as something more than simply disturbing.

In her subsequent book *Dîner fantasma* she also talks about *sekihan* and her grandmother. In her memories of her grandmother making *sekihan*, the movement of her hands is most prominent. Those gestures have become Sekiguchi's own: "When I test the taste of the cooking rice, my grandmother's tongue comes to life again."[57] In other words, by reproducing her grandmother's dishes, Sekiguchi finds it to be the activity of calling back to this world her now-dead grandmother herself, or her grandmother's *fantôme* (spirit). The spirit that resides in these recipes comes to possess Sekiguchi, but no one other than Sekiguchi has the magical arts to call forth her grandmother when these dishes are recreated. It may well follow that the earnestness that accompanies home cooking and regional dishes is because people are individually possessed in this way.

The reason Sekiguchi is so committed to visualizing the loss of hometowns as the loss of regional cooking is very likely the result of what is revealed in the movement of refugees and immigrants throughout Europe. In the section "Eating the Land" in *Manger fantôme*, she gives examples of places with negative connotations such as Syria and Palestine. The reason these areas are no longer places where people who enjoy cuisine think to go is because the image of these locales is paired with the reality of the many people dislocated from those areas: these are the two sides of the same coin. The home cooking and regional cuisines of these places also seem to be in a continual process of decline. Just as the various countries in Europe have been changed by the influx of refugees, Sekiguchi sees a similar fate as evacuees flow out of Fukushima and the communal sense of place breaks down. When these communities collapse and concomitantly experience loss of intangibles and non-concrete items such as flavors and practices, Sekiguchi would also seem to be thinking about her grandmother's *sekihan*. Sekiguchi summons her grandmother's spirit through this discussion of her *sekihan*; she is able to do this because the dishes are, in a real sense, her grandmother. Further, it is because her grandmother is passing on to her the history of the flavors associated with that particular home and family.

Thought about in this way, Sekiguchi's intense focus on these issues relates to issues raised in Anne Georget's 2015 film *Festins imaginaires* (Imaginary Feasts). The film is a documentary about prisoners of Nazi concentration camps, Soviet gulag labor camps, and Japanese prisoner of war camps who made great efforts to write down recipes while imprisoned. The film reveals the enormous number of recipes collected by all these people who were separated from their communities and confined in these camps. The film poses a question: "They wrote secretly on stolen paper. What was told there? Was it hopes? Memories, perhaps? Dreams?" The film examines a variety of detention centers to discover that in all of them prisoners are secretly writing down recipes. All these people from all over the world now in the extreme situation of facing death—men and women both, the elderly and also the young—are secretly scratching out these recipes: what can this possibly mean? Holocaust historian Michael Berenbaum points out in the film that the writing of recipes allowed the prisoners to return to a past when they were in their own homes, in their own kitchens, with their own families. Well-known French chef Olivier Roellinger notes that although knowledge of the backgrounds of music, literature, and art is important, it takes education; the flavor of delicious things is open to all and everyone, and the writing of recipes is universal. At the same time, while Berenbaum has no trouble with the idea that there may be something universal in the writing of recipes for those imprisoned in the Soviet Gulag or the Japanese POW camps, he suggests that the meaning of recipes for those in Holocaust camps was likely quite different. For those in Auschwitz: "It was not only their own extinction, but the ruin of the world itself. Nothing would remain. That is why they wanted to preserve these recipes. That was the essence of existence. The recipes were existence."[58]

Why is it that recipes serve as a proof of human existence? Why would these people, in the midst of starving to death, record for posterity their cuisine in the form of recipes? If putting to paper memories of delicious things eaten in the past, then why not write with a more literary writing style?

Recipes come in a form that, theoretically, if followed faithfully, allows anyone to recreate the precise flavor of the dish. If they were able, in these camps with absolutely nothing, to write down these recipes, it suggests that all of the individual steps required to recreate these dishes remained burned into their physical bodies. Recipes are accompanied in this way by an embodied physicality, even as Sekiguchi's grandmother's recipe for *sekihan*, having been passed down through the generations, could only be transmitted orally within the household. As to the end of the world, the Holocaust could only have been felt to lead to the end of families, the end of tribes. In the face of such loss, the sense that these things need to be preserved in writing no matter what points to something greater than a single individual's memory of eating those things and points to something passed down by mouth across generations. The reason for this is that oral traditions can only be passed down from one living person to another. Recipes are all the more a proof that a particular person lived on this earth. In recipes, as Sekiguchi has written, resides the spirits of particular people. Further, recipes that have been preserved contain the very history of the traditions, not just individuals but entire tribes.

In sum, to inquire "What is Fukushima?" is the same as to ask "What is a nuclear accident?" It is to ask "What was lost in a particular place because of that nuclear accident?" An answer can be found in the scattering of traditions passed down orally, in that place, and based on the physical existence of people who lived there. The most fragile and formless example of this is, as Sekiguchi shows, the tradition of food.

NOTES

1. Elfriede Jelinek, *Hikari no nai* (No Light), trans. Hayashi Tatsuki (Tokyo: Hakusuisha, 2012), 9–10, 60, 61. Original publication: *Kein Licht* (Frankfurt am Main: Rowohlt Theater Verlag, 2011).
2. Kobayashi Erika has had long interest in the history of radiation. Her novels *Madamu kyurī to chōshoku wo* (Tokyo: Shueisha, 2014) and *Hikari no kodomo 1* (Tokyo: Ritorumoa, 2013) form a pair. The latter is technically manga, but given its richness, it would be better described as an art book. In this work, Hikari, born in the same year as the Fukushima Daiichi nuclear power plant meltdown, is able to travel through time and lands in Paris at the time that the Curies are discovering radium. In the sequel, *Hikari no kodomo 2*, the Second World War intrudes, and she traces the history of radiation up to the dropping of the atomic bomb on Hiroshima.
3. Jelinek, *Hikari no nai*, 30, 45, 22.
4. Jelinek, *Hikari no nai*, 37–38.
5. These zones range from areas that are above the annual 20 millisievert level and are designated "hard to return to" (*kikan konnan kuiki*), to areas where they are actively decontaminating and rebuilding in hopes that the limits will drop (*kyojū seigen kuiki*), to areas that are under the annual limit and are preparing to repatriate residents (*hinan shiji kaijo junbi kuiki*).
6. Yasushi Kurabayashi, *Shinsai to āto: ano toki, geijutsu ni nani ga dekita no ka* (Disaster and art: What could art accomplish at that time?) (Tokyo: Bukkendo, 2013).
7. Theodor Adorno, "Cultural Criticism and Society," in *Prism* (Cambridge, MA: MIT Press), 34.
8. See Higaki's essay "Shizen wa ranbō de aru ni kimatte iru," in Ataru Sasaki et al., eds., *Shishō to shite no 3.11*. Tokyo: Kawade shobo, 2011, 131–40.
9. Asada Akira and Azuma Hiroki, "'Fukushima' wa shisōteki kadai ni nariuru ka," *Shinchō* (June 2014): 421.
10. Taki Kōji, *Sensōron* (On War) (Tokyo: Iwanami shoten, 1999), 108. This translation of Adorno is from E. B Ashton's translation of *Negative Dialectics* (New York: Seabury Press, 1973), 362–63.—Trans.
11. Taki, *Sensōron*, 108. I learned about this from Kurabayashi Yasushi's *Shinsai to aato: ano toki, geijutsu ni nani ga dekita no ka* (Tokyo: Bukkendo, 2013). Hosomi Kazuyuki's *Frankufuroto gakuha: Horukuhaimā, Adoruno kara 21 seiki no "hihan riron" e* (Chukō Shinsho, 2014) traces the history of Adorno's intent when he made this proclamation.
12. Taki, *Sensōron*, 119–20.
13. Among non-Japanese works in addition to Jelinek, there is also Ruth Ozeki's *A Tale for the Time Being* (New York: Viking, 2013).
14. Jean-Luc Nancy, in *Équivalence des catastrophes (après Fukushima)* (Paris: Éd. Galilée, 2012), considers "Fukushima" together with the Holocaust. The Holocaust overlaps with "Hiroshima" and "Nagasaki" as a historical genocide of innocent citizens. "Fukushima," however, is understood within Japan as part of "Hiroshima" and "Nagasaki's" history of radiation exposure. Yoshiyuki Satō and Takumi Taguchi,

in *Datsu genpatsu no tetsugaku* (Kyoto: Jinbun shoin, 2016), consider the radiation of Fukushima within the history of environmental pollution.

15. In the terrorist attacks on critical American buildings on September 11, 2011, the planes that hit the World Trade Center in New York were referred to as "kamikaze" in the press. Similarly, the workers tasked with cleaning up after the events at Fukushima Daiichi Nuclear Power Plant in March 2011, the so-called "Fukushima 50," are also understood as "kamikaze" for having risked their lives for the greater cause. Meanwhile, in Germany, Alfashirt sold mugs and T-shirts with the logo "Fukushima 50 Liquidator" written under a picture of a soldier with the Japanese war flag and the Sino-Japanese characters for the Japanese Special Attack Forces. In French, children's author Christophe Léon's *Mon père n'est pas un héros* (Paris: Oscar 2013) is in the form of a letter written to TEPCO's president from a fourteen-year-old boy who relocated to Nara. His father was one of the Fukushima 50 who died six months later. The son writes "my father was not a hero, he was a sacrifice" (p. 35).

16. See the following from the March 24, 2011, *Nihon Keizai Shimbun* morning edition: "Tokyo announced on the 23rd that radioactive iodine was found in drinking water at the Kanamachi water purification plant (Tokyo and Katsushika) in the amount of 210 becquerels per 1 kilogram. It would appear to be an effect of the accident at the Fukushima Daiichi Nuclear Power Plant. This amount exceeds the unofficial limit of 100 becquerels for infants and young children. The metropolitan area issued a warning to refrain from giving tap water to children less than one year old. This was for residents of the twenty three Tokyo wards, as well as the cities of Musashino, Mitaka, Machida, Tama, and Inagi that get water from the Kanamachi and Misato plants, both of which draw water from the Edogawa River."

17. The *Nihon Keizai Shimbun* reported the following in its December 7, 2011, morning edition: "The Meiji Corporation (Tokyo, Kōtō-ku) announced on the sixth that it detected 30.8 becquerels of radioactive cesium per one kilogram of their *Meiji Step* (850 gram can) of powdered milk baby formula for babies nine months and older. Approximately 400,000 cans of this formula were produced; the company is now offering free returns. The Ministry of Health, Labor and Welfare announced that since the levels were below the unofficial limit of 200 becquerels, they are not issuing a recall. They also claim that this is the first time since the disaster that radioactive cesium has been found in powdered milk formula. The Meiji corporation reported that the contaminated formula was found at the Saitama factory in Saitama prefecture's Kasukabe city. The raw ingredients had been dried between March 14 and 20. The company was notified of radioactive particles in the formula by consumers and when they conducted an inspection on the third, they found radioactive cesium ranging from 30.8–21.5 becquerels in formula with sell-by dates of October 4, 21, 22, and 24 of the following year. The powdered skim milk was all processed before the disaster. Some of the milk was from Hokkaido, but the majority was imported from the US and places throughout Oceania. Meiji explained that 'A large amount of heated air is used in the manufacturing process to dry the ingredients, and radioactive cesium that had dispersed in the atmosphere from the accident at the Fukushima Daiichi Nuclear Power Plant was mixed in.'"

18. Sekiguchi Ryōko, in her *L'astringent* (Paris: Argol éditions, 2012), writes about persimmon juice. Persimmons are part of the fall scenery and are often featured in haiku poems. She explains how the persimmon is like a national fruit, cultivated in almost all areas of Japan except Hokkaido and Okinawa. After writing in a number of places about the multiple varieties of persimmons used for drying, Sekiguchi includes the following note in her discussion: "Fukushima prefecture is (was) famous for its production of dried persimmons (over 2,500 tons per annum)" (pg. 25). By including both "is" and "was," one can read Sekiguchi as suggesting that not only are the trees and soil contaminated, but the air as well is thick with radioactive particles, such that areas of Tohoku that had been up to that point well known for dried-persimmon production are now unable to produce them. According to the *Tokyo Shimbun* of January 17, 2015, Fukushima prefecture had again begun producing and selling dried persimmons starting in 2015. The newspaper went on to note that they are conducting a thorough decontamination of the trees and ground and that they will monitor the levels of radioactive cesium before shipping any products.

19. According to the *Nihon Keizai Shimbun* of April 11, 2017, a Ministry of Education, Culture, Sports, Science and Technology study found that "among those who evacuated from Fukushima because of the TEPCO Fukushima Daiichi Nuclear Power Plant accident, there were 129 cases of bullying of school-aged children." Since bullying is often overlooked, there are likely more cases.

20. The *Nihon Keizai Shimbun* of January 21, 2017, reported: "A female student in the first year of middle school at a public school who had evacuated from Fukushima to Niigata's Kaetsu region because of the TEPCO Fukushima Daiichi Nuclear Power Plant accident was bullied and on numerous occasions called 'contagion' by other students. This was discovered on the 20th with material gathered from the Niigata Board of Education."

21. The *Nihon Keizai Shimbun* of March 5, 2014, reported receiving inquiries for advice from "Mothers who voluntarily evacuated and were 'considered by those in their old neighborhoods as having "fled"' and found that 'close friends stopped responding to messages.' They also pointed out that 'they felt the uneasy thinking about the friends and family still back home'."

22. Fujita Naoya argues: "Anxiety and suspicion arises from time to time, at times it threatens reason. This is the situation of life in Japanese society after the nuclear accident. It is the 'harm' that we have received and that has created the environment we now find ourselves in" ("'Sei' yori mo warui unmei," in Iida Ichishi and Yutaka Ebihara, eds., *Higashi Nihon Daishinsai-go bungakuron* [Tokyo: Nan'undō, 2017], 427).

23. *Kentōshi* was first published in *Gunzō* in August 2014, then republished in book form (Tokyo: Kodansha, 2014). English translation by Margaret Mitsutani as *The Emissary* (New York: New Directions, 2018).

24. *Nihon Keizai Shimbun* October 19, 2014, evening edition. In a similar interview about *Kentōshi*, Tawada told the *Tokyo Shimbun* interviewer how her feelings toward Japan changed after the disaster and nuclear accident: "At first I wanted to return to Japan. . . . I was struck by a longing so strong that I was willing to disappear

along with Japan. I had to wonder if some sort of memory of community actually does flow through me." *Tokyo Shimbun* December 2, 2014.

25. "Fushi no shima" was first published in Tanikawa Shuntarō, ed., *Soredemo sangatsu wa, mata = March was made of yarn* (Tokyo: Kōdansha, 2012), and later included in *Kentōshi*. It was translated as "The Island of Eternal Life" by Margaret Mitsutani. Elmer Luke and David James Karashima, *March Was Made of Yarn: Reflections on the Japanese Earthquake, Tsunami, and Nuclear Meltdown* (New York: Vintage Books, 2012).

26. *Sakoku* refers to the isolationist policy of the Edo period government in Japan from the seventeenth-nineteenth centuries.—Trans.

27. Tawada, *Tokyo Shimbun*, February 2, 2014, evening edition. Np.

28. See Jeffrey Angles's translation at the website Words Without Borders, https://www.wordswithoutborders.org/article/the-far-shore.—Trans.

29. After the 2011 civil war, the 5,000,000 Syrian refugees became an international issue. According to the *Tokyo Shimbun* (February 16, 2017, evening edition), as of 2016, Japan had certified refugee status for only seven of the sixty-nine applicants seeking entry.

30. In the summer of 2013, Tawada took a three-night, four-day trip to the disaster area, "meeting with people living in the Iwaki City central temporary housing units," then "traveling to areas such as Iwaki City's Usuiso region, Tomioka Kamiteoka, Tomioka Yonomori, and Naraha Yamadaoka," and listening to stories from "refugees from Namie." She visited her guide's uncle "who had evacuated to Kitakata," and then visited "Miharu" before returning. She had the following to say about how this trip transformed her own writing: "I had planned to expand my short story 'Fushi no shima' into a novel, but my position changed slightly as a result of this trip. In result I wrote *Kentōshi*, which surprised even me in how it turned out" (*Hon*, November 2014, 5).

The disaster damage to the various areas Tawada visited is as follows: Iwaki City's Usuiso region sustained serious damage from the tsunami. Tomioka Kamiteoka was designated an evacuation zone due to the accident at the Fukushima Daiichi Nuclear Power Plant. On March 25, 2013, it was redesignated as an "evacuation area preparing to have restrictions lifted" (*hinan shiji kaijo junbi kuiki*) and an "area allowing limited repatriation" (*kyojū seigen kuiki*). In April 2017, the evacuation order was rescinded (*hinan shiji kaijo*). Tomioka Yonomori, which is famous for its cherry blossom trees, is above the 20 mSv/year limit and is designated as "hard to return to area" (*kikan konnan kuiki*), with the exception of one part that is a "area allowing limited repatriation" (*kyojū seigen kuiki*). On August 10, 2012, as part of the reevaluation of hazard areas (*keikai kuiki*), Naraha Yamadaoka was changed to a "evacuation area preparing to have restrictions lifted" (*hinan shiji kaijo junbi kuiki*), and on September 5, 2015, the evacuation order was rescinded. On April 1, 2013, Namie was split into three zones: *hinan shiji kaijo junbi kuiki*, *kyojū seigen kuiki*, and *kikan konnan kuiki*. On March 31, 2017, the evacuation orders were lifted except for the "hard to return to" areas. Kitakata, near the Aizu region, and Miharu, in the Nakadori region (between Aizu and Hamadori), took in evacuees from the earthquake, tsunami, and radiation damage in Fukushima prefecture.

31. *Tokyo Shimbun*, February 2, 2014, evening edition.
32. Off-line is "written with the Chinese characters meaning 'Honorable-Woman-Naked-Obscenity'" (*The Emissary*, 44).
33. Volleyball was written as 排球 (*haikyū*) and handball 送球 (*sokyū*). Platform became *jōsharō*. "Terminal" is written 民なる.—Trans.
34. This introduces a similar piece of wordplay. Yoshiro's *Kentōshi* (遣唐使) refers to the Tang-era envoys from Japan to China and is the assumed word for this reading. It echoes Tawada's title, but this *Kentōshi* (献灯使) is a neologism that means something like "Lantern-bearing envoy."—Trans.
35. Tawada, *Kentōshi*, 45.
36. Tawada, *Kentōshi*, 50.
37. Tawada, *Kentōshi*, 104.
38. Tawada, *Kentōshi*, 104.
39. *Mumei* means, literally, "no name."—Trans.
40. Tawada, *Kentōshi*, 97.
41. Tawada, *Kentōshi*, 152.
42. Tawada, *Kentōshi*, 14.
43. Tawada, *Kentōshi*, 15.
44. Tawada, *Kentōshi*, 152–53.
45. I discussed this work in Chapter six of my previous book *Shinsaigo bungakuron* (Tokyo: Seidosha, 2018), 177–89.
46. Sekiguchi Ryōko, "Le goût de Fukushima," in Corinne Quentin and Cécile Sakai, eds., *L'archipel des séismes: écrits du Japon après le 11 mars 2011* (Arles: P. Picquier, 2012), 282.
47. Sekiguchi, "Le goût de Fukushima," 276.
48. Sekiguchi, "Le goût de Fukushima," 276–77.
49. Sekiguchi, "Le goût de Fukushima," 277.
50. This is often referred to in English more simply as the "Street cleaning event."—Trans.
51. Sekiguchi, "Le goût de Fukushima," 278.
52. *Sekihan* is made with rice and red (adzuki) beans and is eaten on special occasions in Japan.—Trans.
53. Kariya Tetsu, *Oishinbo 110: Fukushima no shinjitsu (1)* (Tokyo: Shogakukan, 2013), 187. The manga series *Oishinbo* stretches across many volumes, all dealing with food.—Trans.
54. Kariya Tetsu, *Oishinbo 111: Fukushima no shinjitsu (2)* (Tokyo: Shogakukan, 2013), 78.
55. Kariya, *Oishinbo 111*, 88.
56. Sekiguchi Ryōko, *Manger fantôme: Manuel pratique de l'alimentation vaporeuse* (Paris: Les ateliers d'Argol, 2018), 60.
57. Sekiguchi Ryōko and Felipe Ribon, *Dîner Fantasma* (Paris: Manuella éditions, 2016), 24.
58. Anne Georget, *Festins imaginaires*. DVD video (Paris: Montparnasse, 2015), 51:38.

Chapter 3

From Fukushima to Hiroshima and Nagasaki

THE STORY OF CHERNOBYL

The year 2015 marked the four-year anniversary of the Great Eastern Japan Earthquake Disaster, the twenty-year anniversary of the Great Hanshin Earthquake, and the seventy-year anniversary of the end of the Second World War. The international art exhibition *Don't Follow the Wind* has been on display in the "hard to return to zone" (*kikan kon'nan kiuki*) surrounding TEPCO's Fukushima Daiichi Nuclear Power Plant since March 11, 2015. Even so, given current conditions, it will be a long time before anyone can see the exhibit in person. In order to make the exhibit more widely accessible, a version was broadcast via satellite and viewable at Tokyo's Watarium Museum of Contemporary Art September 19–November 3, 2015. I was able to attend the Art Unit's *Grand Guignol Future*: "The Hard to Return to Zone Inside a Cave." For this exhibit, the performer and artist Ameya Norimizu holed up in a cave in Okinawa that had been used as a field hospital seventy years ago during the Second World War. Also participating were art critic Sawaragi Noi and performance artist Yamakawa Fuyuki, who were in the actual "Hard to Return to Zone" in Fukushima, all connected by landline phones to Ameya in Okinawa. This was not a phone conversation taking place in real time, but a prerecorded version, nor were there any visual feeds. The audience gathered in the performance space, lights were turned off to replicate the darkened space of the cave, and one needed to strain to hear the phone exchange. Listening to these sounds in a situation where nothing was visible led one to imagine Ameya standing in the pitch-dark cave in Okinawa, to imagine the artworks on display in Fukushima that no one could see, and the radiation there in Fukushima that also could not be seen: it made for a very powerful performance. Sawaragi later pointed out that we could "see the 'Fukushima' in Okinawa, and the 'Okinawa' in Fukushima."[1] With that, we come to understand that this was an attempt to connect the seventy-year-old battlefields in Okinawa with the current battlefields in "Fukushima." In a similar manner, we see how numerous were the art, theater, film, artistic journals, and other publications produced in 2015 that reflected on the War's seventy-year anniversary.

The seventy-year anniversary of the end of the war simultaneously commemorates the seventieth anniversary of the bombings of "Hiroshima" and "Nagasaki." Looking at Hiroshima and Nagasaki today, in the context of the still-unfinished repairs of the Fukushima Daiichi Nuclear Power Plant, allows me to believe that someday Fukushima too might all be cleaned up. But it is a faint hope, especially given that 2016 is also the thirtieth anniversary of the accident at Chernobyl: my hope is quickly dashed given the conditions in Chernobyl after all these years.

In 2014, Germany's foremost mystery writer Mechtild Borrmann published *Die andere Hälfte der Hoffnung* (The Other Half of Hope), a novel based on material she collected in Chernobyl's exclusion zone. A Japanese translation by Akasaka Momoko appeared the following year. According to the afterword Borrmann contributed to the Japanese version, this novel was "born of the Fukushima nuclear accident."[2] She continues,

> I was shocked to find that these people were forgotten a mere few weeks after the nuclear accident. The story was soon overtaken by other news stories. The world moved on.
> The thing that strikes me with a sadness I cannot shake is to think that if "Fukushima" had not happened, we might also have forgotten about the great catastrophe of Chernobyl.[3]

Thirty years may have already passed, yet we clearly see the overlaps between the two cities and the two events. Bormann recounts "the loss of hometowns, the deaths of people close to oneself, and the high rates of sickness and suicide" that remain unresolved; the "many women worried about genetic issues and who are unable to have children"; "the many people whose roots to their birthplaces have been severed and are now living in housing constructed on the outskirts of town" also remain; and all of this, up until "Fukushima," had been completely forgotten by European society.[4] If we understand that it took "Fukushima" to wake us up, then *Charnobyl'skaia malitva* (*Voices from Chernobyl*)[5] by Belarusian author and 2015 Nobel Prize winner Svetlana Alexievich would also seem related. "Fukushima" completely changed our understanding of the Chernobyl nuclear accident. Up to that point, Chernobyl—a meltdown that led to a reactor explosion and a fire—was written off as having occurred under the leadership of a particular country and the Soviet systems of secrecy, which led to this "impossible" accident. Chernobyl was considered the sort of accident that would never happen again. However, the Fukushima Daiichi Nuclear Power Plant meltdown in Japan—a technologically advanced country, of hardworking people, on an island nation not only accustomed to earthquakes but outfitted with earthquake-resistant construction—forced us to confront the fact that such an accident can indeed happen again, anytime, anywhere. We now find that Chernobyl proves, in the end, to be no different than "Fukushima": both events proved beyond anyone's ability to control in the actual moment of crisis.

Here on the other side of "Fukushima" we once again want to understand the story of Chernobyl. We are especially curious about the lives of those who lived in the so-called "zone" that marks areas as off-limits around Chernobyl; we also want to know the story of how people lived in a Chernobyl without access to reliable numbers or statistics. Such a story will come to illuminate the path that lies ahead for Fukushima in the wake of the disasters. Thus writers, whether Borrmann or Alexievich or someone else, are not looking for the cause of the accident; rather, they are looking at people whose lives were uncompromisingly turned around, out of the blue, as they went about their lives. More than anything, it is literature that provides such knowledge.

A HISTORY OF POLITICAL TRAUMATIZATION

The meltdown at the Fukushima Daiichi Nuclear Power Plant released huge quantities of radioactive particles and gave birth to yet another generation of *hibakusha* (nuclear victims) in Japan. While this shocked most Japanese, those *hibakusha* from "Hiroshima" and "Nagasaki" who participated in the antinuclear demonstrations must have felt the rug being pulled out from under their feet. Kanō Mikiyo, Hiroshima *hibakusha* and women's historian, asked in her book *Hiroshima to Fukushima no aida: Jendā no shiten kara* (In Between "Hiroshima" and "Fukushima": From the Perspective of Gender), "Why did a country that was attacked by atomic bombs become a world leader in nuclear power? Why was 'Hiroshima' unable to stop 'Fukushima'? How did we willingly allow the construction of fifty-four reactors?"[6] Many intellectuals have asked themselves these same questions. Kanō examines representations of the atomic bombings and makes clear how the gendered image of innocence in victimhood has been constructed as female. Her analysis reveals how all that is associated with present-day "Fukushima" was already present in "Hiroshima" and "Nagasaki." Following Kanō's lead, I want to rethink the representations of "Hiroshima."

Let's begin by looking at Sekigawa Hideo's film *Hiroshima* (1953). The film depicts Hiroshima *hibakusha* seven years after the bombing. One day in class, a high school girl displays symptoms of the onset of atomic-bomb disease. Her teacher, played by Okada Eiji, looks into it and finds that one-third of the students in the class are *hibakusha*. The surprise is that *hibakusha* did not make up the majority of the class. Of course, most of the *hibakusha* were given a cold shoulder by society. Another female student begins to explain the symptoms of atomic-bomb disease by recounting how it makes you feel sluggish in the summer months and reluctant to get out of bed. Another student then mocks her:

> "So, like who isn't sluggish in the Summer?" Unable to take the laughter rippling through the classroom, one male *hibakusha* stands up and says: "This is why we stay silent. . . . We may not talk about it, but we tremble every day in fear that atomic-bomb disease will take our lives. That's how we live. But were we to say such things out loud, you'd say we are uppity and boasting; you'd accuse us of milking the disease, laughing as you do so.

Another student states that not a single person can cure themselves of atomic-bomb disease:

> But the minute you say that, the conversation is over. You are reproached for giving in to the disease. There are those like "Mr. First-Atomic-Bomb-victim Yoshikawa" who pulled himself together and went public with his scars as an accusation [to society], or the Hiroshima Maidens relying on public sympathy for treatment, or the vagrants who hang around the Hiroshima train station late at night and live off the pity of travelers. But most people are different. They hide the ugly keloid scars and live lives in the shadows like it was something that we did wrong. Or they cover up the scars with clothes and take jobs as construction workers.[7]

We can assume that lack of understanding and sympathy is in part due to pressure from the General Headquarters of the Occupation forces, which prevented dissemination of information about the bombings. It is also true that young women who refrained from marriage and pregnancy preferred that the information about the atomic bomb remain hidden. Nonetheless, what this film makes clear is that even seven years after the bombing, no one, not even residents of Hiroshima city themselves knew any details about the actual effects of being radiated. Given such ignorance and misunderstandings, the vulnerable *hibakusha* are in the weakest position possible and are attacked for "milking" the disease. The experience of being radiated thus shifted from being a major historical event to being considered an individual problem. *Hibakusha* can, of course, demand a restoration of their rights, but when they do, they are often censured for being "uppity and boasting," for exercising special privileges. This criticism of *hibakusha* is not orchestrated from on high but manifests as a will of the masses. The *hibakusha* have no choice but to seclude themselves. What is more, the victims take on the burden of the radiation as though they themselves are to blame for their afflictions. This in turn dampens any will to press their case. Sekigawa's *Hiroshima* shows how this trauma is not simply internal and individual but is also the result of external forces. If we define trauma as a psychological issue that occurs within the individual, historical catastrophes come to be confined within the individual as well. Moreover, causing the victims to feel that their afflictions result from personal transgression, we will call a political traumatization; that is, the source of the wounds that these people must bear is political, it in no way arises from individuals. It is, rather, a swindle produced from historical trickery.

In a scene at the end of the film, a high-school student who quit school and now works at a factory is interrogated by the police for selling *hibakusha* skulls that he has dug up from an air raid shelter. We learn that one day the factory suddenly ceased manufacturing their usual goods and began producing ammunition for cannons and large guns. Given that this is in the middle of the Korean War, it seems likely these weapons were to be sold to some neighboring country. We then learn that the student, not wanting to be involved in the production of arms for war, had quit his job at the factory. The contradiction inherent in a Hiroshima whose factories produced weapons of war only seven years after the end of the Asia-Pacific War is deeply etched into this film.

Like the surge of a burst dam, early in 2015 the nuclear power plants started coming back online in Japan. Since this took place in the midst of the political confusion surrounding passage of the Legislation for Peace and Security (*Anpo hōsei*),[8] the nuclear restarts are directly connected to this political activity. Further, these two events—nuclear plant restarts and the political activity around the legislation—are part of the process of Japan's postwar development, all of which was undertaken in collaboration with the United States. It was to be a year when all of these issues were once again brought up for review. I anticipate that before long revision of the constitution will be an actual issue for us;[9] be that as it may, preservation of the constitution in the seventy years since the war is not necessarily praiseworthy because, in point of fact, we now come abruptly and painfully to realize that the seeds of constitutional change have been carefully nurtured during those seventy years.

In the midst of these events, the victims of the Great Eastern Japan Earthquake Disaster, and especially those who were radiated, find themselves open to criticism for "milking" their status as victims should they veer from this narrative about successful reconstruction, in a clear repetition of the

"Hiroshima" *hibakusha* experience. As ever, unchanged within Japanese society, the weak are glibly discarded as losers, at times even finding themselves the objects of bashing and harassment. The reality that the film *Hiroshima* holds for us even today is that politicized trauma is the way of doing things in contemporary Japan, and has been, over and over again, from the end of the war to the present.

THE IMAGE OF AN ATOMIC-BOMBED "HIROSHIMA" AND "NAGASAKI"

Another point needs mention in the context of Sekigawa's *Hiroshima*: the attempt in this work to recreate the facts of August 6 as faithfully as possible. Imamura Shōhei's 1989 film *Kuroi ame* (*Black Rain*) also scrupulously recreated the days from the bomb's being dropped to those immediately following. There is no doubt that this film too accomplished this goal. It seems to me that, now more than ever, it is time to assess the result of such obsessive recreating of the events of August 6.

This because what we know of "Hiroshima" and "Nagasaki" comes from accounts in works such as *Genbaku no ko* (*Children of the A-Bomb*),[10] in the displays at the Atomic-Bomb Museum, and representations in atomic-bomb fiction; the world recreated in the films mentioned above are in complete alignment with the museum and fictional accounts: blast-singed flesh peeled and hanging off bodies, swollen faces, voices pleading for water, corpses floating in rivers. The summer of 2015 saw reprints of *The Collected Postwar Novels of Hara Tamiki* (Hara Tamiki sengo zenshōsetsu) and *The Collected Poetry of Hara Tamiki* (Hara Tamiki zenshishū). Hara's "Summer Flowers" (Natsu no hana), which is known for the phrase "Stripped of everything in a flash, the world after," includes the following:

> Within the expanse of the silvery nothingness that stretched out beneath the intense sun, there were streets, there were rivers, there were bridges. And then, here and there, there were piles of swollen, red, and raw corpses. This was a new Hell, one brought about by a precise and elaborate means. All things human had been obliterated. What had once been, for example, the peaceful look on the face of someone dead was now replaced by something standard, and mechanical.[11]

The tragic events of Hiroshima and Nagasaki cannot be forgotten; it is by means of such images that it comes together as a collective memory. But one has to wonder if the repulsiveness of the scenes is inversely proportional to how much the reality is somehow lost. For example, consider viewers who saw Imamura Shōhei's *Black Rain*, in 1989, in the midst of the bubble economy: one wonders if the film, being so far from everyday experience, might have lost its sense of "reality." Then again, even Hara Tamiki, for whom "Hiroshima" played out before his very eyes, described what he saw there as something one might see in a painting from one of the Surrealists:

> The limbs of these corpses, which seemed to have become rigid after struggling in their last agony, had a kind of daunting rhythm. In the scattered electric wires and countless wrecks there was embodied a spasmodic design in nothingness. The burnt and toppled streetcar and the horse with its huge belly on the ground gave me the impression of a world described by a . . . surrealist painting.[12]

Thus, if we consider that even for those who witnessed the actual bombed Hiroshima, it exceeds reality; if we then consider how scenes from the bombed city have been faithfully reproduced many times in the film, then we have to wonder if it is even possible any longer to recall the bombed Hiroshima with any sense of "reality." What has been passed down to the generations that do not know that place, that bombed Hiroshima, seems to be nothing more than some distant historical "mistake" that we "will never repeat." In our post–cold war era, who could imagine that such a thing might come and rupture our everyday lives? It is a fact: no atomic bombs have been dropped anywhere since that time. Even so, in various areas around the world people suffering from radiation continue to be born. Surely we should have understood and imagined these details long before "Fukushima" occurred.

John Hersey's *Hiroshima* came out in a new Japanese edition in 2014, seventy years after the atomic bombing of Hiroshima.[13] Then in 2015, Georges Bataille's "*A propos des récits d'habitants d'Hiroshima*," written as a review of Hersey's book, was also reprinted in a Japanese version.[14] Reading Hersey's words from 1946 and 1947 now forces us once more to confront the fact that memories of Hiroshima now resonate with the countless deaths resulting from the 2011 Great Eastern Japan Earthquake Disaster. In Bataille's words: "We can recognize the life and character of those whom in Hersey's book we see suddenly engulfed in horror. They resemble those men, women and children whom we see every day and with whom we are familiar."[15]

These people thrust into the very center of such a "horror" have already become other than "human"; they have entered Battaille's "animal stupor," the "animal's viscerally cowardly situation of compromised psychology,"[16] and seem just barely able to continue "performing human actions."[17] Hersey's *Hiroshima* collects the accounts, based on interviews, of a number of people who lived through the bombings. As such, we do not perceive those experiences as the historical event we now know as "Hiroshima" but as eyewitness accounts of the chaos playing out before human eyes. Bataille describes the content of "recollections . . . reduced to the dimension of animal experience."[18] The "animal experience" invoked here is, of course, contrasted to the "human" one, namely an experience of being "engulfed in horror" amidst the chaos, an experience unaware of the historical act of the dropping of the atomic bombs. According to Bataille, the account that most captures a "human" representation is the one "given by President Truman" that "situates the bombing of Hiroshima within history."[19] But the fact is that "Hiroshima," as an event that will be known to later generations by that particular name, is one that no one will ever again actually be able to witness. At that time, the horrific scenes of a city attacked without warning had not yet become associated with the event that we now know as "Hiroshima." No matter how many eyewitness testimonies we collect, we remain unable to reach the historical reality of "Hiroshima." A gap opens between the experiences of those who were there and the historical consciousness of those observing from afar.

Having situated this as an "animal experience," Europeans find it possible to link "Hiroshima" to Auschwitz as a similar atrocity. But the ability to connect the historical large-scale massacres of "Hiroshima," "Nagasaki," and "Auschwitz" lies in the ability to see beyond the specifics of any one tragedy to the interconnectedness of all mass fatalities. Likewise, those who were able to grasp the entirety of the calamity that is the tsunami of the Great Eastern Japan Earthquake Disaster were those watching the news on TV; it was not the victims of the tsunami, because they were fighting as hard as they could, struggling with everything they had in this crisis that threatened their very existence. When we consider how multilayered was the Great Eastern Japan Earthquake Disaster, and how that in the damage of the tsunami were so many deaths, we find just how much more it comes to resemble "Hiroshima" and "Nagasaki." This may be the reason that Takaichi Sanae, then-chairman of the Liberal Democratic Party Policy Bureau, who was rushing to restart the nuclear reactors, could carelessly say, "It was not the nuclear incident that resulted in a situation of so many deaths."[20] If the imagery of the tragedy of the nuclear meltdown is dependent upon mass death, then, as I have discussed above, "Fukushima" does not seem to resemble "Hiroshima" or "Nagasaki." At the same time, "Fukushima" has come to be discussed in ways analogous to war. This is how observers have easily come to understand and to accept it.

Sono Sion's 2012 film *Kibō no kuni* (*Land of Hope*) is the story of a post-Fukushima Japan set in fictitious Nagashima prefecture. A nuclear power plant has exploded and hopelessly contaminated the land. It probably goes without saying that "Nagashima" is a conglomeration of "Hiroshima," "Nagasaki," and "Fukushima," a metaphor that captures both the atomic-bombs and radioactive contamination.

In the film, a dairy farmer father and his wife, who is suffering from dementia, force their young son and his wife to evacuate and leave the prefecture. The daughter-in-law constantly reads the books about radioactive contamination that she received from her father-in-law, gradually falling into a neurotic condition characterized by obsessive fears about radiation.[21] Initially, the son is at a loss and does not know what to do; he assumes she is overreacting, but as the tension from the accident fades, he grows uncomfortable with the way others seem to forget the reality of the accident and comes to share her feelings. She tells him: "Do you see this? It's an invisible war! You can't see the bullets or missiles, but they are flying all around us! Invisible bullets!"[22]

At this point, describing radiation contamination via wartime analogies means that the nuclear explosion associated with the nuclear accident at Fukushima, for Japanese who have so long understood the trauma associated with Nagasaki and Hiroshima to be theirs in particular, is again brought to the surface of consciousness. All during the Cold War years, it was assumed that a Third World War was a distinct possibility and that it would be an atomic war resulting in the annihilation of the human race.

So, when Tawada Yōko describes an American military plane falling from the sky and falling into a nuclear power plant in her short story "Higan" ("The Far Shore"), she masterfully articulates this connection between the pipe dreams of an actual world that never stopped to question its furious construction of nuclear power plants and the meltdowns of this postdisaster moment. The description of this fictional accident mirrors exactly the images of damage found in atomic-bomb fiction:

> [w]hen the loud shock of the explosion slapped them across the face. They looked up to see an enormous brown umbrella open slowly overhead, so big that it blocked out half the sky. . . .
>
> But those terrifying scenes lasted only a few seconds. After that came painful burns that inflicted great, lingering suffering on the victims. The skin itself did not look that different, but the burns hurt terribly. The victims felt like their arms and legs had been pierced all the way to the bone with long skewers, and their flesh was being roasted over hot coals. These were strange burns, unlike any that anyone had ever experienced before. . . .
>
> That day, tens of millions of victims stretched their burned arms before them and staggered toward the nearest rivers and lakes, trying to find relief in the water. They didn't notice if they lost their shoes along the way.[23]

The reason that the "enormous brown umbrella" that opened "slowly overhead" brings to mind the atomic bomb's mushroom cloud, and that the image of "tens of millions of victims" who "stretched their burned arms before them and staggered toward the nearest rivers and lakes" brings to mind the atomic tragedy, is because that imagery is so well established. Tawada deliberately employs atomic-bomb imagery here to imply that these explosions, whether at nuclear power plants or from atomic bombs, are exactly the same. In so doing one connects "Hiroshima" and "Nagasaki" to "Fukushima," in effect linking atomic bombs and nuclear energy. In fact, if we allow that there is a direct line of connection between Hiroshima and Nagasaki to Fukushima, we catch the precise image that nuclear bombs and nuclear energy are, in essence, exactly the same thing. This connection forms the critical situation repeatedly portrayed in many films, from *Gojira* (*Godzilla*, 1954) to Hasegawa Kazuhiko's *Taiyō o nusunda otoko* (The Man Who Stole the Sun, 1979). At the same time, this sort of crisis has been consistently depicted as the destruction of the earth, as the annihilation of mankind, and as accompanied by mass death and the total destruction of cities. The same is true for the representative image of the atomic bomb, namely Hiroshima's Genbaku Peace Dome, via photographs taken to foreground the scorched-earth landscape immediately following the bombing and to highlight a dome standing amidst a landscape reduced to dust. Further, the Genbaku Dome was left standing as it was; the result was to cement an image of a restored (*fukkō*) Hiroshima having risen from the damage of the atomic bombs, presenting the illusion that Hiroshima has completely recovered from radiation and its damage.

In this way radiation exposure could be treated as a singular event—very conveniently for both the U.S. military and a like-minded Japanese government. By minimizing estimates of the damage and the number of deaths from radiation, both governments could avoid acknowledging long-term illnesses resulting from atomic-bomb radiation (*genbakushō*). If negative health effects are not the direct result of the atomic bombing, they could argue that the damage is not the result of being irradiated. Further while negative health issues do exist, they cannot be definitively attributed to the effects of radiation. It would thus seem that the imagery with which the atomic bomb and nuclear weapons were discussed—as a single event—work to conceal the long-term negative effects of radiation.

From the vantage point of the radiation victims, "Fukushima" is the same thing as "Hiroshima" and "Nagasaki." Kanō Mikiyo asked herself, "Why didn't 'Hiroshima' stop 'Fukushima'?" In the same spirit, Nagasaki *hibakusha* writer Hayashi Kyōko wrote in the aftermath of "Fukushima": "We who were made *hibakusha* in the twentieth century spoke and wrote of our experience and lived our lives in the hope of being the last of this new race. But in the twenty-first century, our nation, our irradiated nation (*hibakukoku*), has given birth to yet another generation of *hibakusha*."[24]

At present, it is only the *hibakusha* who lived through atomic bombings who can equate "Fukushima" to atomic bombs. This is because they know better than anyone that the term *hibakusha* does not refer only to those who died on the day of the bombing. "Hiroshima" and "Nagasaki" began on "that day" and now, with the parade of days one after the other since then, it has continued for seventy years. If we posit no similarities between "Fukushima" and "Nagasaki" and "Hiroshima," it may be because we are held prisoner by the image of the atomic-bomb blasts on August 6 and 9. The film *Hiroshima* does in fact portray those who died from the radiation of those bombs, but *hibakusha* are not only the dead but also survivors, those who continue to live. That is one thing that this film depicts: the many *hibakusha* who "live every day in fear of atomic-bomb disease taking" their lives. If we cannot picture "Hiroshima" as anything more than a single tragedy of war, we must reread and reposition those depictions.

REREADING *HIROSHIMA MON AMOUR*

In 2014, Kudō Yōko's new Japanese translation of Marguerite Duras' *Hiroshima Mon Amour* appeared, advertised as "The story of Hiroshima and love that you will want to read in the wake of 'Fukushima'." Using the invitation of this advertisement, I want here to reread and analyze anew *Hiroshima Mon Amour* and then use it as a tool for thinking about "Fukushima."

In Alain Resnais' 1959 film of the same title, based on Duras' screenplay, Emmanuelle Riva plays a French actress shooting a film on location in Hiroshima. She spends two nights with a Japanese architect and left-wing activist played by Okada Eiji. The story of these two, referred to only as *She* and *He*, opens with the following conversation about Hiroshima:

He: You saw nothing in Hiroshima. Nothing.
She: I saw everything. Everything.
She: The hospital, for instance, I saw it. I'm sure I did. There is a hospital in Hiroshima. How could I help seeing it?
He: You did not see the hospital in Hiroshima. You saw nothing in Hiroshima.[25]

The man denies everything the woman claims to have seen in "Hiroshima." She tells him about what she saw at the Atomic Bomb museum; she then tells him about what she saw on the newsreels. What she *saw*, of course, did not go beyond the exhibits and the old-fashioned news footage housed in the Peace Memorial Museum, the bombed landscapes recreated in the film *Hiroshima*, and the events written about in John Hersey's *Hiroshima*.

As discussed above, if we posit that those in the midst of it cannot grasp the entirety of the events around them, then we can read the opening two lines of dialogue in *Hiroshima Mon Amour* as the contrast between the woman's seeing of "Hiroshima" as a historical event, and the man's assertion that she did not see it as an experience from within the maelstrom. *Hiroshima Mon Amour* takes this historicized, distant event and fashions it as a tale of the quest for a memory as though from personal experience.

For many people around the world, "Hiroshima" has signified "the end of the war." When the man asks her "What did Hiroshima mean for you, in France?" She replies, "The end of the war, I mean, really the end. Amazement . . . at the idea that they had dared . . . amazement at the idea that they had succeeded. And then, too, for us, the beginning of an unknown fear. And then, indifference. And also the fear of indifference. . . ."[26] For this French woman, "Hiroshima" was not merely the end of the war; she goes on to relate the seemingly bottomless terror in the face of a nuclear weapon used for the first time in human history and continues on to tell of the terror "we" felt in the face of indifference. Those of us alive after "Fukushima" know the meaning of such terrors becoming reality.

It does not need restating, but France also experienced war. The woman of the film also has a past, one in which as a girl in Nevers, a lover was killed. A German soldier, her lover was shot and killed. She was disgraced by the villagers for her transgression of fraternizing with enemy soldiers. They shaved off her hair and locked her in her family's basement.[27] As she tries to remember "Hiroshima," she also tries to share her memories of Nevers with him. As she speaks of Nevers, the pain within her begins to overlap with that of "Hiroshima." She has the Japanese man listen to her story about the German lover; we find that the conversation proceeds with an intentional melding of the two men's identities. For example, the Japanese man draws the story of the German lover out of her by asking questions like, "When you are in the cellar, am I dead?"[28]

Finally, the woman begins to talk about her process of forgetting: "Oh! It's horrible. I'm beginning to remember you less clearly. . . . I'm beginning to forget you. I tremble at the thought of having forgotten so much love."[29] Her story is about the inevitability of forgetting. With that, given the necessity of forgetting, *Hiroshima Mon Amour* becomes a story about the search for the means to remember those things that need to be remembered. How in fact is one to remember the "Hiroshima" (as well as the Nevers) that will surely fade from memory? Here we find one of the themes of *Hiroshima Mon Amour*. Just what is the "Hiroshima" that must be remembered?

Hiroshima Mon Amour was filmed in 1958. The Lucky Dragon Incident, remembered as the third nuclear blast following Hiroshima and Nagasaki, was already in the past. That incident means that less than ten years after "Hiroshima" and "Nagasaki" the Japanese were once again exposed to radiation from American hydrogen bombs. The woman says, "Listen. . . . I know. . . . I know *everything*. It went on."[30] In the March 1954 Bikini Atoll hydrogen bomb test it was not only the Lucky Dragon that was irradiated; other ships were also engulfed. *Hiroshima Mon Amour* also includes images of the irradiated crew of the Lucky Dragon and also of contaminated tuna that had to be destroyed. She continues:

Women risk giving birth to malformed children, to monsters, but it goes on.
Men risk becoming sterile, but it goes on.
The rain of ashes on the waters of the Pacific.
The waters of the Pacific kill.
Fishermen of the Pacific are dead.
People are afraid of the food.
The food of an entire city is thrown away.
The food of entire cities is buried.
An entire city rises up in anger.
Entire cities rise up in anger.[31]

The terror of radiation the woman speaks of here is not the terror of an atomic bombing. Her fear is of being irradiated by radioactive rain; it is the fear of internal exposure from eating irradiated "atomic tuna" (*genshi maguro*); it is fear of the result wherein reproductive functions are disrupted. The film captures scenes of demonstrations calling for the banning of nuclear and hydrogen weapons; it shows how the Lucky Dragon Incident spawned protest movements against nuclear weapons such as hydrogen bombs. Yet while *Hiroshima Mon Amour* shows antinuclear movements, it is not to highlight the issue of mass deaths from nuclear weapons; rather, the issue that *Hiroshima Mon Amour* raises is the fear that accompanies low-level radiation exposure. This was, of course, a concern following "Hiroshima" and "Nagasaki" as well, but the issue gained new visibility with the irradiated tuna from the Lucky Dragon Incident. And now, for those of us who have lived through "Fukushima," concerns over food and anxieties about rain and water feel all the more real. But low-level radiation exposure would seem thus far to have been insufficiently imagined in the imagery of "Hiroshima" and "Nagasaki." Failure to associate the reality of low-level radiation is one way that the imagery of "Hiroshima" and "Nagasaki" has become diminished.

LUXURIANT GREEN

Albert Camus predicted the following in the August 8, 1945, edition of *Combat*: "We can sum it all up in a sentence: the civilization of the machine has just achieved its ultimate degree of savagery. A choice is going to have to be made in the fairly near future between collective suicide and the intelligent utilization of scientific discoveries."[32] Georges Bataille wrote:

> The possibility of seeing the world delivered up to uranium obviously justifies some general reaction. And it is strange that, in the malaise in which it called men to holy war (to conquests, to crusades, to religious wars) or to revolution,

the human voice, formerly so powerful, no longer has the slightest force, even given the most compelling reason ever.[33]

As they predicted in the immediate aftermath of "Hiroshima" and "Nagasaki," there have been no decisions to halt the use of nuclear energy completely. That, despite the fact that we have "Hiroshima," "the most compelling reason ever." We can thus say that Hiroshima was always already "Fukushima." Looking back from our present moment, we know that when the bombs were dropped, the science behind nuclear power plants was fully envisioned, and *hibakusha* were already scattered across the entire world. But reading Camus and Bataille clarifies that it was already understood that we would never be able to give up nuclear energy. Jean-Luc Nancy argued similarly in *After Fukushima*: "The problem posed by the 'peaceful' use of the atom is that of its extreme, and extremely lasting, harmfulness. This harmfulness is the same after Hiroshima as after Three Mile Island, Chernobyl, and Fukushima."[34]

Everyone knows that nuclear weapons and nuclear power plants equally provide harm because of their radioactive particles, but unlike "Hiroshima" or "Nagasaki," the image of mass fatalities associated with "Fukushima" is quite different. So then, what is "Fukushima"? Stated another way, what is it that connects "Hiroshima" to "Fukushima"? To answer such a question we must search within the image of "Hiroshima" itself.

I want to note here that when the woman in Duras' *Hiroshima Mon Amour* insists she saw "Hiroshima," along with representative images of the atomic bombing—the melted iron and bottles, skin with keloid scars, women's hair falling out in clumps—she also relates the state of the vegetation covering the ground: "on the fifteenth day too, Hiroshima was blanketed with flowers. There were cornflowers and gladiolas everywhere, and morning glories and day lilies that rose again from the ashes with an extraordinary vigor, quite unheard-of for flowers till then."[35] Duras in her own notes makes clear that she took this passage from Hersey's book. The relevant passage from Hersey comes from Sasaki Toshiko's testimony. One month after the bombing, on September 9, Sasaki is transferred to a different hospital and for the first time sees "the ruins of Hiroshima."

> Even though the wreckage had been described to her, and though she was still in pain, the sight horrified and amazed her, and there was something she noticed about it that particularly gave her the creeps. Over everything—up through the wreckage of the city, in gutters, along riverbanks, tangled among tiles and tin roofing, climbing on charred tree trunks—was a blanket of fresh, vivid, lush, optimistic green; the verdancy rose even from the foundations of ruined houses. Weeds already hid the ashes, and wildflowers were in bloom among the city's bones. The bomb had not only left the underground organs of plants intact; it

had stimulated them. Everywhere were bluets and Spanish bayonets, goosefoot, morning glories and day lilies, the hairy-fruited bean, purslane and clotblur and sesame and panic grass and feverfew. Especially in a circle at the center, sickle senna grew in extraordinary regeneration, not only standing among the charred remnants of the same plant but pushing up in new places, among bricks and through cracks in the asphalt. It actually seemed as if a load of sickle-senna seed had been dropped along with the bomb.[36]

As if the seeds had been dropped from the sky: this image of green growth pushing up through the city rubble is unsettling. But this was not a green that was desired. This "fresh, vivid, lush, optimistic green" was something brought about by the bomb; it existed because there was an atomic bomb. All this green, every inch of it, was dripping with radiation.

American trauma scholar Cathy Caruth commented on this passage:

Miss Sasaki's return to Hiroshima is a return to a new kind of vision. . . . Returning to the site of the catastrophe—which is also the site of unconsciousness (or the "edge of unconsciousness")—Miss Sasaki now sees something that "gives her the creeps," the flowers "optimistically" growing over the ruins, a form of ongoing life inextricably bound up with the very act of destruction. . . . Marguerite Duras disturbs the second seeing by superimposing it on the first, by "transferring," as she puts it, the line about the sprouting flowers, onto the footage of the "burnt children screaming." In juxtaposing the "optimism" of the flowers growing over the ruins with the documents and reconstructions of the moments of the catastrophe, Duras emphasizes the catastrophic sight that remains disjointed and insistently returning along with the strange survival of life.[37]

The city of death the atomic bomb created was not a place where all life was extinguished. Even with so many dead bodies, plant life grew even more luxuriantly. This eerie green was witnessed by many as the strong force of life, able to continue on no matter what.

Ibuse Masuji described the grass climbing out of the burnt ground in his novel *Kuroi ame* (*Black Rain*, 1970). When the factory boss in the story remarks that "It seems even seventy years from now no grass will grow in Hiroshima or Nagasaki," the narrator Shizuma Shigematsu comments:

The name of the bomb had already undergone a number of changes, from the initial "new weapon" through "new-type bomb," "secret weapon," "special new-type bomb," to "special high-capacity bomb." That day, I learned for the first time to call it an "atomic bomb." But I couldn't believe that nothing would grow there for seventy-five years. Hadn't I seen weeds running riot all over the ruins?

"Now that you mention it," said the manager when I told him, "I saw them, too. I saw a plantain drooping over at the top because it had grown so tall."[38]

The image of irradiation is not one of pure annihilation. Indeed, even in Godzilla's case it is imagined as having birthed an abnormally huge living creature. If Godzilla represents the terror of a life that will survive in a mutated form, then the luxuriant green bursting forth in the burnt ruins can also be understood as a dormant ominousness submerged in the life force.

This image of luxuriant green captures exactly the landscape one now sees in "Fukushima," in the zones now uninhabitable for humans. I can imagine just how many people have memories of feeling strangely disoriented upon seeing the photographs taken of the cherry trees in glorious full bloom just days after the nuclear disasters. These magnificent blooms are in zones where no one can see them. We know from the many photographs of the area that those zones registering high levels of radiation are overflowing with life. This is completely opposite to the images of death and destruction we imagine will accompany the nuclear threat. We find there an expanse of land that is thriving and continuing to live. So then, even though this irreconcilable image of luxuriant green had manifested from the start in the atomic-bomb literature coming out of "Hiroshima," why is "Hiroshima" so strongly stamped with the image as a place of miserable scorched earth? All the miseries of the atomic bomb are handed down to us by all the forms of life that lived through it.

VULNERABILITY (OF LIFE)

As an image of survival, the most striking, for "Fukushima" in particular, is that of the animals left behind in the irradiated zones. Cows wander left and right across concrete roads. Ostriches—imported as mascot for the nuclear power plant—strut about freely. There are no humans; they have died or evacuated. In their absence animal populations have flourished. Many of the animals we see in photographs of the zone look directly at us. French writer and philosopher Jean-Christophe Bailly took this up in his work on animals. Citing Rainer Maria Rilke's opening to *Duino Elegies*—"All eyes, the creatures of the World look out into the open"—he goes on to say the following about the animal gaze:

> The world of gazes is the world of *significance*, that is, of a possible, open, still indeterminate meaning. For the percussive impact of difference that is produced by discourse, the gaze substitutes a sort of dispersal: the unformulated is its element, its watery origin. The gaze gazes, and the unformulated is, in it, the pathway of thought, or at least of a thinking that is not uttered, not articulated, but that takes place and sees itself, holds itself in this purely strange and strangely limitless place which is the surface of the eye.[39]

As Bailly argues, the world animals gaze upon is a world not yet accorded meaning. In *Hiroshima Mon Amour*, this is the Hiroshima that the woman sees, the one the man says she does not see; this is the Nevers the woman remembers, the trauma not yet historicized. Likewise, Sasaki Toshiko's narrative and the luxuriant green in the burnt-out ruins of *Black Rain* record observations in a situation before meaning has been assigned. Bailly calls this "the pensivity of animals," which he explains this way:

> Thus it is even among humans, who compensate, however, thorough discourse for this lack of determinacy and of articulation. But among animals, the absence of language means there is no compensation for the lack, and this is why their gaze is so disarming when it settles on us, which happens, as Rilke's line says, sweetly and soberly. In the face of that which is and can only be for us neither question nor response, we experience the feeling of being in the presence of an unknown force, at once supplicating and calm, that in effect traverses us. This force may not need to be named, but where it is exercised it is as though we were in the presence of a different form of thought, a thought that could only have ahead of it and overwhelmingly, the *pensive* path. . . .
>
> My concern is not that we should credit animals with access to thought; it is that we should move beyond human exclusivity, that we should let go of the eternally renewed credo according to which our species is the pinnacle of creation and has a unique future. The pensivity of animals, or at least what I am trying to designate and grasp with this term, is neither a diversion nor a curiosity; what it establishes is that the world in which we live is gazed upon by other beings, that the visible is shared among creatures, and that a politics could be invented on this basis, if it is not too late.[40]

While this proposal may seem slightly naïve, the argument resonates within a European culture that brought about a civilization by managing nature.

Bailly's "pensivity of animals" is a response to the questions raised in Jacques Derrida's *The Animal that Therefore I Am*. Derrida's discussion begins, famously, after his having been stared at by his cat while naked in his bathroom. There is also a scene in *Hiroshima Mon Amour* where the woman relates her memories of having been stared at by a cat. At the time of being censured by the Nevers villagers after the discovery of her affair with the German soldier, getting her head shaved and locked in the basement, she relates the experience of being stared at by a cat this way: "Sometimes a cat comes in and looks. It's not a mean cat. I just don't know anything at all."[41]

The action of being looked at by the cat is not accorded any further meaning here; the woman is simply in a situation of "not knowing anything." For animals the survival instinct takes precedence over everything else; that is, animals do not find survival to be a choice in some way ominous and threatening. Survival drove the woman's decision to leave Nevers.

Although it may be obvious, the vulnerability of life constantly haunts survivors. For *hibakusha*, survival means not only watching others die but, even more, surviving with the oppressive terror of death that may come at any time from radiation hanging over them. In that sense, this is where "Hiroshima" and "Nagasaki" are continued through "Fukushima."

In the case of "Fukushima," lack of information means one cannot even be sure if one has been irradiated or not: every day is anxiety-filled; radiation could appear at any moment. Radiation does not exist in any concrete way. Generally one traces irradiation retroactively back to the original symptoms, that is, when an ungraspable, imprecise anxiety emerges. More to the point, it proves extremely difficult to determine whether or not feeling out of sorts is the result of radiation. In response to actual occurrences of ill health, one can only be anxious about radiation. It connects to nothing material. In that sense, one always carries the seeds of anxiety. This vulnerable life situation is exactly where the *hibakusha* resides; that vulnerability is not something directly arising from issues of health and injury. This is the same set of issues faced by the *hibakusha* who lived through "Hiroshima" and "Nagasaki." As Hayashi Kyōko has written in her "To Rui, Once Again": "This fear of 'internal exposure' continues, because up until the day that radioactive emissions reach zero, radioactivity continues to be emitted. This has no relation to whether or not we develop symptoms."[42]

Only now, after "Fukushima," have some Hiroshima and Nagasaki *hibakusha* finally been able to get certification attesting to their atomic-bomb disease. We now understand radiation better. After "Fukushima" we can test for different things, such as "internal radiation." Thus, it is only after "Fukushima" that those living with radiation, not just those facing imminent death, are officially recognized as *hibakusha*. "Fukushima" has changed even the way we approach Hiroshima and Nagasaki.

By way of example we have Ishiuchi Miyako's *Hiroshima*, a collection of photographs of belongings of those who died in the atomic bombings. A meticulously embroidered handbag, a carefully laid-out blouse with fancy buttons decorated with embroidery: the beauty of these items takes your breath away. It may have been wartime, but we find that these women were no different than we are now. Such insight cannot be gained from the reconstructions in films like *Children of Hiroshima*, *Hiroshima*, *Black Rain*, and others. They cradled beautiful things, they were enamored of lovely things, no different than us. We come to understand through these items that the death of that day visited them in a manner that no one had foreseen. These fragments of beautiful clothing left behind take us back to the precarity of life experienced by those who wore them. Such beauty and loveliness is, of course, associated with the dead, but it also, surprisingly, is linked to the survivors who lived through it. This is no doubt because of its connection to those still living who carefully kept these items safe and continually thought about them in the seventy years since that day. The living and their manner of keeping alive the memory of those who died is also a prominent theme in many of the descriptions within postdisaster literature.

Hiroshima Mon Amour, as a means of avoiding forgetting and in order to remember, tells the story of Hiroshima and Nevers as the story of two lovers. In the film's last scene, the woman says to the man, "Hi-ro-shi-ma. Hi-ro-shi-ma. That's your name;" he replies, "That's my name. Yes. Your name is Nevers. Ne-vers in France." Duras wrote of this: "She calls him from afar, lost in wonder. She has succeeded in drowning him in universal oblivion. And it is a source of amazement to her."[43]

Duras writes that "She has succeeded in drowning him in universal oblivion," but this cannot be taken strictly literally, since she goes on to say that this "is a source of amazement to her." At that moment the man holds both of the woman's arms and stands in front of her. Given how much she fears oblivion, it seems unnatural that she would "forget" this man right in front of her. Even so, if forgetting means to truly consign memories to oblivion, then "amazement" over this "forgetting" becomes impossible. If one has so completely consigned to oblivion memories that cannot even be recalled, then the fact of having forgotten is itself, and at the same time, erased. After all and everything has been forgotten, one has to wonder what is it that remains. Even if "Hiroshima" is submerged in "universal oblivion," then all the more reason to unravel what sleeps in the depths.

After hearing about what happened in Nevers, the man says: "In a few years, when I'll have forgotten you, and when other such adventures, from sheer habit, will happen to me, I'll remember you as the symbol of love's forgetfulness. I'll think of this adventure as of the horror of oblivion. I already know it."[44] Again, the "forgetting" referenced here is not the complete erasure of memory. Even should one intend to forget something, it will be remembered unexpectedly. It is the same with lovers. Even upon stepping out into a new life with a new person after a breakup, it is unlikely that one will ever completely forget the person they were in love with. There is no complete forgetting in a single lifetime. A phrase like "One can never totally forget the person one loved" seems, upon reflection, quite an amazing human function. Duras, by changing "Hiroshima" into one's lover (*mon amour*) attempts to make forgetting impossible.

Descriptions appearing seventy years after the war, such as those that portray "Hiroshima" and "Nagasaki," need to be reread after the 3.11 disasters: earlier depictions of war and disaster look different now. Likewise, the point of view that immediately likened the disasters to war requires rereading and reevaluation. This does not mean that "Fukushima" was a wartime situation. Rather, since "Fukushima" we read the postwar period in a different way;

we discover "Fukushima" within the postwar. When "Fukushima" occurred, more than a few people felt that "we *already knew* this would happen." Memories buried in the abyss of forgetting are now called forth a second time.

When Hotta Yoshie's 1955 novel *Jikan (Time)* was reprinted in 2015,[45] this astounding novel depicting the Nanjing Massacre from the perspective of the Chinese unexpectedly made an appearance in our time. It seems not too farfetched to think that postdisaster literature is being written with an eye to rethinking situations that have already occurred in the future.

NOTES

1. Sawaragi Noi, "Kikan suru koto ga konnan na basho kara," *Shinchō* (October 2015): 239.

2. Borrmann, Mechtild, *Die andere Hälfte der Hoffnung* (München Droemer, 2014). Translated by Akasaka Momoko as *Kibō no kataware* (Tokyo: Kawade Shobo, 2014), 308.

3. Borrmann, *Kibō no kataware*, 308.

4. Borrmann, *Kibō no kataware*, 308.

5. Translated by Matsumoto Taeko as *Chiyerunobuiri no inori* (Tokyo: Iwanami Shoten, 2016).—Trans.

6. Kanō Mikiyo, *"Hiroshima" to "Fukushima" no aida: Jendā no shiten kara* (Tokyo: Inpakuto shuppankai, 2013), 16.

7. Hideo Sekigawa, dir. *Hiroshima* (Tokyo: Shin Nippon Eigasha, 1953).

8. Kimura addressed this in chapter 1 as well. *Anpō Hōsei* would seem, literally, to be "Peace Legislation." The controversy and subsequent protests were because this legislation would allow Japanese forces to participate in foreign conflicts, thereby abrogating Article 9 of the Postwar constitution which commits Japan to self-defense only.—Trans.

9. At the time Kimura was writing this (2015), Prime Minister Abe was preparing the process for one of his key political causes, the changing of the Japanese constitution, particularly Article 9, to allow Japan to participate in non-self-defensive military maneuvers. When Abe resigned due to sickness in 2020, initiative lost focus and drive.—Trans.

10. Osada Arata, *Genbaku no ko: Hiroshima no shōnen shōjo no uttae* (Tokyo: Iwanami Shoten, 1990 [1951]). Translated by Jean Clark Dan and Ruth Sieben-Morgen as *Children of the A-Bomb: The Testament of the Boys and Girls of Hiroshima* (New York: Putnam, 1963).

11. Hara Tamiki, "Natsu no Hana," in *Shōsetsushū: Natsu no hana* (Tokyo: Iwanami bunkō, 1988), 27. This translation, modified slightly, is from Treat, *Writing Ground Zero*, 148–49. For a complete translation of Hara's story, see Richard H. Minear, trans., "Summer Flowers," *Literary Review* 60, no. 3 (September 2017), 51.—Trans.

12. Hara, "Natsu no hana," 27; Minear, "Summer Flowers," 51. The English translation adds the name of Dali, which is not in the original.—Trans.

13. John Hersey, *Hiroshima*, translated by Ishikawa Kin'ichi (Tokyo: Hosei Daigaku Shuppankyoku, 2014).

14. Georges Bataille, *Hiroshima no hitobito no monogatari*, translated by Takeshi Sakai (Tokyo: Keibunkanshoten, 2015).

15. This translation is found in Georges Bataille, "Concerning the Accounts Given by the Residents of Hiroshima," translated by Alan Keenan, *American Imago* 48, no. 4 (Winter 1991): 499.

16. I have added this phrase to reflect the phrase in the Japanese translation (動物的な臓臓状態)—Trans.

17. Bataille, "Concerning the Accounts," 505.

18. Bataille, "Concerning the Accounts," 501.

19. Bataille, "Concerning the Accounts," 501–2.

20. See, for example, *Huffpost Japan*, updated July 20, 2013 14:31 JST, https://www.huffingtonpost.jp/2013/06/18/sanae_takaichi_n_3463023.html, accessed 11/10/20. – Trans.

21. Kristina Iwata-Weickgennant criticized the film for promoting an image of "female hysteria" and reinscribing gender stereotypes through female characters who are overly sensitive to radiation. In the final scene, just as the wife is finally able to feel safe after evacuating to a distant place, the husband hides from her the fact that the Geiger counter has detected radiation there too. Iwata-Weickgennant criticizes Sono as paternalistic for assigning the acquisition and control of information to the male character. Kristina Iwata-Weickgennant. "Gendering Fukushima: Resistance, self-responsibility, and female hysteria in Sono Shion's *Land of Hope*," in *Fukushima and the Arts: Negotiating Nuclear Disaster*, eds. Barbara Geilhorn and Kristina Iwata-Weickgenannt (New York: Routledge, 2017).

Kanō Mikiyo argues that the image of the *hibakusha* has been gendered female. This would seem to also be true for "Fukushima": Kanō Mikiyo, *"Hiroshima" to "Fukushima."*

22. Sono Sion, dir. *Kibō no kuni* (Tokyo: Third Window Films, 2013).

23. Tawada Yōko, *Kentōshi* (Tokyo: Kōdansha, 2017), 207–9. Translated by Jeffrey Angles as "The Far Shore," https://www.wordswithoutborders.org/article/the-far-shore, accessed 11/10/20.

24. Hayashi Kyoko, *Tanima: Futabi Rui e* (Tokyo: Kōdansha, 2016). Translated by Maragaret Mitsutani as "To Rui, Once Again," *Asia Pacific Journal/Japan Focus* (April 1, 2017).

25. Marguerite Duras, *Hiroshima Mon Amour*, trans. Richard Seaver (New York: Grove Press, 1961), 15–17. These quotations are drawn from the screenplay, but I have deleted the non-dialogue sections.—Trans.

26. Duras, *Hiroshima Mon Amour*, 33.

27. After being liberated from the Nazis, women who had had sexual relations with Nazi soldiers were disgraced by having their hair shaved off. It seems there were more than 20,000 such women across France. The exhibit *Présumée coupables 14e–20e siècle* at the French National Archives (November 30, 2016–March 27, 2017)

displayed the history of women's suffering simply for being female, from Eve's original sin, to Joan of Arc, to the medieval witch trials, to the twentieth-century post–Second World War shaving of women's hair.

28. Duras, *Hiroshima Mon Amour*, 54.
29. Duras, *Hiroshima Mon Amour*, 64.
30. Duras, *Hiroshima Mon Amour*, 21.
31. Duras, *Hiroshima Mon Amour*, 22.
32. Albert Camus, *Camus at Combat: Writing 1944–1947*, edited and annotated by Jacqueline Levi-Valensi, translated by Arthur Goldhammer (Princeton: Princeton University Press, 2006), 236.
33. Bataille, "Concerning the Accounts," 498–99.
34. Jean-Luc Nancy, *Équivalence des catastrophes (après Fukushima)* (Paris: Éd. Galilée, 2012). Translated by Charlotte Mandell as *After Fukushima: The Equivalence of Catastrophes* (New York: Fordham University Press, 2015), 18.
35. Duras, *Hiroshima Mon Amour*, 19.
36. Hersey, *Hiroshima*, 91–92.
37. Cathy Caruth, *Unclaimed Experience: Trauma, Narrative, and History* (Baltimore and London: Johns Hopkins, 1996), 55.
38. Masuji Ibuse, *Kuroi ame* (Tokyo: Shinchōsha, 1970). Translated by John Bester as *Black Rain: A Novel* (Tokyo: Kōdansha, 1969). 282.
39. Jean-Christophe Bailly, *The Animal Side*, trans. Catherine Perter (New York: Fordham University Press, 2011), 14.
40. Bailly, *The Animal Side*, 15.
41. Duras, *Hiroshima Mon Amour*, 59, translation modified. The original French reads, "Je ne sais plus rien"; the Japanese translation has "mō nanimo wakaranai," and the English "I don't remember anymore." The distinction between "not knowing" and "not remembering" is critical for Kimura's following arguments.—Translator.
42. Hayashi Kyoko, *Tanima: Futabi Rui e*, 228. (Interestingly, this line does not seem to appear in Mitsutani's English translation.—Trans.)
43. Duras, *Hiroshima Mon Amour*, 83.
44. Duras, *Hiroshima Mon Amour*, 68.
45. Hotta Yoshie, *Jikan* (Tokyo: Iwanami Shoten, 2015).

Chapter 4

From Disaster to War

STORIES OF WAR FROM THE THIRD GENERATION

Literature of the Asia-Pacific War—"that war"—a war that had been for a time relegated to a place of complete oblivion, began to appear again in a steady stream as though some sluice gate had swung open in 2015 on the occasion of the seventieth anniversary of the war's end. New questions were asked in 2015. There was a sense of urgency not seen on the fiftieth or sixtieth anniversaries. One reason is surely that the Great Eastern Japan Earthquake Disaster caused us to think again about that war because imagery of that war's destructive crisis was used to describe the triple disasters; but even more because the nuclear accident, which once again irradiated land and people, prompted us to examine once again the path we have trod in the years since the war. The Second World War is currently being written about by the third generation, the grandchildren of the war survivors. Further, after the disasters, we find that novels about the war in the South Seas have received numerous new writer awards. I want to examine that connection here.

For example, in 2016, Takayama Haneko's "Taiyō no gawa no shima" (Island on the Sunny Side) was awarded the second Hayashi Fumiko Literary Prize. This work is straightforward in structure; it is comprised of letters between a husband stationed on an island in the South Seas—described in ways that bring Indonesia to mind—and his wife in Japan. In another example, in 2016, the thirty-second Dazai Osamu Prize went to Yozuri Jūroku's "Rakuen" (Paradise). This tale concerns a young man in his thirties and the stories he heard from his grandfather about his war experiences. The descriptions here also suggest that the grandfather was deployed to Indonesia.

Another novel that marks the beginning of the third, grandchild generation taking up the war in the South Seas was Takahashi Hiroki's *Yubi no hone*

(Finger Bone), winner of the 2014 Shinchō New Writer's Prize. The work opens as the protagonist comes upon a group of men walking listlessly along a yellow road. The setting is the war in New Guinea. They seem to be walking to Salamaua; these exhausted soldiers shuffle, they can hardly be said to be marching. As a unit, any military function is completely gone; this is simply a group of men putting one foot in front of the other. The novel does not refer to these men as "soldiers" but as "humans" (*ningen*)—mere life-forms at death's door and on their last faint breaths. The war depicted here is one of "humans" and a fight between life and death rather than "soldiers" for any particular battle. Such would seem to be the novel's main message.

The protagonist carries an "aluminum lunch box, inside of which is a bone, a human finger bone."[1] It is a piece of Sanada's body, someone he had been close to at the field hospital. He feels he must stay alive and return home to deliver the bone to Sanada's son. It was a promise based on their "pinky finger shake."[2] Even so, the protagonist thinks back to that time when "it was me, of course, that should have died in that hole that night," a time before he was carried off to the hospital with his serious injuries, a time when he already felt an unsettling premonition.[3]

He did not die at that time; he now feels his fate was "completely tied to that yellow road, that's what I now think."[4] The present of this tale's narration is our "now," the final scene of the novel is connected to this setting in New Guinea, and we realize that the entire story has been relayed as a flashback. When one thinks about it, war diaries can only be relayed as flashbacks. The reader wants to believe that the protagonist survived to narrate his tale, but the specter of his death nonetheless hangs heavily from start to finish. For the reader who has been following Takahashi's protagonist, the uncertainty about the story's outcome and the exquisite handling of the tale draw them in. And yet, we are also left to wonder when exactly was the time that the protagonist referred to, the time he should have died. Then the tale reverses course and moves to a scene on Mount Isurava right before he was taken to the field hospital. The protagonist believes that this is the scene most closely connected to his death, not because his childhood friend Furuya jumped out of their foxhole, apparently confused, and died there on the battlefield. Nor is it because he was injured as he attempted to run to Furuya's side. No, it is because this is where he shot and killed a young white Australian soldier. The sensation of killing beckons him back to the nights in the foxhole. This is where the exchange of fire between the Japanese and Australian soldiers took place, where he repeatedly fired his rifle. He finally gets the full sense of actually having killed someone in the midst of the exchange of gunfire. It came, to be sure, when he shot the enemy soldier who had killed Tanabe, the division leader he much respected, but even that death for which he was responsible came without warning, seemingly entirely contingent and accidental.

With the sound [of gunfire] the Australian soldiers turned their heads to look in this direction. The young white soldier looked blankly at me as I raised my head over the foxhole's edge; his blue eyes fixed on me. I pulled the trigger. The bullet lodged in the base of that young white neck. He yelled out something in English that sounded like a bird's cry. He fell over backwards, his palm pressed to his bloody neck.[5]

Later, deep in the forest, fleeing an attack by local tribespeople, the protagonist remembers again this earlier killing, probably prompted by the thought that he too will now be killed, as is natural, before too long: "I had no intention to kill. I may have practiced the motions of shooting and killing, but I had no desire to kill. Just like that young man looking at me blankly with his blue eyes, I blankly pulled the trigger."[6] The war depicted in this novel is an accumulation of murders that occur "blankly" and innocently. That is, this is not about brainwashing and the imperial rescript on education, nor about fealty pledged to the emperor, but simply the reality of a young twenty-first-century author imagining the experience of being sent to the front. That is why in this protagonist's experience of the war there is none of expected human ugliness or evil. In this novel, day follows day at the field hospital in a way that calls nothing of wartime to mind. In particular, the exchange activities with local residents, such as Sanada teaching Japanese to the indigenous people in the nearby settlement of Kanaka, or his receiving in thanks food and cowries, are such that readers can almost blissfully forget that this is wartime.

One notes as well that the story clearly depicts the atrophy of feeling required to preserve such tranquility. We read how, in the face of the deaths of two friends from his hometown with whom he was mobilized, and then watching patients in the field hospital succumb to death one after the next, the narrator "was not sad." He explains that he "somehow felt hollowed out back then."[7] He becomes aware of his own lack of "sadness" at these deaths he should mourn. In the last stages of the novel, when the troops have already started their retreat to be repatriated, the military doctor who had treated him at the field hospital shoots himself. Looking down on the doctor's corpse, he tries to pick up the pistol, thinking that maybe it would come in handy as a trade at some time in the future. The now rigid finger being in the way, he attempts to cut the finger from the trigger with his sword. But seeing his face reflected in the point of the sword and comes to his senses at the last moment, "I finally realized how strangely I was acting."[8] At the same time, we might think, was it not a common practice to deliver a finger from a dead body to relatives back home as proof of death? Do his hesitations arise only from his ulterior motives?

Right before reaching the yellow road, one of the soldiers asks that his hair or bones be taken to his wife and children; he then dies. The finger, as usual, is severed and the flesh burned off the bone in an approximation of battlefield cremation. His fellow soldiers, on the verge of starvation, grow restless as the smell of burning flesh wafts through the air. The eeriness of the "finger bone" being carried in the aluminum lunch box on his back grows ever more strong and oppressive. Unable to fully cremate the body, they burn the finger in order to deliver bone fragments to his family; we find this hardly different from cooking human flesh. However, "Standing here and looking on this, that may very well be how one turns to cannibalism," the protagonist thinks to himself; he then "turns and runs for his life."[9]

The final scene of the novel connects to its opening. He is gradually losing consciousness, sitting with his back against a tree, only to open his eyes to find he is actually lying on his side. "In the glow of the setting sun lay the arm of a corpse. The five fingers, as though clutching an egg, were turned in towards the palm. Amidst this world lying on its side I looked with wonder at the corpse's palm which seemed to be clutching something important."[10]

This "corpse" is no metaphor. It is that of Fujiki, whose brains were blown out earlier, a patient who died in the act of eating: his unexpected death echoes all the other deaths in the novel. Life comes to a close before one is even aware of it; this scene is connected to any number of the other deaths in this novel. The narrator himself does not realize that he too is now dead. Now a corpse, the narrator gazes upon the five fingers with eyes that should not be able to see. The narrative has been narrated to the end in the first person: "I . . . am gazing," for example. In other words, the tale being relayed is buried in the memories of the protagonist. It is a war tale narrated by a soldier dead on the battlefield. As he narrates his tale he is also dying. It is the war tale told by a dead man. Stories told by the dead: we see this in much literature following the disasters. This sort of thing can only be accomplished in novels, and *Yubi no hone* is especially adept with this narrative strategy.

Now when it comes to wartime cannibalism, there is no doubt that this is a memory that those who experienced the war would like to seal up tight. Ōoka Shōhei, in his *Nobi* (*Fires on the Plain*, 1952), could go no further than to merely hint at this extreme taboo, no doubt because his readers as well as those who had experienced the war were all of the same generation. It was still too close. By comparison, Tsukamoto Shinya, as both director and actor, takes the cannibalism and enacts it via his own body in his 2015 film version of *Nobi*. He began with Ōoka's vague language and took it to its limit with concrete images. This is likely only possible because nearly seventy years had passed since the end of the war, so viewers with wartime experience were no longer the majority. The sickening scene of maggots crawling in the corpses would surely reawaken the trauma of those who experienced the war, but for the current generation with no knowledge of war it served to foster a strong sense of aversion to war.

In the same sense, even though Asada Jirō is not a member of this third generation, his short story collection *Kikyō* (Homecoming, 2016) is wartime fiction for this new generation. In "Kinshi no moto ni" (Under the medal of the Golden Kite) a military unit is involved in a suicide charge (*gyokusai shi*) on Bougainville Island in present-day Papua New Guinea. The protagonist is the only soldier to survive and return home. He is now regularly praised for his fit body, but this results from his spending a year and a half in the jungle. "The most frightening thing to come out of that jungle," he recalls, "was the soldiers on our side."[11] This because the only way one could survive on the extreme edge of hunger was by eating the flesh of one's friends. Having returned to Japan, where provisions are scarce and work nonexistent, soldiers find they are once again starving. The protagonist comes to know a man who organizes the now-begging, disabled veterans. One of them, a man who seems to have had similar experiences in the South Seas, explains, "All of us, who knows how many soldiers we have packed into our bellies, we returned. No way we gonna starve to death now because the country has other plans. We're gonna stay alive, gonna get through this one way or another"[12] At this point the protagonist, whether to gain employment or to atone for his sins, cuts off his own arm and becomes a beggar. Thinking about it this way, even though Takashashi Hiroki's *Yubi no hone* directly confronts the issue of cannibalism, in his description the protagonist is a single individual in the midst of war's madness who is able to come to his senses and flee; the reader senses in this a total reworking of the world described by Ōoka Shohei and other veterans of that war. In Takahashi's novel, when the finger bone is being burned in preparation for a return to the mainland, we likely assume that his starving comrades, delirious from the smell of roasting flesh, have in fact consumed human flesh. How is it that the protagonist can remain unsullied? The innocence of the narrator, through first-person narration, has long formed the backbone that sustains novels. At the same time, that tradition has been smashed to bits by past works of fiction. If we cannot rely unconditionally on the narrator's innocence, we are required to inquire how such professed purity could be maintained. In particular, it would be these third-generation writers to whom such questions should be put, for they have taken on the special privilege of pursuing the traumas that those with war experience are unable to narrate.

Seirai Yūichi's "*Koyubi ga moeru*" (Pinky finger in flames) would seem to be a rework of his 2010 "*Koyubi wa omokute*" (Pinky finger is heavy); they both describe the war in the South Pacific.[13] The rewrite, however, includes scenes of cannibalism not found in the earlier work; at the point when one of the four surviving Japanese soldiers kills and eats one of the island locals, he proclaims, "boy, was that delicious."[14] This can also be read as a critique of Takahashi Hiroki's *Yubi no hone*. Seirai Yūichi's fictional method is to use the descriptions of catastrophe penned by other writers, such as Hayashi Kyōko, as a base upon which to layer memories of the Nagasaki area. As we come to understand when we read Seirai's *Aibu, fuwa, wakai, aibu no hibi* ("Caresses, discord, reconciliation, and days and days of caresses")[15] the main character, an author, who has been living at the atomic bomb's epicenter, writes how his grandfather, his father, and many *hibakusha* "were all silent, without desire to speak, passing into old age. If you ask what they passed down to their family, well, it was not about the catastrophe clearly told, rather just the shadow of a hazy experience, simply a heavy weight of pressure."[16] By this we come to know of the heavy burden that has been shouldered—more importantly, this positions him in a place different from those who "know nothing of August 9."[17]

For example, at an event celebrating the publication of his collected works, this author/narrator recounts having met Nagasaki author Hayashi Kyōko, referred to here as H-san, for the first time. He says to her that no matter what he might write, given that he has no actual experience of that day, "if I were to hear from you, who had in fact experienced that day, that 'the stuff you have written is wrong, it wasn't like that,' then I would be finished, it would be the end for me."[18] When he relates to her that he has been in turmoil thinking about this, H-san responds, "write what you want. Fiction has that sort of freedom (*shōsetsu ha jiyū desu*)."[19] While this episode is also reiterated in *Koyubi ga moeru*—there it occurs in the company of *hibakusha* with experience of the bombing, the author/narrator's father included, who are about to leave this world—it can also be read as an effort by the author to pass down to future generations the memories of being irradiated. In this way we find, in the end, that atomic-bomb fiction can also be passed on to a generation now far removed from the war.

But the question remains: why is it that the war in the South Seas is being written of anew, now? We know that there is a straight line to be drawn from the reckless tactics in the closing years of the war that resulted in many deaths from starvation; we know this from the many war diaries that serve as tales of heroism. Furthermore, as late as the 1970s there were still cases of soldiers returning from the islands, leading us to wonder how they managed to survive thirty years in the jungle. This only added to the incomprehensibilities of the war in the South Seas. Since so few soldiers survived the South Seas battlefields, there is ample room for the fictional imagination to fill the gaps in knowledge; there are many blank spaces where one wants to fill in the truth via fiction. Now, in our present moment, realities of that war in the South Seas are made clear: the stories of those who did not give in to starvation but sold their souls to the devil and resorted to cannibalism in order to survive; those not few soldiers only faintly visible in the background who were willing to risk their lives by refusing to trample on human dignity and morals.

With all that, we still have to wonder why these stories are being written by this third generation. The Holocaust and atomic bombings imprinted an intense sense of shame on the survivors of those atrocities. One of the things we learn from Tsuchida Hiromi's photography exhibition *"Hiroshima" 1945–1979/2005* at the 2014 Yokohama Triennale was that not many *hibakusha* parents actively spoke to their children about their atomic-bomb experience. On display are photographs of the children who wrote their memoirs of the atomic bomb in *Genbaku no ko* (Children of Hiroshima).[20] In the exhibition, photographs Tsuchida took in the 1970s were displayed side by side with photographs she took in 2005. It is striking to see how many who refused to be photographed in the 1970s gave permission in 2005. The difference overlaps with the passage of time, that those who refused to be photographed in 1970 are now able to pass on their atomic experience to their grandchildren. This difference in generation might also explain the differences we saw above between Ibuse Masuji's publication of *Kuroi ame* (*Black Rain*) in 1965, when memories of the war and the atomic bombing were still fresh, and Imamura Shōhei's 1989 film version, when the majority of viewers were too young to have experienced the war. In the words of Reiko Abe Auestad,

> In other words, when Ibuse wrote his *Black Rain* in 1965, the memory of the war and the Hiroshima bombing were more freshly etched in the minds of the majority of the Japanese people, while in the 1980s, they had long lost that immediacy. . . . And no doubt, the death of the Shōwa emperor in January 1989, which lifted the taboo on discussing the emperor's war responsibilities provided welcome opportunities for "soul-searching over personal war guilt,"[21] as James Orr points out, and unleashed a resurgence of interest in World War II. Imamura's film joined this popular trend in reevaluating the Japanese people's war experience.[22]

Imamura's film features people with first-hand experience of the war; the result is to give viewers floating in the 1980s bubble economy generation an opportunity to hear the voice of someone who lived through the war. Education about the war, from its end right up to the present, has been structured around understanding it through hearing the voices of those who experienced it. To imagine the war oneself and then put it into fiction has been exceedingly challenging for the generation who were not witnesses to it. By contrast, the third generation, released from these constraints, are freer to write about this subject.

For example, Japanese American writer Julie Otsuka's *The Buddha in the Attic* (2016) uncovers the history of Japanese "picture brides" sent across the sea to arranged marriages with Japanese immigrant men in the United States. Then, with the Second World War, these Japanese Americans were rounded up and interred. Otsuka's novel appeared in 2011, but given that war fiction drew renewed attention to the seventy-year anniversary of the war, we are made even more aware of memories from the Japanese American experience, memories which remain very much alive.

Miyauchi Yūsuke's *Kabūru no sono* (Garden of Kabul, 2017) is also a tale of a third-generation Japanese American that pursues the history of being sent to an internment camp during wartime. Set in California, the novel depicts the discord between a second-generation mother and her daughter. The protagonist is a thirty-eight-year-old successful programmer for a venture capitalist firm who nonetheless suffers from the trauma of having been bullied as a child. She is consumed with a computer program that uses virtual reality to enable a person to experience and overcome the past. The protagonist always thought it was her mother's fault that she was bullied on account of something in the wartime Japanese American experience that could not be told. The bullying she received in the wider American society is also deeply connected to her being Japanese American. The search for missing links that shape her present takes her to the wartime internment camp site at Manzanar. She discovers there, in the section of the museum where one can listen to recorded testimonies of internees, a person connected with her own family. This forces her to confront her family's history; she goes on to reconcile with her family and to overcome the trauma of racial discrimination. Within this tale the mother, that is, the second-generation Japanese American, is unable to tell her story. And this is the very reason driving the third generation to bring to light the story of the war.

Other works from third-generation artists include Kyō Machiko's manga about the war in Okinawa, *COCCOON* (2010), which was adapted for the stage by the Mum & Gypsy theater company in 2013. Kyō also took up the Nagasaki atomic bombing in her 2015 *Paraiso*. There is also Kōno Fumiyo's manga *Kono sekai no katasumi ni* (*In This Corner of the World*) of 2008, which depicts the bombing of Hiroshima from the naval port of Kure city, and was made into a film by Katabuchi Sunao in 2016. Although crowdfunding supplied the film's capital, it was a major hit, grossing over twenty-six billion yen. All these new tales of war coming from the third generation of writers depart from the standard wartime educational narrative and are able to raise new questions with more freedom and less rigidity.

HIROSHIMA MON AMOUR SEVENTY YEARS LATER

Jean-Gabriel Périot's film *Natsu no hikari* (*Summer Lights*, 2017) is another story about Hiroshima coming from the third generation. This film, given that it was made by a French director, is essentially a seventy-year anniversary version of *Hiroshima Mon Amour*. Resnais' 1959 film, as discussed in the previous chapter, is the story of a French actress who comes to Hiroshima to make a film for peace and ends up spending two nights with a Japanese man. Meanwhile, in *Summer Lights*, the one coming from France to make a television documentary for the seventieth anniversary of the bombing is a man named Akihiro who lived in Paris for twenty years. His plan was to return to Tokyo via bullet train the day after filming was completed and fly back to Paris. This schedule allows a mere half day in the Hiroshima Peace Park with a woman he meets there by chance.

Summer Lights begins with the filming of the story of Takeda-san, a *hibakusha* played by Yoneyama Mamako. The opening of *Summer Lights* overlaps with lines from *Hiroshima Mon Amour* where the Japanese man tells the French woman, "You saw nothing in Hiroshima. Nothing." To which she responds "I saw *everything. Everything.*"[23] This places Takeda-san's story in *Summer Lights* in complete opposition because as the one who was there she had, in fact, actually seen everything.

Indeed, the scene that Takeda-san saw on the day that the atomic bomb was dropped overlaps perfectly with that described by Hara Tamiki in *Natsu no hana* (Summer Flowers). Takeda-san, fourteen at the time, speaks with great passion about her older sister Michiko, who was working as a hospital nurse in 1945. She was run ragged by attending to the steady stream of patients coming into the hospital and only returned home over a month later, completely exhausted. Stroking the forehead of a sleeping Michiko, Takeda-san found that her hand had become completely wrapped with hair that had fallen out of Michiko's head. Michiko implored her, "Don't cry now," but it was not long before her entire body was wracked with pain and she died of radiation poisoning. Michiko was only twenty years old.

Summer Lights portrays Takeda-san relating her story. When she turned eighteen, she departed for Tokyo. She hid the fact that she was a *hibakusha*. She has now returned to Hiroshima and relates her experience as an official storyteller. The impetus for this would seem to come from walking those streets turned into scenes from Medieval Buddhist hell screens. In the film, she tells us that she "had never been so angry in her life." It seems clear that anger is her motivating force. "Relating this is the only thing that I can do" she says, and ends her tale, "This is the battle I have been called to." Akihiro finds it impossible to listen any longer and heads into the Peace Memorial Park. A woman dressed in an old-fashioned *yukata* sits beside him on the bench and begins talking.

Just as the man and woman in *Hiroshima Mon Amour* wander the streets of Hiroshima, so Akihiro walks the streets of Hiroshima, with this woman as his guide. Viewers of this film, which portrays the streets of a contemporary Hiroshima, will overlay this and compare it to the streets of Hiroshima as portrayed in the *Hiroshima mon amour*. One is made to feel again just how deserted were the streets of Hiroshima in 1958.

At times the woman speaks as though she has witnessed the unfolding of time on Hiroshima's streets, from the moment the bomb was dropped to the present. When she begins to speak of her commute to nursing school, perceptive viewers will likely sense that she is the long-dead Michiko. She only gives her name in the latter part of the film after having led Akihiro to a town by the sea: she says her name is Takeda Michiko. The names "Takeda" and "older sister Michiko" have now been repeated often, and it hits Akihiro that this is the name of the older sister of the woman whose story he was listening to just this morning; in that moment the viewers understand that she is a ghost. This takes place during the day; the Bon-odori festival for returning spirits is scheduled for that night. One assumes that Michiko has returned to Hiroshima for this occasion. Before he fully realizes that she is a ghost Akihiro asks, "Are you really going to go?" This becomes his seeing her off to return to the world of the spirits.

For the benefit of French viewers, Akihiro explains to a child he meets in the seaside town the meaning of Obon, that every year on Obon the dead return to their families. To the boy's reply that "Michiko is not part of our family," Akihiro responds, "Families can always be refashioned like this, as many times as you want." Such a line, even if intended to cheer him up, is much too simplistic an explanation for this child who does not know his father, whose mother works in Tokyo, and who is living with his grandfather in the Hiroshima countryside. Furthermore, one has to wonder how Akihiro met Michiko in the first place. It was she that pointed out to him the Atomic Bomb Memorial Cenotaph in the Peace Memorial Park, the place where the ashes of seventy thousand unidentified victims are interred. Without any family members now to mourn their remains, to where would these souls return during Obon? We have departed souls with nowhere to return to; might they not, like this man who comes all the way from France to Hiroshima to which he has no connection whatsoever and is able connect to a stranger's experiences, also be able to forge connections?

If we accept that, Akihiro, by sharing time with Michiko, briefly serves as the "family" to which she returns, then it follows and comes to mean that anyone at all is able to refashion the place—a family—to which spirits can return. Akihiro, a perfect example of the postwar third generation, sees Hiroshima through the eyes of the dead. And that means that anyone with the volition can do the same; anyone can forge such relations with the departed.

Now, it turns out that Jean-Gabriel Périot's interest in Hiroshima goes back further than the triple disasters. Already in 2007 he had made a video entitled *200,000 Fantômes* (200,000 Phantoms)[24] that casts its eye across the past one hundred years of Hiroshima history. Set to the piano melody of Current 93's *Larkspur and Lazarus*,[25] the image of the contemporary Hiroshima Dome is overlain with a succession of historical photographs, one after the other, starting from the building's initial construction in 1915. Next come the sounds of a plane overhead followed by an explosion, and the screen whites out and fades to black. During the following period of soundlessness a number of post-bombing photographs of Hiroshima play across the screen. The music of Current 93 begins again with photographs of the Dome through the four seasons, and historical photographs that capture the changing streets of Hiroshima and their redevelopment over time are shown chronologically.

The 2017 premier of *Natsu no Hikari* was a double-bill, screened after *200,000 Fantômes*. The Genbaku Dome itself has been preserved as monument to radiation (*hibakuikō*) in order to pass the legacy of Hiroshima's atomic-bomb misery to later generations. Périot gave the title of *200,000 Fantômes* in reference to what the Dome has looked down on, across these one hundred years. We can assume that the number 200,000 refers to the number of people who died from the atomic bomb, but it also refers to the bombed streets and departed spirits of Hiroshima. The music pauses and then, after contemporary images of the dome are overlaid in rapid succession, come photographs of the lantern-floating ceremony that occurs every August 6, in front of the dome, on the Motoyasu River. The video is edited so that it appears the lanterns are floating atop the still images. With a subtle fade, viewers then find that they have moved from looking at the Dome to looking at the floating lanterns. These lanterns are floated to memorialize the dead, each lantern representing a single person. The screen image is now comprised of superimposed color images of the lanterns, then transitions to black-and-white, and a photo that appears to have been taken during a family outing at the end of Spring is superimposed. This is the final photo of the film. One quickly understands that this black-and-white photo was taken in the prewar period, possibly immediately before the bomb was dropped. The photo is edited so that the people in it appear transparent. This is superimposed onto the photo of the floating lanterns: we then realize the people in the photo are nothing other than ghosts. In Périot's work the Genbaku Dome comes to symbolize not simply the historical dropping of the bomb but also the streets of Hiroshima haunted by the ghosts of these countless dead. In *200,000 Fantômes* the dead are obliquely referred to, whereas in *Natsu no Hikari* they are represented much more concretely. This manner of representing ghosts resonates very strongly with the descriptions of departed spirits found in postdisaster fiction and film. Together they point to a new way of facing past histories, as I shall take up more fully in the next chapter.

HIROSHIMA AS SPECTER

For the French, "Hiroshima" has always already been phantasmal. Since the "h" is not pronounced in French, Hiroshima in that language is pronounced "Iroshima." Of course this does not mean that "h" is not recognized as existing in French. A distinction is made as to whether or not there is elision between words, which determines whether or not it is pronounced. Thus, whether the "h" is pronounced or not does not erase it, for there is still a distinction made between the silent and voiced "h." Further, even if the "h" cannot be heard, it does not disappear as a letter in writing. That is, it makes its appearance in the written language and has a distinct existence.

According to Daniel Heller-Roazen, looking across the history of writing we find that some letters have disappeared, but "h" never did. Of great interest to us here is that Roazen explains the disappearance and reappearance of letters using the metaphor of a "ghost": "It is entirely possible for a single letter to disappear multiple times and then after the pronouncement of its death to appear again, exactly as a ghost does."[26] We find that the word for "aspiration" is "spiritus" which is to say, these signs of absent sounds are of "spirit," of "ghosts."[27] The sense of the ghostly (*bōreisei*) expressed by this "h" was carried further when Jacques Derrida created the neologism "hauntology," putting the word "ontology" together with the English "haunting." Regardless of any actual haunting, the existence of something that cannot be seen, such as this silent "h," means that double meanings—"hauntology" and "ontology"—can be expressed at the same time.

"Hiroshima," which becomes "iroshima" in French, is haunted by this "h." This "h" appears and disappears in a manner similar to the atomic bomb. Sekiguchi Ryōko, in her *Ce n'est pas un hasard: Chronique Japonaise* (This was not coincidence: Japanese Chronicle), recalls director Michel Pomaredo, in a 2005 interview covering his radio reportage, saying the following concerning the issue of "Hiroshima":

> I believe I have made comments in the past about the pronunciation of the place name Hiroshima. The "H" of the Japanese [is dropped] in French and it sounds like "Iroshima." Whenever I hear "Hiroshima" pronounced with an "h" as in Japanese, I think about the path that city has trod over the past sixty-five years, of which the atomic bombing is one part, but of which there is much more. When Japanese people say, "I am going to Hiroshima," it is not only the atomic bombing that comes to mind. However, with the pronunciation "Iroshima," it only occurs when evoking the catastrophe. This means that "Iroshima" carries a more deeply-etched historical impression. With the appearance of the slightest amount of breath, the aspirated "h" comes to symbolize the sixty-five years since the end of the war.[28]

In Japanese, "Hiroshima" points first to the town itself, same as "Fukushima" points to the city of that name. However, when these towns are discussed in French, there is never any question but that they refer to the atomic bombs and nuclear power plants. Here are the ghosts and hauntings: the "Iroshima" of French is forever haunted by atomic bombs.

Since Akihiro and Michiko from *Summer Lights* both have an "h" in their names, when pronounced in French, it feels as though something is missing, or maybe that something is added; it sounds clunky. One gets a feeling that in those places with an "h" something ghostly is squirming about. It thus feels perfectly natural that the French directors associated with the third generation would take up ghosts when reassessing the Hiroshima bombing. Périot shot all his works on location in Hiroshima, and all who appear in the film are Japanese. They may all have come from France, but they are also Japanese and can pronounce "Hiroshima" with an "h." For observers in the French environment, the "Hiroshima" of the Japanese can only be perceived as "Iroshima"; this means that the vanished "h"—like these ghosts, like radiation—must be recreated for them. There are multiple layers where these ghostings occur.

HOW GHOSTS MEMORIALIZE THE DEAD

Given that the sounds of "Hiroshima" as they appear in French preserve, in a manner explained by hauntology, the memory of the bombing, where does *Natsu no hikari*, in order to consider "Hiroshima," locate the meaning of placing these ghosts before our eyes (*genzen*)? Memories of this tragedy, whether as history or as everyday reality, are ghosts that float through this world. I now turn to the works of French artist Christian Boltanski to think more about this.

Boltanski's father was a Jew who traced his roots to Russia. Boltanski spent his early childhood amidst the history of the Holocaust and its survivors. Many of his works evoke memories of the Shoah.[29] But when Japanese viewers in the postdisaster period saw his 2013 exhibit *No Man's Land* at the Echigo-Tsumari Triennale Art Field, they surely found the exhibit also to be representing the 2011 disasters. Prior to this in 2010, his installation *Personnes* was on display at the Paris Grand Palais. This work features a mountain of clothing from which a crane grabs a scoopful of material and randomly drops it. In Paris, this installation surely conveyed meaning related to the Shoah. People would know from imagery employed at other memorial Shoah museum exhibits which, in order to prompt people to think about the slaughter in the internment camps, exhibit mountains of shoes of those sent to the gas chambers, for example, or eyeglasses discarded and now piled high, as well as black and white ID photos of untold numbers of victims.

Boltanski's mountains of old clothing are traces of the bodies of those who wore them. Once all of those clothes are piled in one place they are inevitably connected to the memories of mass death.

When this work was displayed at Echigo-Tsumari 2012, viewers most likely thought of the recent mass casualties in Japan. I, at least, understood the large pile of clothing as an image of debris that the tsunami had picked up; I imagined that the owners of that clothing were all casualties of the tsunami.[30] In the context of postdisaster Japan, this clothing is understood as a vestige of those bodies, but one that is separate from the history of the massacres in the concentration camps. Instead, these old clothes return to a more universal meaning, as a ghostly reminder of the dead.

This ghostly manifestation was even more apparent in Boltanski's *Animitas—Les âmes qui murmurent* (Souls Who Murmur) on display from September 22 to December 25, 2016, at the Tokyo Metropolitan Teien Art Museum. According to an interview which curator Tanaka Masako conducted with Boltanski to accompany the exhibit, for Boltanski, "soul" (*fantôme*) does not necessarily mean a concrete appearance of the dead.[31] Rather, in contemporary times, he calls "souls" the traces (*kage*) of the dead that reside in all humans. Boltanski explained this in terms of the particular features found in our faces: a nose resembling your grandfather's, eyes resembling your great-grandfather's. Indeed, just as the words and language we use are nothing more than all the words used by those who lived before us which have been passed on to us, our physical bodies as well are constructed from those things we received from our parents and from all the generations that preceded us in the past. The long-dead continue to exist within all of us.

However, the memories of those who came before are only remembered as far as the third generation, Boltanski continues. He asks, "Who remembers my grandmother?" Today it is Boltanski alone; when he dies, that memory will completely disappear. Pursuing this thought further, Boltanski insists that the dead are not anonymous but are particular individuals with names, existing in the memories of each individual who remembers that person. The practices of mourning the dead are always undertaken by those who remember the deceased. Accordingly, what are called souls in Boltanski's works are connected to mourning. Even so, what prompts these memories are not only hereditary relationships. We know this because while Boltanski's works evoke memories of the Shoah, the fact that in a different context they evoke the Great Eastern Japan Earthquake Disaster shows us that the act of memory is not necessarily comprised only of hereditary relations. In short, by making hereditary relations a stepping stone, his work leads us to a regard for all those who have died; this marks one of the particularities of his work.

On the occasion of the 2016 Tokyo Metropolitan Teien Art Museum exhibition, Boltanski made visits to the tsunami disaster areas and the officially designated "hard to return to zones" (*kikan kon'nan kuiki*), thinking he would make an artwork taking the disaster as theme, but he relates that he abandoned those plans when told by Japanese that it was too soon and the memories too fresh. Those opposed because they felt it was too soon were very likely concerned that such artwork would again bring trauma to survivors of the disasters.

Margaret Iversen argues that artworks concerning the Shoah in Europe—parallel to artworks after the Japan disasters, as well as the response to them—are works that might incite trauma, and that artists therefore found it difficult to reconcile this crisis of conscience.[32] Iversen explains this by quoting Peter Weibel, who argued that the concept of trauma and memory in the twentieth century exists under the shadow of the history of the Holocaust, that Postwar Germany is deeply connected to the trauma of the Holocaust, and that one finds this reflected in artworks.[33]

Weibel is mainly concerned with art since the 1970s related to the radical West German group RAF (Red Army Faction), but what is in question here is the issue of Holocaust memory. It is a question about whether the experience of trauma and violence can be represented without theatrical embellishments, without beautification; can it be represented, that is, not in the manner that the imagery of violence within Hollywood films is made to provide pleasure. Trauma refers to experiences inexpressible even by those who experienced them; in the end the representation of trauma is impossible. Perhaps trauma means being sealed off from memory; it may reside in inciting and calling it forth only to question whether it is right or wrong to do so. Iversen quotes the following from Weibel: "How can we represent what is, by its own definition, by its very nature unrepresentable, (without denying the traumatic experience and the cause of this experience, the evil, the terror) without banalizing it, trivializing it, spectacularizing it, finally repressing it for a second time?"[34]

The Japanese *hyōshō* correlates to the English word "representation" meaning "to make visible," to "place again before one's eyes" (*genzen*). This is easy to understand if we consider whether one can or cannot present, vividly before one's eyes, the trauma. What Iversen is making an issue of here is photography used as art. The photographic medium, just like survivor testimonies, easily gives the illusion of an actual reality. Iversen, by discussing Gerhard Richter's and Boltanski's art, attempts to deny the directness of photography. Iversen selects Richter's *Atlas*, created under the influence of Aby Warburg's *Mnemosyne*, to show that the photographs in Richter's work are not a medium that points to and reveals facts (*jijutsu*) but rather deconstruct the relationship of reality to the referent.

Whereas Richter leaves the referentiality of the photograph to the interpretation of the viewer, Boltanski's use of photographs is more strategic. In an interview with Catherine Grenier, Boltanski explains the distortions in his *Monument*. This installation features black-and-white photographs of children's faces surrounded by lightbulbs, meaning the work looks exactly like photographs lit by candles on an altar. When this was displayed at the New York *Lessons of Darkness* exhibit, viewers apparently understood them as pictures of massacred Jewish children. However, they were photographs of children from Dijon, from a school where Boltanski taught in the seventh arrondissement of Paris; not a single one was Jewish.[35] Iversen quotes from a 1989 interview with Irene Borger where Boltanski says, "If people know the material is from the Holocaust, they are unable to think about anything else." Given that, in order to have people feel that, "Yes, this is a work about the Nazis, but at the same time it's a work about all of us," he used pictures of the children from Dijon for the *Lessons of Darkness* exhibit.[36]

Even photography, which seem to be a documentary media, does not necessarily produce documentary, in this case of the Nazi genocide. Nonetheless viewers, looking at an installation that casts light onto the faces of children in black-and-white photographs, think of the Shoah. While nothing depicted in the photographs was connected to the genocide, the images in the photographs were, in fact, connected to things now vanishing. As Boltanski explains, the children in the photos are still living but have now completely grown up, meaning that the faces captured in the photographs have already disappeared from this world. In this sense, photographs always project that which has been lost. When you photograph a human body, it records the moment-by-moment aging of a body. The medium of photography is always a ghostly existence. Boltanski's works are a method to call forth memories of those who have died, a liaison to those who still exist in this world; their charge to us is to think hard, in the midst of the disappearance of all things, and as all humans move toward death, about mortality.

In the interview with Tanaka Masako, Boltanski said that he welcomes a reinterpretation of his art that connects the mass deaths of the Shoah atrocity in the European context to the 2011 Great Eastern Japan Earthquake Disaster in Japan. The reason is that the completion of an artwork, in the end, lies with the viewer: interpretation of the work is completely free (*jiyū*). If the Great Eastern Japan Earthquake Disaster can be interchanged with the Holocaust, then the reverse is also possible. Works about the Great Eastern Japan Earthquake Disaster likewise have the ability to trigger thoughts of the Holocaust. In that sense, the ghosts that haunt our present are traces that evoke the history of the Holocaust at times, and at other times the atomic bombings and still other times the disasters. It is we who respond to the calls of these ghosts, no matter where we might live, living in a present that is already engraved by world history.

NOTES

1. Takahashi Hiroki, *Yubi no hone* (Tokyo: Shinchō bunkō, 2017), 4.
2. Takahashi, *Yubi no hone*, 4.
3. Takahashi, *Yubi no hone*, 4.
4. Takahashi, *Yubi no hone*, 4.
5. Takahashi, *Yubi no hone*, 6.
6. Takahashi, *Yubi no hone*, 107.
7. Takahashi, *Yubi no hone*, 79.
8. Takahashi, *Yubi no hone*, 105.
9. Takahashi, *Yubi no hone*, 111.
10. Takahashi, *Yubi no hone*, 122.
11. Asada Jirō, *Kikyō* (Tokyo: Shūeisha, 2016), 191.
12. Asada, *Kikyō*, 212.
13. Seirai Yūichi, "Koyubi wa omokute," *Bungakkai* 64, no. 11 (November, 2010): 62–89. Seirai, "Koyubi ga moeru," *Bungakukai* 71, no. 1 (January 2017): 58–130.
14. Seirai Yūichi, *Koyubi ga moeru* (Tokyo: Bungei Shūnjū, 2017), 174.
15. Included in Seirai Yūichi, *Kanashimi to mu no aida* [The space between sadness and nothingness] (Tokyo: Bungei Shūnjū, 2015).
16. Seirai, *Kanashimi to mu no aida*, 23.
17. Seirai, *Kanashimi to mu no aida*, 18.
18. Seirai, *Kanashimi to mu no aida,* 18.
19. Seirai, *Kanashimi to mu no aida*, 19.
20. Arata Osada, Jean Clark Dan, and Ruth Sieben-Morgen, *Children of the A-Bomb: The Testament of the Boys and Girls of Hiroshima* (New York: Putnam, 1963).
21. James J. Orr, *The Victim as Hero: Ideologies of Peace and National Identity in Postwar Japan* (Honolulu: University of Hawai'i Press, 2001), 15.
22. Reiko Abe Auestad, "Ibuse Masuji's *Kuroi Ame* (1965) and Imamura Shōhei's Film Adaptation (1989)," *Bunron: Studies in Japanese Literature* 4 (2017): 4.
23. Marguerite Duras, *Hiroshima Mon Amour*, trans. Richard Seaver (New York: Grove Press, 1961), 15.
24. The eleven-minute video is available at https://www.youtube.com/watch?v=-ZZhgzLB1xw, accessed December 9, 2020.
25. This song can be found on the 2005 album *Soft Black Stars*, recorded in 1998.
26. This is my translation of Kimura's translation from the French translation. Heller-Roazen, Daniel. *Écholalies: Essai sur l'oubli des langues* (Paris: Éditions du Seuil, 2007), 36. The original can be found in Heller-Roazen, Daniel, *Echolalias: On the Forgetting of Language* (New York: Zone Books, 2005), 34.—Trans.
27. This section differs slightly from the original text. Kimura bases her argument on the Japanese translation of "aspiration" as "kionbu" and refers to the French word "esprit." I have streamlined for clarity.—Trans.
28. Sekiguchi Ryōko, *Ce n'est pas un hasard: Chronique Japonaise* (Paris: POL, 2011), 100–101.

29. In English and Japanese, the Nazi massacre of the Jews is usually referred to as the Holocaust, but in French it is more common to use the word Shoah. Since Boltanski himself uses Shoah, I defer to him.

30. Tanaka Masako also had the following to say about this exhibit: "Even if there were people who see this and associate it with the Holocaust, it is possible that today someone else could look upon it and see a landscape scraped clean by the tsunami, or even see a completely different set of ruins overlaid on this piece." Christian Boltanski, Hatakeyama Naoya Hatakeyama, Kobayashi Yasuo Kobayashi, and Sekiguchi Ryoko, *Kurisuchan borutansuki: Animitasu sazameku boreitachi* (Tokyo: Pai International, 2016), 112.

31. http://www.teien-art-museum.ne.jp/exhibition/160922-1225_boltanski.html, accessed December 13, 2020.

32. Margaret Iversen, *Photography, Trace, and Trauma* (Chicago: University of Chicago Press, 2017), especially chapter 6, "The Unrepresentable," 83–84. According to the exhibit *Shoah et Bande Dessinée* at the Paris Shoah Memorial (January 19, 2017–January 7, 2018)—extended past the original close date of October 2017—concrete depictions of the massacre at Auschwitz were taboo for many years after the war. In this way Art Spiegelman's 1986 *Maus* representations of the memory, the trauma, and the rupture between generations marks the start of a new era. Assaf Gamzou, "La mémoire visualisée: discours de la Shoah et bande dessinée," in Didier Pasamonik and Joël Kotek, ed., *Shoah et Bande Dessinée: L'image au service de la memorie [exposition, Paris, Mémorial de la Shoah, janvier-octobre 2017]* (Paris: Denoël, 2017), 7.

33. Weibel's essay appeared in the catalog accompanying the exhibit *Art of Two Germanys: Cold War Cultures*, which opened at the Los Angeles County Museum of Art in 2009 (January 15–April 19) before touring Nuremberg and Berlin. Peter Weibel, "Repression and Representation: The RAF in German Postwar Art," in Stephanie Barron and Sabine Eckmann, eds., *Art of Two Germanys: Cold War Cultures* (New York: Abrams, in association with the Los Angeles County Museum of Art, 2009), 257–59.

34. Weibel, "Repression and Representation," 257.

35. Christian Boltanski and Catherine Grenier, *La vie possible de Christian Boltanski* (Paris: Seuil, 2007), 146.

36. Iversen, *Photography, Trace, and Trauma*, 98. Also see the interview at http://bombmagazine.org/article/1148/christian-boltanski, accessed December 13, 2020.

Chapter 5

The Hauntology of Postdisaster Literature

One of the singularities we find in fiction written after the 2011 Great Eastern Japan Disasters is how often the dead, whether appearing as characters or narrators, go on to narrate their own stories. For example, in Itō Seikō's *Sōzō rajio* (Imagination Radio, 2013), the narrator DJ Ark is now dead, a man washed away in the tsunami whose body remains entangled high in the branches of a cedar tree. In this tale we find DJ Ark broadcasting over the radio to listeners who are also all dead. However, given that we find this radio broadcast is also perceptible to a small group of living persons, the broadcast also seems intent on conveying something to all of us still alive in this postdisaster world.

To take another example, Okada Toshiki with Chelfitsch, the theatrical troupe he leads, performed two works deeply influenced by the disasters. *Genzaichi* (Current Location, 2012) was followed by *Jimen to yuka* (Ground and Floor, 2013). The dead people portrayed in these works—sometimes existing only as voices, sometimes in corporeal form—manifest themselves, in every case, in the contemporary present of living persons. Further, none of these dead are portrayed as having already disappeared from this world. They are still here, beings that insert themselves into the lives of others and seem intent on disturbing the world of the living. Stated another way, while one would assume these dead persons would be relegated to times past, they suddenly appear in the present, in the present tense, still clinging to existence. Which is to say, these dead persons have not returned as revenants from the past; rather, they are portrayed as continuing to exist in a situation where the past continues into the present. Further, these dead do not remain in the progressive past tense but continue within our present tense. We are made aware, yet again, of a narrative method where the dead are yanked back into the narrative present. Given this, I want to use, as a hint, the critical concept of "hauntology" in order to think about this distinctive way of being (*arikata*) found among the dead persons-as-characters in postdisaster literature.

HAUNTOLOGY: A CRITIQUE OF "MOURNING AND MELANCHOLIA"

"Hauntology" is a term invented by Jacques Derrida.[1] It is a portmanteau word constructed from English "haunt" and the philosophical "ontology." As discussed in the previous chapter, given that "h" goes unpronounced in French "ontology," "hauntology" and "ontology" sound the same to the ear in French. Even so, given that the silent "h" is nonetheless there, alive and existing, we can say that something is "haunting" this exquisite term.[2]

Derrida's "specter" refers to the opening statement in Marx's *Communist Manifesto*: "a specter is haunting Europe, the specter of communism." Derrida posits that "everything begins with the appearance of the specter" and that in order to contemplate this "specter" he created the word and idea of "hauntology."[3] As to why we should consider the "specter" he answers that it is necessary for "living" (*ikirukoto*).

> If it—learning to live—remains to be done, it can happen only between life and death. Neither in life nor in death *alone*. What happens between two, and between all the "twos" one likes, such as between life and death, can only *maintain itself* with some ghost, can only *talk with or about* some ghost. So it would be necessary to learn spirits. . . . And this being-with specters would also be, not only but also, a politics of memory, of inheritance, and of generations.[4]

Of course, Derrida is here thinking about the specter of communism within capitalist society, but it would be too simplistic to place "specters" between the dead and the living in order to "learn to live." Yet, as we think about the fact that there indeed exists in the present "ghosts" (*bōrei*) and "specters" (*yūrei*)—that is, those who were believed to be dead and buried in the past—the process that Derrida proposes with the term "hauntology" serves as a helpful point of reference to analyze the issues involved with appearance of souls of the dead (*tama*) in postdisaster Japanese literature. This because Derrida's "hauntology" is being used as critical apparatus to critique Freud's ideas about "mourning" and "melancholia." Even though we see many postdisaster stories that confront death directly, Freud's "Mourning and Melancholia" never enters the discussion; it does not really work here. Derrida's concept of "hauntology," however, is useful in this analysis.

British critic Mark Fisher shows us how. He opened the path for using Derrida's hauntology within cultural studies.[5] Fisher considers Derrida's haunting (*bōrei*) as derived from a failed process of mourning and names it "hauntological melancholia." Fisher's aim in his project was to explain contemporary culture, in particular by arguing that the music scene of the twenty-first century has been haunted by twentieth-century Modernity. Thus Fisher's use of the term "hauntology" does not refer to the relation between dead people and ghosts. I want to note that I understand Fisher's "hauntological melancholia" as distinct from Wendy Brown's "left melancholy" and Paul Gilroy's "postcolonial melancholia." I am discussing a situation where the disappeared past haunts the present, not one like Fisher's where melancholia aims for a cure. Whether in Derrida or Fisher, hauntology and haunting are metaphors for the ghosts of a past that haunt the present. As far as thinking about hauntology as it occurs in postdisaster fiction, here I want to bring back and free these ghosts from the past and from metaphor so that I can take up hauntology as a method to consider the issue of the hauntings and ghosts (*bōrei*) that appear in postdisaster fiction and to consider it as an issue of grammatical tenses.

According to Freud in "Mourning and Melancholia," should one fail at the work of mourning following the loss of a loved one, then one falls into self-blame and depression (melancholy). Further, this melancholy becomes a medical condition requiring appropriate treatment. One may lose a love object and may then go through an appropriate period of grieving, but this does not mean that one can easily pivot one's affections toward another love object. Derrida is positive in his assessment of a pathological mourning that includes the process of introjection for the normal work of mourning and that rejects the process of incorporating the dead into oneself but one where the individual carries with them a "crypt" which serves, as a space within and without of oneself, to preserve the other as other and the dead person as one still living.[6] In other words, he proposes that rather than consign a loved one to a page in their own personal history, a mourner might continue embracing the cold gravestone that marks the crypt in their heart. A crypt, in Christianity, is a stone chamber underneath or in the vicinity of a Church that holds the remains of saints and others who had been associated with the church. Holding the crypt in one's heart, although it does not usually rise to the level of consciousness, is an image of burying the physical body of the other within oneself, enveloped in the solid stone coffin, never becoming integrated into the mourner's heart, carrying an image of that person which may come to mind at any time. Such is a failure of mourning, since the normal work of mourning is introjection where the other melts into oneself.

However, not everyone hopes to quickly complete the work of mourning and speedily return to normalcy. Take, for example, Michel Deguy in *To That Which Ends Not: Threnody*, who writes of his adamant and ongoing refusal to take up the normal work of mourning for his wife, who passed away in 1994.

Soon enough the deep sigh, that dismisses as it evokes the memory, the haunting, will come and substitute for the tears. I don't like it that ex-intimates "do their best" to not even pronounce your name, to relate a shred of the past, and everything to bury in amnesia, to bring on Lethe.[7]

A few weeks after his wife's death, he wrote: "I want to protect this desolation; so as to not 'get my mind off it,' to get in tune, to resonate with these sorry times." In this way he continued his resistance to the completion of the mourning process because it meant forgetting his wife and burying her as something in the past. "The deceased of our ages is expulsed; more completely than I believed."[8] For Deguy, the work of mourning was "mourning's magic trick"; "they were made to vanish, the dead completely disappeared." It was nothing more than "their surviving friends crossing them off the list." The act of the dead "disappearing" or "vanishing" was the same as consigning them to death once more. Deguy could not force his lost wife to die once again.

Sekiguchi Ryōko's "Koe wa arawareru" (*La voix sombre*/The Dark Voice, 2015)[9] also shares this desire to preserve a loved one in the present and not to force them into the past. Sekiguchi contemplates the voices of the dead whose voices suddenly appear before the still-alive. She writes that their voices always appear in the present tense. Even after the owner of the voice and their vibrating vocal cords have departed this world, the voice of the dead and what they have to say, when played back via a recording, for example, does not reappear in the past, but leaves one feeling that one is being addressed in the very moment of listening; it is occurring in the "present" of the listener, she writes. In contrast to the physical body which no longer exists, the voice which continues to exist—or, more precisely, the voice that inhabited the body which produced that voice—comes to us as *fantôme* (*bōrei*) writes Sekiguchi. "Phantoms come and go. In the space between two tenses [temporalities] not knowing themselves if they are in the present or past."[10] In this way they "stir up the tenses." "Koe wa arawareru" closes with the following:

> Voices exist and continue in the present, they do not know death,
>   At least as long as that voice exists.
>   They are gone, the person is no longer here, this appearance is partial, relentless
>   Still, after their lives are over the air continues to reverberate.[11]

This manner of voices appearing in the present seems to intentionally take us back to the "hauntological melancholy" that impedes the normal work of mourning. In short, voices exist *ghostlily* (*bōreiteki*) in the present. It is precisely while considering this "living dead" that we cannot then completely consign the dead to the past where we perceive a space for the *fantôme* (*bōrei*) to make an appearance.

Derrida, in his *Specters of Marx*, touches on the appearance of a ghost (*bōrei*) in the first scene of Shakespeare's *Hamlet* to point out that "this haunting thing, this obsession [*hantise*] is historical, to be sure, but it is not *dated*, it is never docilely given a date in the chain of presents, day after day, according to the instituted order of a calendar."[12] Further, when considering Derrida's quite careful analysis of the line "Time is out of joint," together with Sekiguchi's line that the ghosts "stir up the tenses," we find an overlap of a "hauntological" manner of being.

In Japanese postdisaster fiction, communication with the dead is not established in order to recollect the past but to construct links to the present. In chapter 4 of Itō Seikō's *Sōzō rajio*, the character S, who went to Tohoku as a volunteer, uses writing as a means to communicate with a lover from an illicit affair who died before the disasters. S writes:

> The dead are no longer of this world. One needs to forget and get on with life. Of course they should, no question about it. If those left behind are forever ensnared by this death then time is only stolen from them. But really, can that be the only correct path to follow? Surely we can take the time to listen for the voices of the dead, sadly, in mourning, and move forward little by little, together with those who have died. We can, can't we?[13]

S wants to keep listening to the voice of his dead lover. The lover's voice is not simply being imagined as conversations in S's head. There is mutual communication with the land of the dead. On this point we find that S thinks to himself,

> The memories of those who were left behind would not exist if it were not for the dead. I mean, if no one had died, if they were still alive, you know what I mean? Then no one would be thinking of them. It's a give and take between the living and the dead. This is no one-way relationship. There cannot be just one or the other; the two of them are as one.[14]

This kind of worldview, one that includes the dead, is one connected to the text of Noh Drama (*yōkyoku*), usually intoned by the chorus. In *Sōzō rajio* the people listening to the "imaginary radio" of the title are, all of them, "in the manner of ghosts (*konpaku*) trapped in this world" and as "having resentments [towards those in this world) which prevent them from making their way to the world of ghosts."[15] This condition resonates with sentiments oft-repeated frequently expressed in *mugen* Noh.

Okada Toshiki, discussing his play referenced at the head of this chapter, *Jimen to Yuka* (The Earth and the Floor), explains that "There is a degree to which I am always referencing the style of Noh. I've already discussed how the ghosts appear in *Jimen to Yuka* and I know that you all know that Noh is a theater performed by ghosts."[16] Indeed, his stage makes one think of the Noh stage, with its simple floor of unfinished wood. In performance, Okada places mirrors in the wings of the stage in a spot where they are invisible to the audience. The actors, at certain points, are looking at the mirror while moving their bodies on stage, but this is not revealed to the audience. Thus, when the actors look intently at the mirror, to the audience it seems the actors are gazing intently at something not of this world. In this way the actors perform the appearance of a ghostly appearance in their line of sight.

While it is well known that within Noh ghosts often appear, especially in the genre of *mugen* Noh perfected by Zeami Motokiyo in the fifteenth century, Itō Seikō and Okada Toshiki both deliberately and consciously follow the traditions of Noh, to good effect, enlivening their works in this century. That being the case, when considering the issue of ghosts (*bōrei*) appearing in postdisaster fiction, it becomes necessary to reconsider hauntology, starting with Noh drama. In his research on classical Japanese literature, Takagi Makoto uses the texts of Noh (*yōkyoku*) to construct a theory of ghosts. Takagi distinguishes among the variety of ghosts that appear in *Mugen* Noh as being vengeful ghosts (*onryō*), ancestral spirits (*sorei*), and ghosts of the dead (*bōrei*). This last type "refers to dead person's latency within the text able to disturb time and space."[17] In the next section I will turn to a consideration of the ways that ghosts are described in Noh as a step in reconsidering hauntology and applying it to postdisaster literature.

GHOSTS ON THE STAGE

Noh is a theatrical craft performed by actors, so the ghosts who appear before us usually take human form. In most *mugen* Noh a traveler (*waki*) arrives in a particular place, meets a person (*shite*) from that place, and after they speak to each other in the first half of the play (*maeba*), the local person departs (*nakairi*), and again in the second half (*nochiba*) the *shite* arrives again and discloses their identity, either through narration or dance performance (*mai*). There are cases when the chance meeting with the ghost is in the second half of the play, as in *Taema*, and occurs as if in a dream—"Appearing to you in the midst of your dream, I am the spirit of Princess Chūjō"[18]—but in many cases the dead person actually reappears before the traveler's eyes.

The play *Tomonaga*, for example, features a traveling monk who visits the grave of Tomonaga, a warrior who committed suicide during the Heiji Rebellion of 1160, to pray for the repose of Tomonaga's soul, and there meets Tomonaga's ghost. After hearing about the conditions at the end of

Tomonaga's life from the local resident, the monk chants sutras at his grave, whereupon Tomonaga's shade (*kage*) appears vaguely in the dim lantern light.

Waki: How strange! While a prayer to Kannon is chanted
  In voices clear,
  In the lantern's flickering light
  Unmistakably we see Tomonaga
  Shadow-like appear.
  Could this be a dream, a vision?
Shite: Truly a dream, a vision is this transient life.
  Cease your wondering and continue your recitation of holy verse, I pray
Waki: Indeed, that you appear like this is all by the virtue of Law's power,
  Thinking thus, in devotion, on the rosary beads I count off prayers
Shite: By the voice guided, now comes
Waki: The real form?
Shite: A vision?
Waki: Now seen,
Shite: Now hidden,
Waki: The image[19]

Although the monk queries "could this be a dream, a vision?" by using phrases such as "the real form?" (*makoto no sugata ka*), "now seen" (*mietsu*), and "the image" (*omokage no*), we know that when the monk apprehends Tomonaga's appearance, he does not take it as a simple phantom of his delirium; he does not let go of the feeling that Tomonaga has in fact appeared in this world. According to Tomonaga, the reason he was able to appear in this place with a physical form is because, "Of my two souls, one (*kon*) to the Blessed Place has gone, the other soul (*haku*) still in Asura's Hell remaining, for some time it must undergo tortures there."[20] While *kon* and *haku* both refer to spirits (*rei*), if one is taken to refer to the spirit and the other body, then the latter (*haku*) is the one that governs the physical form. Thus, should *haku* lose its way to the spirit world, a ghost (*yūrei*) can appear in this world with a physical body.

Another example is in *Sanemori*, where the *shite* announces himself as a ghost (*yūrei*). This becomes clear in the exchange between the itinerant priest (*waki*) and Sanemori (*shite*):

Waki: How strange! The story about Sanemori's past
  which I heard, I thought was about another person.
  But how strange, it was about you.
  So then, you are the ghost of Sanemori, are you?

Shite: I am the ghost of Sanemori. While the soul (*kon*) is in the
other world, part of the spirit (*haku*) remains in this world.²¹

Sanemori, a character from a two-hundred-year-old tale, now appears in the present. This is because, as we read above, "While the soul is in the other world, part of the spirit remains in this world." We should note that it is to the itinerant priest alone, who is in conversation with him, that Sanemori's form is visible. Anyone else would only see a priest talking to himself. Announcing of one's name in dialogue, a construction found in all Noh, is likely a ritual necessary for souls and spirits (*konhaku*). We can think of this as being the most important aspect of the ritual mourning, not for an unnamed dead person but for those listening to the tale of the particular named individual.

In any case, what is important here is that we have a tale being told by a ghost (*yūrei*) and one written in such a way that the fact of an appearance by a ghost is not deserving of special comment. If ghostly appearances were not central to the story, there would be no need to reference them specifically as "ghosts" (*yūrei*). So there are also examples where the *shite*, who is always assumed to be a ghost, appears without being explicitly identified as such. In cases when they are not identified as a *yūrei*, even though they be characters associated with an earlier age, the fact of their appearing in the present makes the confusion of tenses even more pronounced.

For example, *Kureha* is the tale of two female weavers who came to Japan from China many years before during the reign of Emperor Ōjin. The traveling courtier (*waki*) who witnesses this knows that the two weavers, Kurehatori and Ayahatori, from the age of Ōjin, are "making themselves visible once more, here in our present," and thinks "this may sound very strange indeed." He does not, however, think of them as *yūrei*. Following the *nakairi*, when the actor leaves the stage, the two weaver maidens return and deliver a pronouncement as gods. Here too, as we have seen, in medieval societies which believed in the manifestations of gods on earth, they always appeared in the present, not as having come from the past. Among the Japanese gods—a good example being Sugawara no Michizane, who became a god after being sent down to a post at Dazaifu—there are numerous cases of actual persons of an earlier age who became gods after their deaths. Thus, while the actual Sugawara no Michizane is now long dead, he also lives on as the god Michizane at the Tenmangu shrine. Here we have an actual historical person who continues to live in the present as a god and is known to make physical appearances in front of people. Therefore we see that the important point here is that, if we can think this way about those who are dead, then with *yūrei* as well it is not so much that they have come from the past but that their appearance is in the present.

Another extremely interesting aspect of Noh is that the dead do not necessarily appear to those with whom they have a connection; rather it is to itinerant monks and other passersby met by chance whom the dead relate their tales. In that light, one begins to feel that the ghost stories relayed in the Tohoku region after the triple disasters also conform to Noh traditions. Kudō Yuka reported on this in her Tohoku Gakuin University dissertation, "Shishatachiga kayou machi—takushii doraibaano yūrei genshō" (The Town of Commuting Dead: The Taxi Driver Ghost Phenomenon).[22] She reports on several instances where taxi drivers in the ravaged town of Ishinomaki picked up fares who turned out to be *yūrei*—they are taxi drivers, yes, but they are also much like the itinerants (*waki*) always on the move, as found in Noh—traveling ghosts with whom the dead had no prior connection. In one reported case, in the middle of summer, a woman dressed in heavy winter clothing wanted to be taken to Minamihama—a region that no longer existed, literally washed from the face of the earth by the tsunami. When she was told that the area was essentially vacant land, she asked with trembling voice, "Have I died?" When the driver turned to inspect the rear seat, he found nobody there.

Ghostly appearances were also reported in the *Kahoku Shimpō* (Kahoku Newspaper) series "Banka no Atesaki: Inori to Shinsai" (Address for an Elegy: Prayers and Disaster). We find that all across the Tohoku region, where female mediums (*kuchiyose miko*) still exist, many people requested their services in order to contact missing and presumed dead family members.[23] We can surmise that they were motivated by a desire to find the resting places of missing family members. Which is to say, this is more like a desire to search for someone who is still in this world, albeit someone they can no longer meet on the street, rather than the desire to make contact with the spirits of the dead as such. Or, it would also seem to be an attempt to search the space between this world and the next (*awai*), to make contact before the dead have irretrievably passed on to the next world. Indeed, as Okuno Shūji reports, in many of the instances of disaster victims seeing ghosts, the experience is one where the dead appear in the present of the living.

Some works written after the disasters describe the dead as writhing in agony, unwilling to accept their own deaths. DJ Ark in Itō Seikō's *Sōzō Rajio* is unable to recall his last moments, and it is only through hearing from other dead people who witnessed it that he learns what happened. The reason DJ Ark is unable to die completely and why he continues his radio program is because his wife and son remain missing and unaccounted for. Not unlike the manner in which the living rely on *kuchiyose* mediums to search for family members who remain missing and unaccounted for, DJ Ark uses his network of dead people in an attempt to find his family.

TALES TOLD BY THE DEAD

One novel that follows the dead to the point at which they can understand and accept their death is Ayase Maru's *Yagate umi e to todoku* (To Finally Reach the Ocean, 2016). *Yagate umi e to todoku* consists of two interwoven narratives. One is told from the perspective of Kotani Mana, who cannot come to terms with the loss of her close friend Sumire who traveled to Tohoku at the time of the disaster, three years earlier, and never returned. The second part is described from Sumire's perspective. Mana's survivor guilt and the grief after Sumire's death get interwoven as these stories unfold. There are many novels that tell of survivor guilt. Atomic-bomb literature, war fiction, and fiction written about 9.11, all share the narration of survivor guilt as a prominent theme. However, fiction in which the dead speak and mourn their own deaths is a different theme, one that we can say appeared in postdisaster Japanese literature. In this sense, Maru Ayase's *Yagate umi e to todoku*, which combines the themes that have been seen in previous fiction about calamity with 3.11 fiction, is a rare example that brings all those themes together.

After Sumire goes missing her mother quickly begins to file the paperwork connected with her daughter's death, even though the body has not yet been returned. She marks the date of the disaster as the day of her daughter's death and visits her grave on that anniversary. Mana is uneasy with this because she wants to believe Sumire will return: she is convinced that Sumire herself wants to return home. Knowing that Sumire's relationship with her mother had been strained, Mana can only think that the mother is "creating an image in her head of her daughter that is convenient for her," and that "the most honest way for her to deal with Sumire would be to continue her care and concern just as she did when Sumire was alive, and not with explanations that only serve herself [the mother]."[24] Mana's way of thinking mirrors the process of mourning described by Derrida and discussed above, a process, that is, that rejects the normal manner of introjection that is part of the normal work of mourning, and strives instead to "preserve the object *as other* within oneself (one living as though dead=as a person dead but still living)."[25] Mana is not in a Freudian state of melancholia. Rather she is trying to continually feel Sumire's existence; she is, in short, in a state of hauntological melancholia.

One day three years after her disappearance, Sumire's boyfriend Tōno is cleaning up Sumire's belongings. He asks Mana to choose anything she might want. Mana thinks, "What will Sumire do when she comes home? Imagine the sadness. We just don't [know what happened to her]," but she is unable to verbalize it.[26] Three years have already passed, and there has even been a funeral. Mana understands that Tōno's request is not at all unusual, yet she remains unable to accept it and questions herself: "Why is this? Why can't I make a break and let it all flow cleanly away? . . . I can't tell you why, I don't know why, but I want to meet her again."[27]

Now, in the section narrated from the dead Sumire's perspective, it is not immediately obvious that Sumire is the narrator because the narrator herself does not know what she is, and has even forgotten who she is. It opens as follows:

> The gossamer curtain of purple night fell away layer by layer and light shone in from the eastern sky. The morning light poured into my open eyes like cold water, filling every crook and cranny in the cavern of my skull, overflowing, spreading through my ears, mouth, and every other opening, and on through my body. "Oh," I then recalled, "this is what my face, my body, is like." The thick grass around me sang drily every time the wind blew. I could hear the sound of water running quietly underground.
> "The bus isn't coming."
> I turned toward the voice and saw a familiar looking older woman standing nearby. With well-worn cardigan and sweatpants, she looked as though she had just walked out of her living room. Her hands were pressed against her stooped back. The socks sticking out of her rubber sandals were an eye-stopping lavender.
> . . .
> "But I gotta get back home."[28]

At first glance, this looks like the most normal of mornings, but this person (Sumire) is clearly out in an open field, lying down in a field of grass. She has probably already turned into a skeleton. Sunlight illuminates the inside of her skull. Because she is lying down she can hear the sound of the grasses and the "sound of water running quietly underground." The "old woman" who says that "the bus isn't coming" is, we find later, her grandmother. We learn this later when Sumire's mother says the following to Mana:

> At the time of her grandmother's funeral Sumire was still in elementary school. She got all worked up at the funeral, yelling that she had to put this pair of socks into the casket. They were just regular thick purple socks, nothing special. She was upset about the white *tabi* socks, worried that granny's feet would be cold, and she would complain if we changed them to white ones.[29]

Sumire is unable to recall that this old woman in sandals with the "lavender" socks is her own grandmother who wore "thick purple socks." And then, even though this old woman called out to Sumire numerous times and she "understood this to be a girl's name,"[30] she could not catch the details of it. Even though the old woman says to Sumire, "I wonder if you got lost coming here. Come over here by me" and then leads her to "a big two-story house" with "blue roofing tiles," Sumire feels that she must quickly get home and charges out the front of the house. At the time of their departing it is suggested that this old woman is also dead.³¹

> The old woman stood as before with her hands on her lower back. But where her face had been was now a gaping hole filled with small flowers growing thick. Her eyes and nose were buried in the grass and could not be seen. Even so, I had the feeling that a pair of eyes glimmered at me as they peeked through gaps in the grass.
> The one in front of me is no longer the old woman from before. Because I turned my back on her did the old woman cease being an old woman? My instincts scream "You should not look at this." Here was the form of a living creature after the shell of flesh was stripped away. Fighting down the nausea, I opened my mouth.
> "Who the hell are you?"³²

She does not know that she too is "a living thing stripped of its flesh." Hence her fear upon simply sensing the "rising nausea." She does not think of herself as dead. That is why she so desperately starts walking back home.

Sumire's next section is chapter 4. She cheats on Tōno and is now on a date with another man. Following dinner they step outside to find that "the area in front of the train station was like a muddy stream"³³

> The man with clear eyes grabbed my hand with a force that suggested protection. I grabbed fast to his hand, hard enough to make my fingers numb, and we pushed into the stream. Our bodies were jostled, pushed forward and back, and pulled from side to side.
> The pressure was too strong and our linked hands were abruptly separated. I gasped as our eyes met. His body was completely swallowed by the black wave, no longer visible. He was gone. It was like, you know, this person one day was snatched from my life, like a piece of fruit. In response to my hand becoming suddenly light, I spun and spun, tossed around in the black crowd.³⁴

Following this she remembers the words that someone had once said to her: "I want someone to deeply, deeply love me—say, if god were to ask that person after death, 'choose a single special someone,' the person would choose me before anyone else,"³⁵ and then in the middle of the muddy swirl of water she collides with a man whose "eye was blemished by a mole that resembled a tear."³⁶ Readers who have read Mana's earlier section will know that the person who wants a person to "deeply, deeply love me" is in fact Mana, and the man with an "eye blemished by a mole that resembled a tear" is Tōno. Sumire is left feeling that "I so want to call out the man's name but no matter what, I cannot remember it."³⁷

In the next section we find Mana, having received Sumire's things from Tōno, heading home, when all of a sudden she is possessed by Sumire.

> I feel I need to call out his name. But what was it, that boy's first name? What did we call him? I used to call him by his family name but right now I can't remember his first name.
> . . .
> The shushed and quiet town flowed like a river outside the train's rounded window.
> "A-chan."
> I called out someone's name, so suddenly, it seemed a hard candy had flown from my mouth. It was a voice crisper and brighter than mine. The sweet and painful attachment to the one called out to glittered like a wet thread in a spider web.
> An unrooted sadness churned slowly in my gut. This was something that had been ripped from her, something no longer hers. Yanked away like a straw hat, or a necklace, or a sneaker. In the moment after I realized this, the recollection that had pulled forth that memory, all those things that had flowed into me, now rushed out from my body.[38]

During the moment that she looked at Sumire's things, right before coming back to herself, something had "flowed into" her. That thing called out the lover's name that she had been trying to remember. That voice "crisper and brighter than mine. The sweet and painful attachment to the one called out to" is Sumire's voice. It was in this moment that, via Mana's physical body, Sumire appeared as a manifestation. Mana cannot apprehend Sumire's visit. The act of calling out that name itself, for whatever reason, is now completely forgotten.

In chapter 8, Sumire's section, Sumire returns to the moment she was overwhelmed by the tsunami.

> Lost in the shadows from the trees I couldn't see that well. Even so, deep in the forest, a large something was moving.
> From the underbrush about ten meters away came black water, as though licking the earth. What might it be? Oil? Don't be ridiculous. Yet that man with the marigolds, in the station building, was talking about tsunami warnings. But surely, here, we are far enough away from the coastline, aren't we? Within a space of seconds the blackest of muddy water erupted out from another wood nearby. My heart jumped with a sound.
> Gotta get out of here, gotta escape, but there's no path. . . .
> No way; I cannot die. I don't want to leave like this. Everything I was protected by, all of it, is being ripped away. Finally, little by little, I was able to be happy. Getting to this point took a long time. I cannot die, I mean, because . . .
> . . .

> Why didn't anyone tell me? Life is so fragile. Why didn't anyone tell me that? Why?
> I want to go home. This is wrong. I'm scared. My feet are trapped by the cold water. My upper body is unsteady. In a flash I have fallen forward into a wave of the water now above my knees.
> . . .
> I can't go home. All those people, never again, I'll see them never again.
> But no, that's a lie. I close my eyes in forceful rejection.
> . . .
> "The bus isn't coming."[39]

She hasn't given up. She does not accept the fact of death. That's why she proclaims it a "lie" and "close[s her] eyes in forceful rejection" and is again returned to the meeting with the old woman, her grandmother, who proclaims that "The bus isn't coming."

In chapter 11, Mana's section, Kunikida, whom she had grown close to through the crazy days they shared after their boss's suicide, invites her to come stay at the mountain inn his family runs. Mana is in a dreamlike state as they walk in the mountains when she senses Sumire's presence. There they are walking together, holding hands as they used to in the mountains. "I must not let go of this hand," she thinks. "I cannot remember the details but if I let go, I'll regret it forever,"[40] when "suddenly a black, muddy current surged in from the side and swept her body away."[41] When she opens her eyes, she realizes she is crying. Then comes a small noise and the thicket shakes. "She sees a white arm slip away into the darkness," she pursues it, and falls down a slope.[42] Kunikida then grabs her arm and she snaps out of it. In the space (*awai*) between dream and reality Sumire has revealed her body. While talking with Kunikida that night, words that seem to be Mana's own thoughts suddenly come from her mouth. Remembering that the words were something Sumire had said, she relates the following:

> You are in a place like this, I called out from within myself. One drop of blood, one fragment of bone, pushing me in the direction of living, the momentary swelling of thought that does not even rise to consciousness.
> After a long time, such a very long time, I am able to meet her.[43]

Even while she thinks she is relaying her own words, something feels amiss, and she comes to realize the words are not hers. The Sumire within Mana was never completely internalized and introjected completely as something of Mana's own; Mana comes to feel, just as though Sumire has appeared from out of the crypt, that she exists as Sumire. That is why Mana feels like she was "able to meet her." Sumire exists hauntologically within Mana.

In Sumire's part in chapter twelve, she finally remembers her own name.

> Utsuki Sumire. These are Utsuki Sumire's shoes. I turned reflexively to look at the river behind me. . . . Birth, death, right up to this water's edge: I could see everything on the path that Utsuki Sumire had trod. By removing my shoes I have moved one step farther away from her.
> There in the middle of the path I could see all the people I had left and gone far away without a goodbye.
> All of a sudden warm air was sucked into my body, bloated I rose to float. I wanted to be with them. I wanted to see them once more, I wanted to say at least one word of goodbye, and that's the reason I came as far as this place.[44]

At the moment she remembered her name as Utsuki Sumire, her consciousness had already diverged from Utsuki Sumire's. If we speak in terms of Noh theater, this is much like the separation of soul (*kon*) and spirit (*haku*). She turns around and the people she wants to meet are visible. It is not clear at the time who they are, but in the next section, which is Mana's, we find that Mana and Tōno both first dreamt of Sumire at the same time; we come to understand that Sumire has come to both of them, in their dreams, in order to say goodbye.[45]

Sumire walks with a tote bag on her shoulder. From this bag comes, from time to time, the slight sound "pichi," the sound of fresh cleanness coming from the fish swimming in the bag. Sumire reaches the shore and releases the fish into the lapping waves and at the same time she too is reborn as a new soul.

> The little fish jumped out as though happy to be free. In the next instant the eye of the fish became my eye. The vibrant, brand new spirit, the voice calling from deep within the ocean, the vessel of flesh just beyond, was, all of it, mine.
> Spinning and circling around, confirming the taste of fresh seawater, not bothering to look back, I took off swimming at the speed of lightning. I was being called. My other shoes had already been prepared.
> . . .
> Suddenly the smell of the water changed. The land comes closer and closer. The calling voice grows louder and louder.
> I'm home! Finally home! Crying loudly, I flew into the hands that were there to scoop me up.[46]

The woman who had returned to the land was no longer Sumire's ghost (*bōrei*); more, she was no longer Sumire. This last scene should probably be read as Sumire's soul (*haku*) leaving her corporeal body behind in this world, while the "I" of this "brand new soul (*kon*)," is being reborn, reincarnated perhaps, into this world. In that case, the ocean (*umi*) in Ayase's title *Yagate umi e to todoku* is the place of reincarnation, or perhaps it is the place where a new spirit is reborn.

This novel, via Mana's sections, depicts Mana as having failed in the normal work of mourning and describes her as have succumbed to hauntological melancholia. However, this novel does not proceed in a straight line: there are numerous depictions of Sumire hauntologically existing within Mana; moreover, Sumire, who is surely dead, is made to speak, and the work closes in a section narrated by Sumire. In this ending, since it describes a way out (*sukui*) for those victims who cannot finally take their place among the dead, this novel itself becomes a story about a repose for these wandering souls. Only in fiction can the words of those now dead be written. But thinking about this via the traditions of Noh we find that a situation in which dead people narrate their own stories has been told numerous times throughout the traditions of Japanese literature.

TALES OF THE POSTDISASTER DEAD

Why is it that we must make the dead speak following the disasters? One reason is that since those lives were cut off so suddenly and unexpectedly due to the tsunami, those of us who remain feel as a community that, surely, there were many things left unsaid. Therefore the dead—as we saw with the taxi drivers in Ishinomaki—make appearances to people to whom they may or may not have any connection.

Death without a corpse and the difficulty of accepting that death is also an issue associated with the many soldiers who have died on overseas battlefields. Following the tsunami there were also many deaths without a corpse. Tendō Arata's *Mūnnaito daibā* (Moon Night Diver, 2016) is tale of divers who, in the "hard to return to areas" near the Fukushima Daiichi nuclear power plant, slip through the security barriers in order to search the ocean for leads to the bodies submerged there. People who have heard nothing about the deaths of those close to them, have heard nothing from those who have died and cannot accept it, is one of the main themes in depictions of the tsunami damage. But might it not also be the case that those who were abruptly enveloped in the massive wave are also unwilling to accept their own death?

Ano hi kara (From that Day, 2015)[47] is a collection of short stories by authors from Iwate Prefecture. It was only after five years had passed that these missives from the very center of the disaster could be published. There are a variety of depictions of dead people in this collection. In Takahashi Katsuhiko's "Saru no yu" (Monkey Hot Springs) we meet a man who cannot comprehend his own death and who is suspicious about the dead people who keep appearing in his photographs. In the end he makes use of a hot spring as his path into the hereafter and departs this world. In Kikuchi Yukimi's "Umibe no kauntā" (Counter by the Sea), a professor known to have died shows up at a bar and, having drunk his beer, sticks a clammy, wet one-thousand-yen bill on the counter and disappears.

It is not only grief and regret that calls the dead back to the present. Rather, we read of characters wanting to repair relations with the dead, to hear their voices again, to call back into the present those consigned to the past; such, however, is an issue for those on this, the living side, who want once more to fully think about death and those who have died. The seventy-year anniversary of the war came while memories of the disasters were still fresh; for many, the disasters became the thing that called forth memories of regret for those who died in the war.

Take, for example, director Yamada Yōji's *Haha to kuraseba* (*Nagasaki: Memories of My Son*, 2015). The film is about the Nagasaki atomic bombing, but the film can easily be read as being deeply colored by the disasters as well. The film was preceded by Kuroki Kazuo's *Chichi to kuraseba* (Living with Father, 2004), a cinematic adaptation of Inoue Hisashi's play of the same name. In Kuroki's film, the daughter, who is wracked with feelings of guilt that she didn't do enough to prevent her father's death, says "I'm sorry I'm still alive, but I don't have the courage to kill myself." The father's ghost then appears before her and encourages her to take the first steps toward living again. Now, survivor's guilt, as in this daughter's inability to move past her guilt, is a central theme in atomic-bomb fiction, war fiction, and literature in general. In contrast to this, in the postdisaster film *Haha to kuraseba*, it is the son who disappeared from this world in the flash of the atomic bombing and who reappears as a ghost. In the process of remembering how he died, he can come to terms with his death.

In the film, Kōji, a medical student, dies while listening to a lecture at his university. In this film the atomic bombing is depicted as a flash of light that traverses the classroom, after which the shot focuses on a glass inkpot that slowly twists and melts atop a desk. There is no depiction of dead bodies, yet with this shot alone we easily imagine the things that happened to bodies in Nagasaki. As there is no corpse nor any ashes, Kōji's mother and his girlfriend Machiko continue to feel that he might someday breeze in, but after three years their hopes fade and grow faint. Finally, the mother, thinking young people need move on with their lives, says to Machiko, "We have to give up." With this acceptance of her son's death his ghost seems able to appear.

One concern of this film is whether the dead can necessarily easily accept their own deaths. Why did I die? Did I have to die? The obsession of the dead with their lost lives is shown in various scenes. In one scene Kōji cries a single tear while listening to the Mendelssohn record he liked. Upon finding a picture of his medical school professor, he wonders "what is he doing now?" In that instant, he remembers that during that professor's lecture the bomb fell. Another scene shows him unable to accept Machiko's getting on with her life with a new partner. These are all examples of various ways the dead continue to struggle.

The central theme of *Haha to kuraseba*, at first glance an atomic-bomb work about Nagasaki, overlaps with themes that are taken up in postdisaster fiction. In that sense, the "Nagasaki" described in Yamada's film contains a worldview that would not have been possible if there were no Great Eastern Japan Earthquake Disaster. To illuminate this point I focus on an important line in the film about the atomic bombings that makes one associate it with the recent disasters.

Koji's mother assumed that his being in medical school would get him a military deferment, or, even if he were called up, being a doctor would mean that he would return. But he didn't return. At the moment she laments that he ended up dying nonetheless, Kōji's ghost appears and says to her, "Not a thing anyone could have done about it. Just my fate. That's all." In response his stunned mother shoots back: "Fate? Things that we cannot prevent, like earthquakes and tsunami, they are matters of fate, but this could have been prevented. Humans planned and carried out this terrible tragedy. How can you think this was fate?" To us these days, the often-heard phrase "earthquake and tsunami" directly evokes the Great Eastern Japan Earthquake Disaster. In the original text on which the film was based, the phrase was not "earthquake and tsunami" but "typhoon and tsunami." One assumes that during filming this was deliberately altered to allude to the disasters of 3.11. In contrast to the phrase "earthquakes and tsunami," the demonstrative "this" of the "this could have been prevented" refers to the atomic bombing of "Nagasaki" in the context of the original work, a tale about Nagasaki, but here, with the disasters of 3.11 superimposed, "atomic bombing" (*genbaku*) of Nagasaki comes also to mean the "nuclear meltdown" (*genpatsu*) at Fukushima Daiichi. With this single utterance this work changes from being one written with a focus on "Nagasaki" to a work that connects the irradiation of "Nagasaki" and "Fukushima."

We have seen how ghosts and spirits (*yūrei*) appear in postdisaster fiction in a manner that resonates with the narration of war; in the same way, I want to stress here, postdisaster fiction also invokes memories of war in the midst of disaster. To think again about the experience of war, or perhaps the history of war is, metaphorically speaking, to hear again the voices of people who lived in the past; it is to turn our ears to the voices of the dead. The concept of hauntology is necessary at just such a time because it reminds us to be on guard against too-easy self-serving interpretations, because it provides a critique of the "introjection" resulting from interpretations that are advantageous to those still living, and because it provides a means to square off against the tendency to relegate anything foreign to the past.

I argue thus because tales of the *Tokkōtai* kamikaze as the brave and beautiful youth who were scattered like the cherry blossoms in defense of the nation have already been internalized (introjection) in self-serving ways by postwar Japanese society. Instead, we had best now turn our ears to tales of regret for those youth who, having no way to flee, died in despair. Noda Hideki's 2016 play *Gekirin* (Human Torpedo) allows the young men being sent to their deaths as human torpedoes to voice doubts about battle strategies they could not, would not, have agreed to. Likewise Tsukamoto Shinya's 2014 cinematic remake of Ōoka Shōhei's *Nobi* (*Fires on the Plain*) shows the battlefield as a dark, gloomy place where soldiers kill their own comrades in order to stave off starvation.

When we reconsider the war through the lens of the disaster, the existence of ghosts arises as an issue of memory. For example, in Medoruma Shun's novels, set in an Okinawa onto which an unending postwar has been forced, the dead from the battle of Okinawa often appear. In "Denreihei" (Dispatch Orderly) a youthful soldier who ran messages for the military amidst the chaos of war is unaware that the war is now over and that he is dead. He continues to run through the Okinawa streets, and in this tale aids a character who appears about to be assaulted by American soldiers. This young boy, whose head was blown off by a bomb, has been running around, headless, from wartime into our present day. He was there for the uprising in Koza, and he was there when an elementary school girl was raped by American soldiers; this dead person *lived through* it all. When one of the characters says, "You have to wonder what message that orderly is still trying to deliver?" another replies, "Nobody knows," and both of them understand that a dead person continues to live through all these postwar years and has something to deliver.[48] This seems to suggest, quite pointedly, that here in Okinawa the war is far from over, that the war is far from forgotten. What is resurrected by the existence of ghosts is not the dead, but the memories of the living. So, in conclusion, I say we had best not fail to listen to tales from the disaster dead: we need to refuse the normal work of mourning and stand firm within hauntological melancholy. That is what these tales are telling us; we need to listen.

NOTES

1. See his *Specters of Marx: The State of the Debt, the Work of Mourning, and the New International*, translated by Peggy Kamuf (New York and London: Routledge, 1994).

2. In French the term is *hantologie*.

3. Derrida, *Specters of Marx*, 4. Translation modified to reflect the Japanese phrasing.—Trans.

4. Derrida, *Specters of Marx*, xviii–xix.

5. Mark Fisher, *Ghosts of My Life: Writings on Depression, Hauntology and Lost Futures* (Winchester: Zero Books, 2014).

6. Jacques Derrida, "Fors: The Anglish Words of Nicolas Abraham and Maria Torok," in Nicolas Abraham and Maria Torok, *The Wolf Man's Magic Word: A Cryptonymy*, translated by Nicholas Rand, xi-xlvii (Minneapolis: University of Minnesota Press, 1986).

7. Michel Deguy, *To That Which Ends Not: Threnody* (New York: Spuyten Duyvil, 2018), unpaginated.

8. Deguy, *To That Which Ends Not: Threnody*, n.p.

9. Sekiguchi Ryōko, "Koe wa arawareru," *Bungakukai* 71, no. 3 (March 2017): 140–198.

10. Sekiguchi Ryōko, *Katasutorofu zen'ya: Pari de san ichichi o keiken suru koto* (Tokyo: Akashishoten, 2020), 152.

11. Itō Seikō, *Sōzō rajio* (Tokyo: Kawade shobō shinsha, 2015), 180–81.

12. Derrida, *Specters of Marx*, 4. Translation modified to reflect the Japanese.—Trans.

13. Itō, *Sōzō rajio*, 132–33.

14. Itō, *Sōzō rajio*, 132–33.

15. Itō, *Sōzō rajio*, 99.

16. "Kunsten no tame no 'chimen to yuka' nōto 0509," accessed July 12, 2021, http://jimen.chelfitsch.net/journal/okada/.

17. Takagi Makoto, "Bōrei no toki/ bōrei no uta, arui wa intātekusuchuaritii no naka no *Gikeiki*: mirai no 'kioku'/mirai kara raihō suru 'bōrei'," in Takagi Makoto, Kimura Saeko, and Andō Tadao, eds., *Nihon bungaku kara no hihyō riron: Bōrei, sōki, kioku* (Tokyo: Kasama shoin, 2014), 326.

18. This translation from Thomas Rimer, "*Taema*: a Noh Play Attributed to Zeami," Monumenta Nipponica 25, No. 3/4 (1970), 443.

19. Shimazaki Chifumi, ed. and trans., *The Noh* (Tokyo: Hinoki Shoten, 1987), 192–195.

20. Shimazaki, *The Noh*, 198. The terms for these two souls vary by translator. While Shimazaki uses "soul" for both terms, Smethurst translates *kon* as "soul" and *haku* as "spirit." I have added the Japanese terms to the translations for clarity.—Trans.

21. Smethurst Mae, trans., "Sanemori," in Elizabeth A. Oyler and Michael Watson, eds., *Like Clouds or Mists: Studies and Translations of Nō Plays of the Genpei War* (Ithaca, NY: Cornell East Asia Series, 2013), 151.

22. This appeared in book form in Kanebira Kiyoshi, *Yobisamasareru reisei no shinsaigaku* (Tokyo: Shin'yōsha, 2016).

23. The terms for these mediums vary by region: *itako* (Aomori, Akita, Iwate), *ogamisama* (Miyagi, Iwate), *onakama* (Yamagata), and *mikosama* (Fukushima). Kahoku Shimpōsha, ed., *Banka no atesaki: Inori to shinsai* (Tokyo: Kōjin no Tomosha, 2016). Reports of such meetings with ghosts are reported in Richard Lloyd Parry's *Ghosts*

of the Tsunami: Death and Life in Japan's Disaster Zone (London: Jonathan Cape, 2017). Okuno Shūji's *Tamashi demo ii kara soba ni ite: 3.11.go no reitaiken wo kiku* (You may be Spirit, but please stay close by: Listening to Ghostly Experiences after 3.11) (Tokyo: Shinchōsha, 2017) reports on experiences with ghosts by survivors of the tsunami where the dead appear in the living person's present.

24. Ayase Maru, *Yagate umi e to todoku* (Tokyo: Kōdansha, 2016), 89–90.

25. English translation can be found at Derrida, *Specters of Marx*, 71; translation modified to reflect the Japanese.—Trans.

26. Ayase, *Yagate*, 25.
27. Ayase, *Yagate*, 27.
28. Ayase, *Yagate*, 28–29.
29. Ayase, *Yagate*, 72.
30. Ayase, *Yagate*, 33.
31. Ayase, *Yagate*, 30.
32. Ayase, *Yagate*, 37.
33. Ayase, *Yagate*, 76.
34. Ayase, *Yagate*, 76.
35. Ayase, *Yagate*, 16.
36. Ayase, *Yagate*, 78.
37. Ayase, *Yagate*, 82.
38. Ayase, *Yagate*, 100–101.
39. Ayase, *Yagate*, 126–28.
40. Ayase, *Yagate*, 181.
41. Ayase, *Yagate*, 182.
42. Ayase, *Yagate*, 183.
43. Ayase, *Yagate*, 195.
44. Ayase, *Yagate*, 202.

45. This sense of "meeting in dreams" will likely resonate with Japanese readers to the Heian period sense that meeting in a dream is more "real" than meeting in the physical world.—Trans.

46. Ayase, *Yagate*, 221–22.

47. Michimata Tsutomu, ed., *Ano hi kara: Higashi Nihon Daishinsai chinkon Iwate-ken shusshin sakka tanpenshū* (Morioka: Iwate Nippōsha, 2015.)

48. Medoruma Shun, "Denreihei," in *Sensō shōsetsu tampen meisakushū* (Tokyo: Kōdansha bungei bunko, 2015), 223.

Chapter 6

Post-Fukushima Sublime and the Anxiety of Hauntology

THE SPECTACLE OF CATASTROPHE

In 2016 the Centre Pompidou-Metz held the exhibit *Sublime: Les tremblements du monde* (*The Sublime: World Tremors*) which focused on natural and manmade disasters around the world—earthquakes, storms, volcanoes, natural gas burn off, tsunami, and nuclear tests.[1] It included dioramas of the Great Lisbon Earthquake, Turner's storm paintings, as well as Kawamata Tadashi's *Nami no shita* (*Under the Water*), a large installation constructed of doors and chairs washed up by the tsunami and arranged and hung overhead to suggest the undulation of a wave.

Why name an exhibit like this "Sublime"? The answer becomes clear while viewing the video installation of volcanologists Maurice and Katia Krafft. The Kraffts had filmed numerous eruptions and lava flows around the world before they went missing in 1991 while working on Japan's Mount Unzen. We assume that they sustained injuries, as did many other news and data collection personnel, in the lava flows as they were never seen since. The exhibited images taken by the Kraffts were of spellbindingly beautiful landscapes of bright red burning lava flowing across the ground. Extremely hot lava is a frightful thing, of course, that can bring instant death with a single misstep. Even so, the sight of the lava's red luminescence flowing down a bare mountain side appears as a magnificent and beautiful natural phenomenon. From this we can deduce that the central concept of the exhibit would be how Nature's power, which has no concern for human death, can fill us with such sublime beauty.

An approach such as this—one that considers horrific events and the resulting dreadful, widespread human death to be "sublime"—will seem unsavory to those who have just come through the experience of the Tohoku disasters.

Even so, as Kobayashi Erika, for example, reiterates and emphasizes through her *Hikari no Kodomo* (Luminous) series of art books or her novels such as *Madamu Kyūri to chōshoku wo* (Breakfast with Madame Curie),[2] there may be no contradiction between beauty and the deadly, even a death close at hand. We recall that at the time the Curies discovered radium, the objects emitting green light were found to be simply beautiful; it crossed no one's mine that it might be an evil substance. The Curies blithely placed the radium in their bedroom; it was used to make chandeliers and other accessories and decorations.[3] Those enthralled by its beauty were unknowingly exposing themselves to the dangers of radiation. Humans seem unable to imagine evil within beautiful things; at the same time beautiful things are not necessarily good for humans. If it can be said that this is the nature of the "sublime," then this fact is made clear in this exhibit.

The most problematic section of the exhibit was one about nuclear disaster, entitled "Nucléaire: Le sublime ultime" (Nuclear: The ultimate sublime). The exhibit included a section on the "most recent" example of nuclear calamity, namely the accident at the Fukushima Daiichi Nuclear Power Plant in March 2011. To be precise, there is a cogent point being made here, at least from what we read in the explanation accompanying the exhibits, for while there is no beauty to be found in nuclear calamity, "nuclear" can be ambiguous. Even in the "nuclear" in antinuclear movements we can find the sublime: a thing deadly and calamitous while also magnificent and sometimes even beautiful. We read in the accompanying exhibit panel:

The imaginary of a nuclear holocaust haunts the second half of the 20th century. It contributes to forge a new sublime, nourished by the fascinating beauty of the tests, the power of the blasts, the terror generated by the arms race or the catastrophes tied to civil nuclear [sic]. In particular, the Cold War context fuels a fantasy of imminent destruction and sustains a climate of international terror. Since the 70's and the 80's, activists, intellectuals, feminists and artists converge and speak out to express their rejection of the civil and military threat posed by this technology on the world. New art forms are invented, often modest, and widely distributable to call for vigilance. The emergence of nuclear power has also generated a new kind of disaster with multiple consequences: "They aren't any more natural catastrophe [sic]: there is only a civilizational catastrophe," voiced the philosopher, Jean-Luc Nancy.

The "modest" artworks referenced above would seem to be such pieces as Louise Odes Neaderland's *Nuclear Fan*. Mushroom clouds are printed on long, thin pieces of paper that collapse into a pink hand-held fan. On the edge is printed, "THIS IS ONLY A TEST." Another example would be Dona Ann McAdams' photograph of three women juggling in front of the Turkey Point Nuclear Power Plant in Miami Florida. The photo was made into a postcard with "They're Juggling Our Genes!" printed across the top. In short, the works gathered for the exhibit can be considered antinuclear protest art. We also find here artworks about the accident at the Fukushima Daiichi Nuclear Power Plant, which I turn to next.

THE SUBLIME OF RADIOLOGICAL HARM

Maurizio Lazzarato and Angela Melitopoulos's *Two Maps* is comprised of an interview in October 2011 with photographer and art theorist Minato Chihiro. Minato presented two radiation contamination maps, one from the Japanese-language *Tokyo Shimbun* and one from the English-language *Japan Times*. We find that, while the latter makes visible a wide area of the country, from Aomori in the extreme north to Shizuoka just south of Tokyo, the former displays a much more limited area—indeed, the entire northern part of Japan is omitted from this map. While both maps cover the same circumstances, Minato in "Two Maps" argues that the psychological effects on those who relied on different maps—one with limited coverage and one with a much broader purview—are surely very different. This because readers of the Japanese-language newspapers, in contrast to those reading the English-language paper, are manipulated into holding a minimalized image of the disaster because of the pared-down map. Furthermore, Minato points out that both maps use concentric circles to indicate every ten kilometers' distance from the nuclear power plant at the center, which suggests that the radiation damage is confined within these circles and never extends beyond them. Such concentric circles were also used in Hiroshima to measure distance from the atomic bombing epicenter and to determine the distance from ground zero; allocation of compensation was determined by where one was at the time of the bombing. Minato goes on to show how these lines, on which such decisions are based, are purely political with no relation to actual radiation damage.

In the case of the Fukushima Nuclear Reactor accident these concentric lines were employed not only to determine compensation but also to control people's anxiety about the radiation. Demarcating areas by these lines meant that the people of Tokyo and farther south, at least, would be able to carry on without the fear of radiation. In the face of extreme uncertainty, these maps might provide a sense of safety—providing what we wish to be true although there is no credible base for such hope—that Minato describes as a "visual animism" (*Vijuaru animizumu*) or as an "icon" (*ikon*). Because the maps shape our psychology in this way—which is to say these concentric circles, in the sense that they reduce our estimation of the damage, all questions of compensation aside—they are then exceedingly political.

One of the most intriguing parts of the interview was Minato's response to the question of why, given that radiation is invisible, he takes photographs. Among the pictures he took in Fukushima was one of a field of red flowers blooming in wild profusion, one of the Yokogawa Dam, and one of the seascape. About this we hear him say, in this interview, "The catastrophe is indeed visible in magnificent beauty that can be filmed and represented."[4] While Minato speaks of the ways that radiation can be seen and is visible, the fact remains that humans are unable to perceive radiation by sight, smell, touch, taste, or hearing. So, whether irradiated or not, the fields and forests retain their form and beauty. This is precisely the reason that humans cannot even consider the evil that is housed there, cannot apprehend the crisis there: radiation's threat of damage, being present in the midst of this blameless magnificent beauty, is rendered invisible.

I bring us back to thinking about the meaning behind naming an exhibit *Nucleaire: Le sublime ultime*. The harm from radiation is not, as we have come to think, only found in devastated and desolate areas. In the same way that within the beauty of Mount Fuji lurks the danger of eruption and therefore our dread in the face of it, radiation lurks unseen within the beauty of the natural world; it cannot be apprehended by human senses. We can only apprehend radiation via the sounds and numbers of a Geiger counter, the sole way to "see" where this threat to human bodies resides, thus the anxiety about radiation's destructive power, the source of which cannot know on our own. Furthermore, this destruction resides in a place that cannot be sensed or fathomed, meaning this anxiety has no sensible source; it could therefore be called sublime anxiety.

In *Sacrifice*, Ikebana master Katagiri Atsunobu's collection of photos of arrangements using flowers in full bloom gathered within the twenty-kilometer zone of the Fukushima Daiichi Nuclear Power Plant, we read the following:

> Within Fukushima prefecture, in the area of the relatively warm Minamisoma city, snow had fallen for days. The mountains of debris strewn across the expanse of seashore were now covered in purest white. The whiteness of the snow that covered, however briefly, this painful landscape left me feeling thankful. In the distance of the dancing snow I could just make out the shapes, and hear the calls, of, seagulls. In that distance remained a single blooming paper-white daffodil clinging to its blooms.[5]

This image adorns the cover of *Sacrifice*. Looking through the pages we find images such as one taken inside a building with a toppled boat jammed through an upper story window; one where a rusty, mangled, folding chair is in the foreground on top of which is arranged a single pure white magnolia flower, large and unnerving; one of a black leather backpack of the type that elementary schoolchildren wear, now abandoned, out of which poke the faces of rapeseed flowers, dandelions, and marguerite daisies. We find many such photos, horrifying and appalling. Katagari lived in Minamisoma for close to a year after the disasters and continually made arrangements from flowers that bloomed naturally in the contaminated areas in this town now emptied of people. With the tsunami damage as backdrop, one comes to think and feel just how every flower, every rock and stone, everything that has fallen, everything before one's eyes, all of it, is clothed in radioactive particles. Yet none of it can be perceived by the five human senses. The flowers remain beautiful, so much so that one wants to bury one's nose in them and enjoy their scent. We are brought up against the contradiction that the most beautiful things are pure evil. Again, human beings live lives where they are unable to apprehend radiation. Katagiri probably felt compelled to capture this in his works via flowers arranged amid the scars of disaster, in the mismatch and the ominousness. Katagiri speaks of ikebana, as we see in the full title of the collection, as a "Sacrifice." We read that "that single English word 'Sacrifice' and its multiple meanings—living creatures offered in sacrifice (*ikinie*), offerings to the gods (*kumotsu*), and sacrifices offered (*sasagemono*)—resided within me for a very long time."[6] The sparkling brilliance of the flower's life force in this contaminated off-limits area means it is a life that was destined never to be seen by humans. Such beauty and such life force would not remain in this world if it were not for artists such as Katagiri who are willing to sacrifice (*gisei*), literally, their own lives to make works of art where we can see them. Going to those lengths means that what is captured and displayed in the photos is, of course, the world we are not meant to see, a world polluted with radiation, a world "off-limits."

In the eighteenth century, Edmund Burke spoke of "delightful horror" and Immanuel Kant of "negative pleasure" when theorizing the Sublime. In doing so they created the groundwork for an aesthetics of fear. The Centre Pompidou exhibit explains how this led to the development of images depicting the end of the world on a planetary scale, the sorts of images we now see in science fiction, for example. Lars von Trier's 2011 film *Melancholia* was presented in part of a section of the "Sublime" exhibit titled "Le fantasme de la disparition." The film was discussed as a work that gives expression to such fantasies and to the anxiety and the fear in the sublime.

The film depicts the last few days on earth as a planet named Melancholia threatens to collide with Earth and destroy it. The first half of the film depicts Justine on her wedding day, describing her anxieties and eccentricities. The second half describes Justine's sister Claire and her breakdown during the period of Melancholia's closing in and expected collision with Earth. Knowing she cannot escape death, one wonders—the viewer and Justine herself—if she will kill herself as Claire's husband did, or if she should follow Claire's continuous weeping from fear: given the circumstances, this would all seem to be a very normal response. But during all of this the one who occupies the center of things is Justine. On the day of the wedding, her attention should be elsewhere but she repeatedly looks at the sky, worried about the collision of the planets, and her disturbing premonitions of the collision and her fear permeates everything. She tries to put on a happy face, at least for the duration of the ceremony, but the anxiety returns again and again and she is unable to be calmed. Possessed by her anxiety, she falls into a state of melancholia.

The lush green earth feels none of Justine's anxiety and disquiet; it could not care less. The forests, rivers, and even oceans are filmed to look exactly like a painting with lush natural landscape. As we draw closer and closer to the end of the second section of the film, the planet Melancholia, which we fully expect to completely destroy the Earth, is depicted as sparkling in brilliance like a night moon, beautiful and blue, as exquisite and real to the viewer's eyes as any other time the Earth is illuminated by the spotlight of the sun.

With no future save extinction, the anxiety and despair of those who can find no way to proceed is all placed amidst great beauty: it is exactly this contradiction that characterizes the "Sublime." Further, as Minato Chihiro discussed, it is within magnificent beauty that radiation's danger resides. We can read this film as analogous to Minato's point. In short, the danger from radiation is nothing other than the fathomless anxiety Justine struggles against.

In the latter half of *Melancholia*, Justine seems to regain a sense of calm. She has moved well beyond panic. When she sees the fear in the eyes of Claire's young son, she tries to comfort him by explaining that a magic cave will protect them. She braids tree branches to form a dome. They await the end of the Earth in this space. This is, quite literally, a trick to deceive the boy, but from the child's point of view it works because he likely believes in magic. This eases his anxiety. It also replicates the postdisaster mentality that saw those concentric circles as fully containing the radiation within their borders, like an amulet or pentacle. Humans cannot bear to be continuously subjected to a shapeless, unfathomable anxiety. One option is to continue on as though giving it no thought, flatly refusing to consider it, but this is denial without supporting logic: there is simply no way to forget it. The anxiety bears down on us. This oppressive anxiety possesses us like ghosts. This I call the "hauntology of anxiety."

THE SUBLIMINAL EFFECT OF *SHIN GODZILLA*

The catalog for the *Sublime* exhibit has a glossary at the end with an entry for items not in the exhibit. Godzilla is one of them.[7] It explains that the impetus for the first *Godzilla* film (1954) was the March 1, 1954, American hydrogen bomb testing at Bikini Atoll that exposed twenty-three crewmen on the Lucky Dragon no. 5 tuna trawler to radiation. It suggests that, for the Japanese, this was a continuation, a third instance, of nuclear damage, with Hiroshima and Nagasaki being the first and second. With that lineage in mind, we know that this series of nuclear threats gave birth to this huge monster. I want to note, however, that had the *Sublime* exhibit been open a little later, Anno Hideaki's film *Shin Godzilla* might well have been included in the display section entitled "Nuclear: The Ultimate Sublime."

It was not included in the exhibit, but it is *Shin Godzilla*, more than most artworks, that stimulates "delightful horror" and "negative pleasure" but remains nothing more than a science fiction fantasy film in the context of the radiation threat. What envelops the streets of the capital city Tokyo in catastrophic destruction? Godzilla's radioactive breath. Highly contaminated, three wards of Tokyo become "hard to return to" areas. Presented with the same phrases that became well-known after Fukushima—"damaging rumors" (*fūhyō higai*), "decontamination" (*josen*)—viewers experience a Tokyo that has become one of the "difficult to return to areas" (*kikan kon'nan kuiki*)—another phrase associated with Fukushima. When the Americans in the film decide to use an atomic bomb to bring down Godzilla, the decision means that 3,600,000 residents of Tokyo, as well as Chiba and Kanagawa prefectures, are forced to evacuate. The acting prime minister grumbles that "evacuation means that those who live there have their lives pulled up by the roots and thrown away"; this is exactly the same lament of those in Fukushima forced to abandon their homes by the evacuation orders. As the film progresses, we get much talk about skyrocketing land prices in the western part of Japan and learn that many have relocated to that part of the country. Here again, this exactly mirrors the route used by those who chose to self-evacuate after Fukushima, from Tokyo and the north to the west—and also, as Kirino Natsuo portrays in her novel *Baraka*, to which I turn next, this also describes the worst possible outcome that could be imagined of the Fukushima Daiichi Nuclear Power Plant accident.[8]

In the end, bringing the situation "under control," here by means of a cold shutdown of Godzilla, nuclear-reactor style, is clearly a quote from the nuclear accident at the Fukushima Daiichi plant. Likewise, having Godzilla stopped and literally frozen in his tracks in front of Tokyo Station reflects the still-unfinished state of cleanup at the Fukushima plant. Such images of recognizable disaster clearly embedded within *Shin Godzilla*, a film which garnered record box office revenues of more than eighty billion yen in summer 2016, suggest that for easing the suppressed anxiety in the aftermath of the disaster, it was as effective as *Melancholia*'s "magic cave."

After all this, *Shin Godzilla* winds up with a happy ending. Following the complete and thorough destruction of Tokyo, with no glimmer of hope to be seen anywhere, a discovery is made: the radiation dispersed and scattered across Tokyo has a half-life of a mere twenty days. This forecasts a city soon to be restored to its previous state. The fantasy that radiation can be made harmless is now more than ever a story we wish to believe. It is a swindle constructed on despair, based on structuring a narrative to lead to a happy ending; as such, the more it qualifies as the kind of trick that would fool a child, the more that it arouses people's hopes in what they wish to believe.

However, the euphoria that *Shin Godzilla* brings to viewers does not rely solely on such optimism in narrative construction. Rather, it is through visual material equipped to stimulate the postdisaster anxiety buried deep in our unconscious. Godzilla inhabits a discrete body, albeit one that is forced to evolve. We have a scene in *Shin Godzilla* where Godzilla is forced to swim upstream. The scene is followed by shots of boats and all matter of material being borne aloft by the waves he creates—a sequence, that is, where he becomes the visual image of a tsunami. The film includes here a shot of a man running up a hill to escape boats being pushed behind him by the onrushing water. There are scenes of people who, having fled to high ground, cannot really think that this will be sufficient to escape Godzilla, and who watch the ground below them intently. This tracks precisely with many YouTube videos from survivors of the 2011 disasters. Godzilla is here nicknamed Kamata-kun; the creature thus differs from the one usually thought of as "Godzilla" and provides a means to recall the memory of the tsunami of the Great Eastern Japan Disasters. Even more important are the images of the damage wrought in this second stage of Godzilla's development. In one shot, an upside-down, crumpled car lies atop a mountain of tsunami debris, while a human leg pokes out from the bottom of the pile. As those residing in Japan know, television and newspaper coverage of the tsunami damage was very reserved. It was careful to make sure that images of the dead were never displayed on screen or in the media. Even so, while looking at these media depictions, one could not help envisioning the numerous dead bodies that must be scattered about within them. This all means that the reality of the disasters so cleverly left out of media reports was to reappear in fictional form in a film such as *Shin Godzilla*. It would not be just for those who had seen the dead bodies that these memories were reignited. Rather, while we were all aware of this situation, we all denied it only to have those repressed memories called forth later. The denial festered in our subconscious. *Shin Godzilla*, by means of this extremely quick shot, subliminally stimulates that anxiety.

Later in the film the creature takes on a form more like what we usually think of as "Godzilla": radioactive breath streams from his mouth and turns Tokyo into a scorched expanse of ruin. Shots of evacuees in school gymnasiums, of people lined up to receive curry rice cooked and distributed by the Self-Defense Forces, for example, recall images of the ravaged areas following the disaster. Likewise, when the United States decides to employ a nuclear weapon against Tokyo in order to stop Godzilla, the film cuts to archival black-and-white photographs of Hiroshima and Nagasaki immediately after the 1945 bombings in order to show that this nuclear attack is a continuation of "Nagasaki."

While this film progresses at a quick pace, individual scenes are really too long to be considered "subliminal." Yet subliminal it is, with various extremely quick shots; lacking famous actors, containing images that are somewhat peripheral to the storyline, none of them likely to remain in the memories of viewers in the way the same scenes acted on a live stage might. All the more reason, then, that these scenes stimulate the subconscious and repressed anxiety rises to the surface, whether desired or not. Even while this follows the well-worn narrative path leading to the defeat of Godzilla, the fact is, given that this repressed anxiety is called forth by the subliminal effect I have described, it incorporates a system wherein, the higher the level of anxiety rises, the greater the degree of catharsis. For the people of Tokyo, the most earnest wish was to recover from the radiation and return to normal as though nothing had ever happened: they desire a return to their former way of life. The reality is that, as long as one stays within Tokyo where news coverage of the disasters is waning, one is able to push from memory that not only is there no expectation of successful clean-up at the Fukushima Daiichi Nuclear Power Plant but that the area remains one of large black plastic bags of "decontaminated" dirt piled high, with no permanent disposal site to speak of. But this so-called forgetting continues subconsciously to haunt us in the form of anxiety. No Godzilla story is complete without an appearance in a capital city not named, but one that resembles Tokyo. If one takes the 1954 *Godzilla* as one that draws on memories of "Hiroshima," "Nagasaki," and the carpet-bombings of Tokyo, then this postdisaster *Shin Godzilla* is one that revives the horror and fear of "Fukushima." In the final shot of *Shin Godzilla* Godzilla stands frozen in a spot near Tokyo Station. As the camera pans from his back down across his tail, we see what seems to be a pile of black and burned human bodies at the tip of his tail. This film presents corpses completely burned by Godzilla's heat-ray breath, but at the same time they seem to be the dead bodies resulting from the atomic bombs of "Hiroshima" and "Nagasaki." We find then that this series, starting with the first-generation *Gojira* in 1954 through successive generations through to the 1984 *Godzilla*, has been haunted by the nuclear attacks on "Hiroshima" and "Nagasaki." This is one visible representation of this. Further, in those years, in the context of the Cold War between the United States and the Soviet Union, a period in which nuclear annihilation was a legitimate fear, we encounter scenarios in these films where nuclear bombs are to be used again in Japan, this time against a Godzilla who appears in Tokyo.

Aleida Assmann has written about the issues of memory in German history and of Auschwitz in particular. She arranges quotes from an exhaustive range of texts, such as those from Heiner Müller and Ruth Klüger, to reveal how repressed memories driven from consciousness are replaced by the imagery of ghosts.[9] The ghost in this case is Godzilla, the very embodiment of postdisaster anxiety. Even now the representation of destruction is haunted by the Great East Japan Disasters. This is because the film spectators are themselves haunted by a ghost which is in fact radioactivity and from which they can get no distance. Audiences may wish to surrender themselves to the spectacle of *Shin Godzilla*; it is nonetheless a film about radioactive contamination, a crisis that threatens the existence of the human race. They may be concentrating their efforts via such spectacle in an attempt to wipe away deep-seated anxiety of radiation, but it, in the end, is an ineffective exorcism.

THE LITERATURE OF ANXIETY: ITŌ SEIKŌ'S *DONBURAKO*

However ineffective the exorcism was, the memories of anxiety deeply rooted in the experience of the Great East Japan disasters will, sooner or later, fade. Aleida Assmann makes "generational concept" a key mode of analysis in looking at the history of Auschwitz and Germany, a country split into East and West during the Cold War, to show distinctions based on experience. Of course, as Assmann herself argues throughout her work on cultural memory, theorizing by generation does not equate to History. Nonetheless, for Assmann, when looking at memories of the experience of Auschwitz, for example, and its transfer across generations, rather than being entwined with a single person's life, the pressing question becomes how to prevent the loss of those memories. Memories are lost with the death of particular individuals. In contemporary Japan as well, memories of war continue to disappear, moment by moment, as individuals die. At the same time, since wartime memories are recognized as being important, one can say that, via oral histories and other methods, historical preparations are already in order. But what of memories considered to have no value?[10] Among works of fiction asking these questions, we have Itō Seikō's 2017 novel *Donburako*.[11]

Donburako is a collection of linked short stories concerning the past and present of a man called "Young S." In addition to the title story "Donburako," the stories continue through "Ga" (The moth) and "Inugoya" (The doghouse). These three works treat the same theme but from different angles. While "Donburako" describes issues of anxiety, "Ga" and "Inugoya" describe the issue of memory as passed down across generations.

"Donburako" opens with a giant peach floating down a river making the onomatopoetic splashing noises of the title, "Donburako, donburako. Donburakokko, sukkokko,"[12] and is a variation of the Momotarō tale. While the story is as calm in tone as the folktale, this is a very strange tale. Young S's eighty-three-year-old father experiences a sudden seizure and is rushed by ambulance to the hospital from the old-age home where he resides. En route to the hospital, from deep in his consciousness now peeled back from reality, he has a vision of a peach-like object floating down river. The story begins in the summer of 2011, following the disasters. In response to the calls to reduce energy consumption, he had not been using his air conditioner and subsequently collapsed. From that time forth his dementia progressed and he became like a different person. The old man's consciousness in which a peach is floating down the river links up with a separate story of a woman who, having been abandoned by her husband at fifty-one, moves in to take care of her parents. The tale is intertwined around descriptions of Young S's father and the tale of this woman.

The woman's daughter left home in February 2011. Then in May of the same year her husband also left and moved in with another woman. Throughout the work are such repeated phrases as "Why did this happen to me?" and "Why did this happen to us?" leading us to wonder if these expressions might be the laments of the many old people who find themselves stuck with an end-of-life experience that they could never have imagined, queries that reverberate with the collective experience of many victims after the disasters.

Abandoned by daughter and husband, the woman returns to her family home. Her father's dementia advances and he eventually commits suicide. Money is tight. She stops feeding her invalid mother, who dies from neglect. Wanting to flee this life, she puts her mother's corpse into a large pink packing trunk and floats it down the river. The peach that S's father sees as he is losing consciousness in the ambulance is this trunk: "The body of someone with hands clasped around their knees. I'm tired of these complaints, over and over again. Why is it me alone meeting such troubles?"[13] S's father's consciousness has become intertwined with that of the mother cruelly starved to death by her daughter.

The father then goes on to say the following, as though channeling the consciousness of all the elderly people who die neglected:

> S-chan, humans will not so easily go extinct. Suffering goes on for a long time. Much longer than any words you might say in this life. Think about it, in that long period of suffering you have become like I am now. You know how water flows downhill? Well you, my son, you been living your life and here we are, you turned out like this. No good laughing at me; no good scolding; you can't

get away. That's just how it is. Water flows downhill. And here we are, you just like me.[14]

When did death become so pitiful? After working his whole life wisely and well, through all the vicissitudes of the Showa era, he now finds that at the end that he will be cast off like worn-out goods. Since when has death become something not to be mourned; since when are those approaching death to be neglected so? As a novel about elder care (*kaigoshōsetsu*), of which we are seeing something of a boom in Japan, it is timely, but that is not all. We see here the ways that the disasters pulled back the skin and laid bare what Judith Butler has termed "precarious life,"[15] of which I will have more to say below.

Ever since the disaster, S's father has had in his ear an earpiece connected to a radio that makes no sound; relatedly, the cause of his ill health is his ongoing anxiety that the stones and ground beneath his feet will suddenly slide away. That anxiety: it is the same anxiety felt by those of us who lived through the disasters. These elders symbolize the anxiety symptomatic in society since the disasters and the precarity found at the disaster's core.

The father sells his beloved home for a pittance and moves into elderly housing that S has arranged for him. Against expectations, he is not anxious and unsatisfied, but grateful to his son, saying, "I've got no complaints here, son. I'm not the sort of man who mumbles about trivialities."[16] He continues feeling a need to express gratitude to his son: "I don't blame you for any of this. Your mother and I talked all the time about how grateful we are, as parents, that you, our son, told us he wanted us to spend our last days close by."[17] Such oppressive feelings haunt these elderly people so close to death. "Donburako" can be read as a hauntology of this anxiety.

In Itō's "Ga" (The Moth) and "Inugoya" (The Dog House), the narrator referred to as S has spent a long time studying abroad in Europe. He now recalls returning home in 1999 to visit his uncle Gento, and again in 2010 to see his sick uncle Kensuke. Halfway through "Ga" S's name is revealed to be Karimikan Sankichi. This is also the name of a mysterious translator who shows up in a different novel by Itō Seikō titled *Sonzai shinai shōsetsu* (A novel that does not exist). The premise of these two short novels is that they were first written in a mixture of English and German and later translated into Japanese. Karimikan, long away from Japan, had not until now taken any interest in his place of birth or his own personal history.

In "Donburako" we find S completely absorbed in caring for his father. It is now 2014 and he is writing down the stories his uncle Gento told of his childhood when S visited him fifteen years earlier, in 1999. His parents and relatives were young and full of life at that time, his uncle Kensuke an intellectual studying German. S was influenced by Kensuke and went on to study abroad in Germany. Now he wants to know how his grandfather made his fortune during the Second World War. We are reminded that it is in this way that a family history disappears, if no one remains to remember it: if not transmitted, not written down, it dies with the elders. So it is with the story of the grandfather's fortune. When he tries to trace the history of the Shōwa period accurately, even S, born in 1967, finds there are many things he cannot recall. What he writes is no more than fragments of memory scraped together. This tale follows the flow of S's consciousness and is related as the thoughts come to him. The tale then turns to narrating the story to his wife, Junko Stange. They married in 2008; five years later she set off with two men for Gaza, which had recently been bombed by the Israeli army. She was never heard from again. S's tale is thus addressed to a person who may already have died. It is a tale for those who lived through the Showa period Japan, which no longer exists. We also find here that, as with memories of wartime, if the memories are not connected to grand narratives of history, our past is already in the process of fading.

Here again we can say that, as a continuation from *Sōzō rajio*, Itō Seikō has given us a new postdisaster literature. One thing that has become clear in the context of radiation damage is the differentiation and discrimination (*sabetsuka*) that has become operative in the assigning of value to human life. For example, children and young women able to birth and raise children are the first to be protected in government edicts, on the logic that they are highly susceptible to radioactive damage, whereas by contrast elderly people, even those living in areas with high radiation readings, are not thought to face health risks. Given that the damage from radiation surely affects all bodies the same, the result is that the elderly are already being treated as dead bodies. Disparities such as economic status determine where one can evacuate to, just as preferences for and availability of water and food items are determined by economic status. That being the case, the very fact that there is discrimination in the valuation of life is a source of anxiety. It is anxiety haunted by the precarity of life.

THE MANY *FUKUSHIMA MON AMOUR*

That this sort of anxiety is felt not only by those living in Japan or in Eastern Japan is made clear simply by looking to all the countries that, one after the other, steered toward abolishing nuclear power production following the Fukushima Daiichi meltdown. For example, the July 6, 2017, *Tokyo Shimbun* ran an editorial from Barbara Hendricks, the German Federal Minister for the Environment, Nature Conservation and Nuclear Safety; she wrote that the German government would begin a change in policy and "suspend operations at eight reactors and to phase out operations at the remaining nine" as a direct result of the March 2011 accident at the Fukushima Daiichi Nuclear Power Plant. According to the *Nihon Keizai Shimbun*, on January 11, 2017, neighboring Taiwan "passed a bill to reform the Energy Law that would be central to a revolution in energy production and would move the country away from nuclear energy production," eventually to become nuclear-free by 2025. Further, the new Korean President Moon Jae-in announced energy policies aimed at ending nuclear power production.[18]

The accident at "Fukushima" was of global impact; it has thus become an issue of profound importance that no one can ignore as someone else's problem. "Fukushima" is a problem for everyone. For example, we find even in a pro-nuclear state such as France a recent plethora of books with "Fukushima" in the title.

This is particularly true in fiction where the large-scale experience of radiation exposure in Fukushima readily brings Hiroshima to mind; perhaps also because this experience evokes images from Alain Renais' film *Hiroshima Mon Amour*, a variety of books with the title *Fukushima Mon Amour* have appeared.[19] Gérard Raynal's novel *Fukushima Mon Amour*, set in Kamaishi, follows Kaede, who is still waiting for word from her husband Kiyoto after the tsunami cut off all communications, and continues on to their eventual reunion at a Sendai hospital where he is recovering. Kamaishi was widely damaged by the tsunami and is therefore appropriate to position this couple alive but separated, but it is difficult to incorporate the Fukushima Daiichi accident because Kamaishi is actually quite distant from the nuclear plant; that is, Kamaishi was ravaged by the tsunami but mostly untouched by radiation. In the end, this narrative problem is overcome as Kaede feels oppressed by the incessant flow of news coming from Fukushima, and the issues of the nuclear accident become interwoven with her anxiety.

Likewise, we have German director Doris Dörrie's film *Fukushima Mon Amour* (*Grüße aus Fukushima*, 2016); although the original German title translates into the English "Greetings from Fukushima," I assume that the English gloss as *Fukushima Mon Amour* was chosen with an eye to Resnais' film and international audiences. Like Resnais' film, Dörrie's is filmed in black and white and describes the relationship between a foreign visitor to Fukushima and a Japanese person living there.

The film starts with Marie, a German woman broken-hearted after her fiancé left her, who has come to Japan to bring some comfort to evacuees from the Fukushima nuclear disaster now living in temporary housing. It appears to have been made with cooperation from individuals actually living in the temporary housing, so that, as the film unfolds with images of individual residents, the fictional tale is imbued with a documentary realism. While Dörrie brings that sense of realism to the forefront, the fact is that the setting is rather odd because Satomi, who has impetuously returned to her former home in the "Zone" (*kikan kon'nan kuiki*)—a place now deserted because of the threat of radiation damage—is also presented as the last geisha in Kamaishi. The international press reported that the character of Satomi was based on Kamaishi's last geisha, Ito Tsuyako (Fujima Chikano), and although Kamaishi was in the tsunami zone, it is as we have seen far from the nuclear power plant. One is struck by how the film has the same geographical problem as Gérard Raynal's novel, namely the desire to write about Fukushima radiation but set the narrative in Kamaishi, a town largely washed away and far from the nuclear meltdown. Dörrie's *Fukushima Mon Amour* never explains why a Kamaishi geisha is in Fukushima, only that she is a victim of the tsunami. The answer may simply be that viewers with an unclear sense of the geography would not see the contradiction.[20] Even so, it seems more than coincidence.

Satomi asks Marie to give her a ride to the seashore because she wants to return to her house that was partially destroyed by the tsunami. She wants to go because her beloved apprentice Yuki died there in the tsunami. Having dropped her off, Marie finds that she cannot leave Satomi alone in the zone, so she remains and helps clean the mud and debris from the house in order to return it to minimal livability. They go on to live together in the house. During the night come the sounds of a traditional Kamaishi shore song. As though led by the voice Marie steps outside to see Yuki up in a tree singing the Kamaishi song. As she looks across the beach, she can also see ghosts of others who disappeared in the tsunami.

What comes to the fore here is the question of who is able to see these ghosts in this contaminated place where human habitation has been rendered impossible.[21] In this case only one ghost among the many crowding the shore goes by a recognizable name—Yuki—and the one who can witness that ghost's presence is not Satomi, overwhelmed by a sense of guilt that she allowed Yuki to die, but rather Marie, a German, who has randomly met Satomi a number of times. As I laid out in chapter 5, this parallels the tradition of *mugen* Noh, where ghosts are not met by someone they know well but by traveling strangers who happen by. Marie sees these ghosts in a manner that accords with Japanese literary traditions. Satomi complains that Marie's unhappiness is what summons these ghosts. Again, it is curious that this film made from outside the Japanese tradition so successfully captures so many of its aspects. The overlapping themes and situation in so much postdisaster literature are striking.

An important aspect of this film lies in the fact that the ghosts are not visible by people in this world with guilty consciences over the interactions with those who have now passed, as tradition might lead us to expect, but rather, these ghosts are of people for whom traces of the past continue to exist in this world. Marie's unhappiness stems from her fiancé's having left her because she slept with his friend on the eve of the wedding. In the simplest terms, one could say the cause of her unhappiness derives from a mere lover's quarrel. In the context of the sorrow by those who lost loved ones in the tsunami and by those forced from their land following a nuclear meltdown's radiation, one is inclined to see in her story a mere youthful indiscretion that in no way compares. Nonetheless, the issue does not lie in the weight or the source of the sadness. Sadness differs among individuals and should not be flattened or weighed or compared. Even Satomi, who relies on Marie—who wants Marie to live with her, but continues to treat her coldly throughout—does not, upon hearing of Marie's sorrow, do anything to compare it to her own or to make light of it. For Marie, the breakup was an event of such import that she contemplated suicide. The tale is thus one of resonances born from Marie, herself cloaked in despair, and the occasional meetings with Satomi thinking of Yuki and wishing to die. Marie's sorrow resonates not only with Satomi's sorrow but also with the unhappiness of the land itself. It is because of this that Marie comes to call forth ghosts. It is only via these sorts of encounters that one can draw close to the sorrow of the other. It is possible to resonate/sympathize with even an extreme Other to the degree that the ghosts can be seen. Before she realizes it, Marie comes to desire for Yuki to successfully cross over to the next world and for Satomi to be able to return to her former self. It is the random traveler, haunted by the spirits (*rei*) of the land, who can see them. This tale is in these ways "hauntological," at the same time, because the setting of the tale is one in which the witness is a young German girl, it also clearly shows how the anxiety that comes from the postdisaster spirits (*bōrei*) is one not simply based on memories that followed the experience of the disasters and a land ravaged by the disasters. While *Fukushima Mon Amour* may in fact include that last geisha of Kamaishi, it could only be set in the disaster area of the Fukushima Daiichi Nuclear Power Plant, rather than the actual Kamaishi, because the spirits (*bōrei*) in that destroyed place also represent anxiety felt by the entire world. In short, what we call "Fukushima" is an anxiety haunting the entire world; postdisaster literature is haunted by this anxiety as well.

NOTES

1. Exhibition presented February 11–September 5, 2016. For the catalog, see Hélène Guenin, ed., *Sublime: Les tremblements du monde* (Paris: Centre Pompidou-Metz, 2016). See also the exhibition website (https://www.centrepompidou-metz.fr/sublime-les-tremblements-du-monde) and press packet (https://www.centrepompidou-metz.fr/sites/default/files/issuu/dp_sublime-.pdf).

2. Kobayashi Erika, *Madamu kyurī to chōshoku wo* (Tokyo: Shūeisha, 2014). Kobayashi Erika, *Hikari no kodomo 1, 2* (Tokyo: Ritorumoa, 2013, 2016).

3. In the 1920s the Radium dial company manufactured and sold wristwatches with numbers on the dials painted with green-light emitting radium. As a result, the female factory workers who painted the numbers began to suffer long-term physical afflictions and died one after the other. The remaining workers sued the company and the ruling went in favor of the women. The documentary film *Radium City* (dir. Carole Lange, 1986) investigates this issue.

4. Maurizio Lazzarato and Angela Melitopoulos, *Two Maps* (2012). Video installation.

5. Katagiri Atsunobu. *Sacrifice: Mirai ni sasagu saisei no ikebana* (Kyōto-shi: Seigensha, 2015), 90.

6. Katagiri, *Sacrifice*, 91.

7. Hélène Guenin, *Sublime: Les tremblements du monde*, 198.

8. Kirino Natsuo, *Baraka* (Tokyo: Shūesha, 2016). The morning edition of the February 10, 2016, *Tokyo Shinbun* reported that at the time of the disasters conversations were conducted at the prime ministerial level of the need for a plan of evacuation for the greater Tokyo area, and that playwright Hirata Oriza, who had worked with Prime Minister Hatoyama Yukio as a speechwriter, was told to prepare one, which they then published. It reported that they requested [in a manner that cannot be refused (*aogu*)] the support of local governments in the western part of Japan and charged them to "give women who are pregnant or nursing preferential access to trains."

9. Aleida Assmann, *Cultural Memory and Western Civilization: Functions, Media, Archives* (Cambridge and New York: Cambridge University Press, 2011), 163.

10. Starting with documentary recordings such as *3.11 wo kataritsugu—Minwa no kataritetachi no Daishinsai* (Passing on 3.11—The disaster according to narrators of folktales) produced by Higashi Nippon Broadcasting (KHB), we find a variety of activities aiming to archive memories of the disasters.

11. Itō Seikō, *Donburako* (Tokyo: Kawade Shobō Shinsha, 2017). "Donburako" is onomatopoeia.—Trans.

12. Itō Seikō, *Donburako*, 9.

13. Itō Seikō, *Donburako*, 10.

14. Itō Seikō, *Donburako*, 86–87.

15. Judith Butler, *Precarious Life: The Powers of Mourning and Violence* (London: Verso, 2004). Related to this theme is Anne Allison's *Precarious Japan* (Durham, NC: Duke University Press, 2013) which begins by describing a 2007 event where a fifty-one-year-old man was found in his home, mummified, after having starved to death. A note was found nearby which read "rice ball, please." There have been any number of such events in recent years. There have also been more than a few instances of people who rely on their parent's pensions to live and, when that parent dies, continue to live together with the corpse in order to continue receiving the payments. There has even been a film that treats this issue: Kobayashi Masahiro's 2012 *Nihon no higeki* (*Japan's Tragedy*). I read in this Allison's suggestion that the

warped nature of a national structure that casts off its weakest members in this way can also be seen in the treatment of victims following the disasters.

16. Itō Seikō, *Donburako*, 12.

17. Itō Seikō, *Donburako*, 17.

18. This according to the *Nihon Keizai Shimbun* of June 19, 2017, which reported that "Korea steers toward abandoning nuclear power production and making renewable energy central."

19. While not a work of fiction, there is also a collection of essays in English written by five different authors on their thoughts of Fukushima: Daniel de Roulet, Anne Waldman, Silvia Federici, Constantine George Caffentzis, and Sabu Kohso, *Fukushima Mon Amour* (Brooklyn, NY: Autonomedia, 2011). Roulet's contribution, "You Didn't See Anything at Fukushima: Letter to a Japanese Friend," takes as its title the well-known line from the Resnais film, "You didn't see anything at Hiroshima." Roulet writes the following about his experience in Japan in a letter to a woman named Kayoko:

> Talking about my novel *Kamikaze Mozart*, [Mori, a literary agent] explained to me that the Japanese don't like to have foreigners talk to them about their history, I shouldn't meddle in the fate of the kamikaze. You supported his point of view. Our misfortune is none of your business, you said. I thought you were being harsh. And now, doesn't your misfortune really concern us, despite what you might say? Aren't those employees at the Fukushima plant acting as kamikaze, atomic samurai? (10).

20. I take Kimura to be understated here. There are numerous logical problems with this film that Japanese viewers would not need to have spelled out. In addition to these geographical issues, having the main character be a geisha, in contrast to (for example) a bar hostess, smacks of Orientalism. Likewise, it is hard to imagine an experienced geisha, given the tough-edged, no-nonsense qualities associated with older geisha, having any patience with this clueless western woman whose story also smacks of colonial fantasy, in the trope one might call "Coming to Japan from Europe to help/save it from its troubles."—Trans.

21. As we have seen earlier, DJ Ark, in Itō Seikō's *Sōzō rajio*, has died in the tsunami, but the narration in that work comes from the body of a person that has been left behind after the disasters, still entangled high in the branches of a tall tree because of the high water of the tsunami, in the zone that is off-limits because of the radiation.

Chapter 7

Radiation and Precarious Life

THE REAL POSSIBILITY OF EVACUATING THE ENTIRE EASTERN PORTION OF JAPAN

The destruction at the Fukushima Daiichi Nuclear Power Plant in March 2011 resulted in numerous parts of Eastern Japan being labeled "hard to return to areas" (*kikan kon'nan kuiku*), that is, places rendered inhospitable to human habitation. There are of course other areas within Japan, such as U.S. military bases, where regular citizens are not permitted to enter, but for areas where people had been living since the beginning of time, to be unexpectedly and suddenly rendered dangerous to life—that is a different order of off-limits. Further, when an area is suddenly declared "hard to return to," it also means that the usual sense of moving and changing one's lifestyle is also off-limits: one's entire life to that point must be abandoned and left behind. For a time, there was a real possibility that entirety of Eastern Japan, from Tokyo to Hokkaido, would be designated "hard to return to."

For example, the *Tokyo Shimbun* reported on February 20, 2016, that at the time of the Fukushima Daiichi nuclear accident, a draft of an evacuation plan for the entire capital metropolitan area was drawn up. Then-Prime Minister Kan Naoto seems not to have been aware of the discussions undertaken, but on March 18, MEXT (the Ministry of Education, Culture, Sports, Science and Technology) Vice Minister Suzuki Kan requested playwright Hirata Oriza to formulate a draft, and the document was submitted on March 20. (Hirata was tapped because he had previously worked with Prime Minister Hatoyama Yukio as a speechwriter).[1]

As we saw in the last chapter, this draft proposal projected that the citizens of the capital would overwhelm the westbound trains, appealed for "everyone to stay calm and proceed with a calm demeanor," and directed that "pregnant women and persons accompanying babies and young children be given priority for seats on the trains to Western Japan."[2] As reported in the aforementioned article in the *Tokyo Shimbun*, according to Japan Atomic Energy Commission Chairman Kondō Shunsuke and based on a separate simulation that was run on March 25, the "worst-case scenario" for mass evacuation of the capital metropolitan area was based on the assumption that "the holding ponds for spent fuel at the Fukushima Daiichi reactors one through four would run dry, and the fuel would then melt down, meaning that some tens of millions of people from the Tokyo metropolitan area would need to evacuate."[3]

On March 18, 2011, the *Nihon Keizai Shimbun* reported former Prime Minister Kan Naoto saying, "The sense of crisis was low at TEPCO regarding the situation at Fukushima Daiichi plant, a situation where in the worst possible outcome Eastern Japan would collapse." The same paper on September 21, 2011, reported Kan thinking back on the period of the accident as saying, "we could not avoid consideration that in the worst possible outcome Eastern Japan would collapse." When this drew criticism, he elaborated on the process as follows:

> Right after the nuclear accident I instructed my staff to run a simulation for the worst possible outcome. The worst prediction came up with an evacuation zone stretching out to 200–300 km. While the evacuation of 100,000–200,000 people would be difficult indeed, if we had to evacuate 10–20 million people the country would then cease to function. At the very least, the Diet would be required to relocate. All men, women, and children would be gone from the area around the central government buildings. Everyone working at the Prime Minister's Residence would go to the western part of the country.

THE POSSIBLE WORLD POST-3.11

Within Japanese fiction following these events, there are many works set in a near-future world where there have been even more nuclear accidents. In contrast to these is Kirino Natsuo's *Baraka* (Baraka), which takes as its method a retracing of the earthquake, tsunami, and nuclear accident of March 11, 2011. In her novel, however, all four of the Fukushima Daiichi reactors have exploded and evacuation orders have been ordered for the entire eastern region of Japan, including the capital metropolitan area. As we have just seen, this was hardly baseless fabrication, no mere fiction. In the world described in *Baraka*, only immigrants live in Eastern Japan and all government functions have been transferred to the west of the country; indeed, we now know that at the time of the disasters, this was precisely an outcome that was being feverishly planned for. Fortunately, such a worst-case scenario was avoided; nonetheless the world described in *Baraka* is one that, for a moment, seemed a plausible reality.

What would become of Japan if the entire capital metropolitan area needed to be evacuated? *Baraka* presents a world eight years after the disasters, one where the capital has moved to Osaka and plans to host the Osaka Olympics are proceeding without a hitch. In place of all the former Japanese residents of Eastern Japan, including Tokyo, are foreign laborers who have moved there in search of work. This is the logical endpoint of the production that takes place at nuclear power plants, itself premised and operating on societal disparities (*kakusa*). In essence, given that nuclear power plants are known to come with extreme risk, only depopulated and poverty-stricken municipalities will accept them. Desperate last-ditch plans for subsidies and employment schemes aimed at bringing back areas from the verge of death are built into the plans devised by local governments angling to site a nuclear power plant. Local governments with financial reserves will never choose such risks. Moreover, since the employment comes with the threat of radiation, one has to find labor willing to work for mercenary wages. This entire nuclear industry has been constructed within an economic and social structure that sets up the weak to be sacrificed. Further, every time there is a nuclear incident, it is none but the most financially constricted people who are scraped together and sent to deal with the problem. Nuclear accidents expose yet again the preexisting disparities in a societal system that Giorgio Agamben has called "bare life," where relative values of individual lives are weighed and parceled out.[4]

Baraka is connected to the above issues, not least because it takes as its central theme the buying and selling of human babies. A career woman in her mid-forties suddenly has doubts about her life and feels she wants to have a child, but it is difficult for unmarried women to adopt in Japan. While shopping in a mall in Dubai, she comes across a "baby souk" and purchases a baby. All of the children for sale there are given the name "Baraka," a word which means "By the grace of God." She then goes on to marry a classmate from college and neglects this child who never bonded to her.

At the same time, Baraka's Brazilian Japanese birth parents are frantically searching for their child. There is an episode in the novel involving a Brazilian Japanese church known as the "Voice of the Holy Spirit," which provides another angle on the Great East Asia Disasters, and within which events unfold in unexpected directions. In the chaos of the disaster, Baraka runs from the adoptive mother who bought her in Dubai, only to be discovered in a highly contaminated evacuation zone where she lives as Toyota Baraka, the name "Baraka" now being represented by characters that read "scent of roses." The irradiated Baraka contracts thyroid cancer and bears a necklace-like scar around her neck from the surgery. Because of this she gets tossed about like a political football among both the pro- and antinuclear factions. This is a completely fictional action-adventure tale, but the setup and details overlap with actual circumstances with an unnerving sense of realism.

The combination of these two seemingly unrelated themes—human trafficking and nuclear meltdown—shows the degree to which radioactive contamination is an issue of human life. This is why Baraka's adoption ends in failure. Even if it becomes possible to buy and sell all and everything, the fact that this cannot be applied to human life (*inochi*) is the conclusion that this novel brings us to.

PRECARIOUS JAPAN

The fact is, however, that even before the disasters, the Japanese nation was not protecting the lives of its citizens; the threat of bare life was persistent. Director Kobayashi Masahiro's *Nihon no higeki* (*Japan's Tragedy*, 2012), as a postdisaster film, takes on the issue of fraudulent pension payments. By 2010 it had become clear that many young people without employment were unable to get by without relying on their parents' pension payments, as well as many elderly whose existence or addresses could not be verified. It turned out that, as a result of this situation, a significant number of people were living with a corpse in order receive pension benefits.

Japan has long been thought of as a rich society but is now seeing a steep increase in the "precariat" class. The neologism "precariat," referring to those in an unstable situation, combines "precarious" and "proletariat" to denote the working class without capital resources. The issue is hardly limited to Japan's working poor. It is a term that since the 1990s has been used to refer to the expanding differences across economic classes. Anne Allison, a scholar who has discussed the issues of Japan's precariat and the societal structure in depth, in the opening chapter of her *Precarious Japan*, "Pain of Life," recounts the 2007 case of a fifty-two-year-old man who starved to death in his own home and was found mummified. He left behind a note saying "Please, *onigiri*." Allison is trying to show the shocking situation of Japanese society, where food is plentiful and large amounts are wasted, and yet there are also people dying of starvation because they cannot even get a single *onigiri* rice ball. After introducing the issues of poverty in Japan that followed the 1980s economic bubble, she follows them up to these issues in the context of the March 11, 2011, disasters. She shows that the disasters made clear a wide variety of issues within Japanese society. Allison refers to a July 24, 2011, *Asahi Shimbun* survey showing that, in a society where people dying alone is an everyday experience, in the immediate wake of the disasters, 80 percent of people felt anxious about the future.[5] On the other hand, according to Furuichi Noritoshi's *Zetsubō no kuni no fukō na wakamono tachi* (*The Happy Youth of a Desperate Country*), Japan's young people do not think or plan for the future. They are satisfied enjoying the ephemeral moment. Further, he notes that most twenty-somethings in Japan responded to surveys that they are satisfied with their lives. But as Furuichi himself points out, "these youth were raised by parents whose generation benefitted most from the high-growth era and are known as the generation of 'winners' (*kachigumi*)."[6] The children can thus be said to have been supported by a sort of "family welfare system" under which the well-off parents supported the lifestyles of their children. If so, when that system disappeared, there began to appear the kind of situation depicted in Kobayashi's film: when the parents died, children who had come to rely on their pensions to live faced losing the income; they thus chose not to report the death and found themselves entangled in a situation where they had to continue living with the corpse in order to keep the payments flowing. Either that, it would seem, or starving to death with a note by their side, begging for *onigiri*. As Allison asks, how is one to live with the present ever slipping away and with no sense of any real future? She further laments that there are no plans to solve the many issues facing society.

Now, as though this was not sufficient, the conditions brought on by disaster also force people to confront the true value of their lives. As we found in the draft evacuation plan drawn up by Hirata Oriza for the Prime Minister's office, the fact that "those who are pregnant or those accompanying babies" are to be given priority because young children and babies in utero more easily absorb radiation and are at higher risk of actual harm entails that those past middle age and no longer able to bear children as well as young people who have not married are lower on the priority list, and therefore forced to wait for evacuation. For example, when radioactive iodine was discovered at a Tokyo metropolitan water purification plant on March 23, 2011, an advisory was issued warning to not give tap water to infants and young children; bottled water quickly sold out. In this situation as well it quickly becomes apparent how economic levels and the availability of supplies separated the lives of those able to escape radioactive contaminants and the lives of those who continued to drink water with radioactive particles. The fact of this strict separation of those whose lives should be protected and those whose need not be leaves people in a state of latent anxiety (*senzaitekifuan*).

In *Precarious Life: The Powers of Mourning and Violence*, Judith Butler writes about our various bodies—bodies that are proceeding toward death (mortality); fragile bodies that are easily harmed (vulnerability); bodies that can act (agency)—and how these bodies are "constituted as a social phenomenon in the public sphere."[7] This also means they are never quite exactly our own. After the 9/11 terrorist attacks in America in 2001, the American military turned to the conflict in Afghanistan and the war in Iraq, about which Butler argues that there is a "hierarchy of grief" by which we determine the relative status of mourning. Those whose lives were extinguished in a terrorist attack have a different status of mourning compared to those whose lives were taken from them in war. She further argues that humans distinguish between those whose lives we mourn and feel sadness for (grievable)[8] versus those we do not. Butler's questions—"Who counts as human? Whose lives count as lives? And finally, What *makes for a grievable life?*[9]—are not, of course limited to 9/11 and war, but are increasingly relevant within the competitive neoliberal societies on the rise across the globe. What we call the precariat develops from the issues that accompanies the condition of people cast off and forgotten at the lowest strata of society.

Neither the state nor society offers to save the weak, and in a situation where preference will always be given to those in the topmost levels of society, the weak become anxious about even existing. This leads to a latent anxiety, a sense of foreboding about the-not-yet-occurred. Upon this existential anxiety, where people try to elevate their own value, is built the devaluation of others through exclusionism, xenophobia, racism, and hate crimes. Shōno Yoriko, who has been criticizing neoliberalism for some time, published *Hyōsube no kuni: Shokumin hitokui jōyaku* (The country of all speech: A pact to cannibalize colonials) in 2016, writes of how in the months following the disasters the many empty pronouncements calling for economic revival were nothing but profiteering opportunities for the biggest industries.[10] She goes on to urge a movement against the international system of profit to which Japan has prostituted itself in the form of the Trans-Pacific Partnership. In the time since the disasters, there has once again been a proliferation of hate speech, and, concomitantly, calls for "freedom of speech"—which in this case really only serve to prop up the existing system rather than to change it at its core. Shōno calls this "all possible expressions" (*hyōgen ga subete*), then abbreviates it to *hyōsube* and writes of Japan as a country where hate is rampant, a *"hyōsube no kuni,"* a "Country of all possible expressions." The TPP flows on while hate pumps with ever more vigor. This does not come from the realization of the TPP necessarily, but from the neoliberal system of economic prioritization and its disdain for human life.

In Shōno's 2017 work *Sā, bungakude sensō wo tomeyō: Neko kicchin kōjin* (Let's stop war with literature: The cat kitchen god), she takes on the question, "What is exclusionism, What is racism?" She writes in answer, "What makes a racist? It is the result of the systematization of slander of the Other and the seizure of power in order to legitimate the cover-up of economic exploitation. It is the compact made by an economic system between discrimination and exploitation; they are two sides of the same coin."[11]

In other words, the exclusionism/xenophobia that runs rampant in the world is born from economic exploitation. Ironically, that which by economic exploitation makes prey of and drives into a corner the lowest classes does so by hitching a ride with hate acts (*heito koui*).¹² Why is this? Because hate acts are actions taken by people trying to raise their own class position by looking down on and then excluding those even lower in the class hierarchy. Those lower in the hierarchy include foreigners and immigrants; hate acts make them an "Other" and, further, makes them aware of this othering. Considered within Butler's "hierarchy of grief," these Others are those whose lives are so outside the system that they may not be "grievable." Those engaged in hate acts seem to feel that they can reach up to join hands with the upper strata and gain access to some of their privileges, but it is never sufficient: there is no actual possibility of being elevated into a higher class. This means that they themselves, at the end of the day, begin to doubt and ask themselves whether they may not also be among those whose "lives will not be mourned." This, of course, leaves them stuck with latent anxiety, in the same condition as when they began.

DISPERSAL AND A FUTURE WHERE JAPANESE DISAPPEARS: OKADA TOSHIKI'S *JIMEN TO YUKA*

Okada Toshiki's theater group Chelfitsch performed *Jimen to yuka* (Ground and Floor) from December 14 to 23, 2013, at the Kanagawa Arts Theater. This positive run followed an opening in Brussels, followed by a successful tour of seven European cities.

The setting is not so much "Japan in the far future" as "not-so-far future Japan": this is a tale that predicts the path of postdisaster Japan. The older brother (Yutaka) is an elite businessman whose wife (Haruka) is pregnant. The younger brother (Yukio) used to work in a factory, but that was closed down and relocated overseas, leaving him out of work for two and a half years. He lived on money borrowed from his older brother until eventually landing a job in construction.

Even though the setting is "future Japan," at the mention of two and a half years the audience begins to imagine that Yukio lost his job because of the disaster. If so, the new job is very likely reconstruction work in the disaster zone. He begins by saying, "all these collapsed, warped roads are going to be restored, step by step, to what they were before. Yes sir, so many little cracks, they all need to be repaved." He continues, "Nothing miserable about this work, this is fine work indeed!" But his boasting suggests the opposite, that this is work nobody really wants and, along with other clues, we are given to understand he is in a highly contaminated area.¹³

Yukio and Yutaka's mother (Michiko) has already died, but she returns as a ghost and criticizes her daughter-in-law Haruka. She is visible only to Haruka. Michiko wants no one but Haruka to hear her complaints. When the ghost appears on the simple floor of the kitchen it looks exactly like a Noh stage. Given the traditions of *mugen* Noh (see chapter 5), a ghost speaking on stage is not the least bit unnerving.

Haruka considers leaving Japan on account of her coming child. Although her reasons are not clearly explained, audience members will recall all the people, including the mothers and children by themselves, who left their homes behind and fled to the western part of the country because of the radiation following "Fukushima." Okada himself fled west with his family and now lives in Kumamoto; given that he has friends overseas, we can be sure that he has had the experience of being told "Get out of Japan as soon as possible."

Haruka thinks of leaving her husband behind and fleeing Japan with her child, just the two of them. She also feels sure that his dead mother will entangle her husband and hold him back. Indeed, the mother says, "My desire is to peacefully lie under the surface of the earth forever. For that to happen I want you to come by—just once in a while is fine—and take care of the ground covering me, some of the ground around me, keep a clean grave. That is my only wish. That's not too much to ask, is it?"[14]

We have heard many conversations after the disasters among the people who showed no intention of leaving, even with the disaster damage, because of the strong sense that the family graves must be taken care of. Watching over graves is, almost without exception, a masculine obsession. For a woman who marries into a man's family and moves into the house, those graves are not the graves of her ancestors but of his. One hears of many cases where the woman wanted to evacuate with the children and the husband wanted to stay in the family home; unable to reach agreement, husband and wife begin living separately. Haruka responds to this in similar fashion: "The dead ones' demands on the living are indeed too much to ask, I think. So, I won't listen, I don't want to hear, I will pay no attention to the existence of any ghosts that may be here."[15] Now, the father does not "exist" in the context of this tale; it may be the most distinctive aspect of this tale is the father's nonexistence. Even though it takes up the subject of graves, the most patriarchal thing there is, they are described via the resistance of the women: this is a tale of the *mother*-land, a tale of the *mother* tongue, a tale whose theme, in every sense of the word, is the mother.

There are those that leave Japan. Evacuating one's motherland means going to live in a place where you cannot communicate in your mother tongue. Moving outside the country means abandoning the language of that country. This is all the more the case for a language like Japanese, one that really is only spoken within Japan, but the same thing happens at the level of regional dialects too. The people of Fukushima are now dispersed throughout Japan, and therefore the regional dialect of Fukushima is dispersed as well. The dialect cannot therefore be passed down to the next generation. I have to wonder if all those people who say "come evacuate overseas" think about this. As long as Japan the country exists and remains habitable, it matters little how many Japanese are living overseas. But what would happen if nearly all Japanese people were forced to evacuate to other countries? What if they were never again able to return? It is not hard to imagine, given that swathes of Fukushima can never be returned to and people have been forced to disperse.

The following words appear on a monitor on the stage:

You, have you ever considered
Japanese, and if it should disappear?
Thousands of years from now
(The word "Thousands" is replaced)
Hundreds of years from now
You, have you ever considered
Missiles, flying towards us across the ocean?
You, have you ever considered
Japan, becoming a war zone?[16]

Radiation is not the only reason to leave the motherland. Exile is usually a product of war. There is a long history of people abandoning their homelands and being scattered across the globe. After the disaster, with the indiscriminate and agitated fanning of racial hate flames among Japan and its neighbors, already tense relationships flared into flames of hate speech. A mother who wants to protect her son will not want to see him go to war; Okada shows here the possibilities of a different sort of scattering.

While all of this is going on the Japanese motherland disappears and the mother tongue becomes one spoken only by small numbers of people. In this play, the very existence of the character Satomi forces this point. Satomi is a friend of both Yutaka and Haruka. Seeing that in fact nothing has changed after the disasters, Satomi loses all hope and shuts herself in her room (*hikikomori*). Those who are *hikikomori* have cut all relations with society to the point that it is as if they do not exist in this world. This is another kind of evacuation and of separation from the mother tongue. *Hikikomori* nurture and keep alive within themselves their own mother language, yet it is a language of the communication which they have already ended because they no longer speak to anyone, and also, because they get none of the linguistic changes that occur as time passes, that language becomes ossified. This is the situation of

Latin and other dead languages. This is how Okada imagines the end of the road for Japanese language.

Yukio, with his new job in public construction, visits his mother's grave to report:

> If I keep working like this then it means, at least for the part I can contribute, I can help get this country back to where it was. I have been made part of that project. . . . There's no doubt about it, we are going to get this country back to where it was, actually, no, we can make it even better than it was before. An incredible amount of energy has been gathered together and I can really feel it, like I too am part of that force, I really feel it.[17]

But even as he is relaying all this, his body is continuously wavering, as though something is overpowering and forcing him to curl in on himself. Yukio's body displays nothing proud and fluid as he speaks; this suggests that the future of rebuilding the country is not bright in the least. The play gets to the heart of and crystallizes what the country of Japan is now experiencing.

THE IMAGINATION OF DISPLACEMENT (REFUGEE): FUKADA KŌJI'S *SAYONARA*

Fukada Kōji's film *Sayonara* (2015) is based on Hirata Oriza's play of the same name.[18] Hirata's original, performed in 2010, was a very short play about a woman on the verge of death from sickness, and the android that comes to read her poetry at her side. Perhaps more than the short play itself, it was the spectacle of a human actor interacting with an actual android on stage that initially drew attention. The performance following the Greater East Asia Disasters adds a section where, following the woman's death, a delivery person comes to gather up the android and transport it to its next job. The next stop is "Futabamachi." Futabamachi, the town where the Fukushima Daiichi Nuclear Plant is sited, is well known to Japanese as a town completely evacuated; when performed overseas, the titles projected onto the stage included a supplemental "Fukushima." The delivery person explains things to the android this way:

> You're going to a place with no people. We want you to continue reading poems there. Many people have died over there. None of us can enter or read poetry for those who have died. So, please, take this on. I cannot get any closer than the 5 km radius, so you'll be delivered by some other robots, same kind as you.[19]

"Many people have died": we assume this is a place ravaged by the tsunami, and since entrance is forbidden to humans, it is surely also damaged by radiation. Those who died from the tsunami waves in areas now off-limits get no memorial services. That must be why they are sending in androids to read poetry and pacify the dead. In the postdisaster version, the contrast between the woman who is dying and the android which does not die is transformed into one where the human body, in Butler's sense, is both heading toward death (the mortal) and easily harmed (vulnerable), in contrast with the radiation-resistant android. Indeed, at present, clean-up work for the Fukushima Daiichi Reactor, especially the reactor core and other areas where radiation remains too high for humans and entrance is forbidden, is being undertaken by robots lowered into the center.[20]

At this point in his film adaptation, Fukada Kōji adds to the story that thirteen nuclear power plants have exploded, spewing radioactive contamination widely. Japan has been rendered uninhabitable, and because of this inhabitants from throughout Japan are being systematically evacuated to other countries. The protagonist Tanya, who is white, was born in South Africa. At age ten she came as a refugee to Japan with her parents. Tanya has an incurable illness, in response to which her father has bought her an android companion, Leona, and they live together. Leona had formerly been able to walk, but a section of her legs is now broken, and, following the nuclear explosions, she has not been able to find a repair person and must use a wheelchair. Tanya speaks Japanese, English, French, and German, and Leona responds as best as possible to match whatever language Tanya uses. The result makes for Japanese film unusual for its flow of multiple languages.

In the opening scenes of the film we see television footage of people heading toward Narita airport in order to evacuate from Japan. This is followed by one shot after another of mask-wearing families lugging heavy bags as they trudge along the railways. This sequence comes at the opening of the film, before we understand the narrative, and suggests that people are already, one by one, leaving Japan.

Leona has gone to do shopping on Tanya's behalf. She returns with news that an acquaintance, Mr. Kobayashi, has been assigned to the Philippines for evacuation; however, Kobayashi's grandparents, because the grandmother is no longer able to walk, will be staying behind. Despite the fact that Japan has become uninhabitable, those who have no options but to live there anyway are, as always, the weakened elderly.

Residents are assigned an evacuation number, and when a country to take them in has been decided on, it is announced in a businesslike manner. Family members are provided consecutive numbers, and care is taken to have them all evacuate to the same country. It is not hard to see in these dialogues Hirata Oriza's evacuation plan as drafted for the prime minister's office: "Pregnant women and those accompanying nursing children" should be given precedence in evacuation. Next in line would be those especially susceptible to radiation damage and their families. It seems possible that the well-off would have already crossed to other countries before the evacuation orders were handed down. This is why Tanya's friend Sano-san says, "A middle-aged single woman like me doesn't have a chance. I'm at the back of the line." When Sano-san invites Tanya to go to hear the announcement of the "Seventh Wave of Evacuees" a man stands up and starts shouting, "This selection process is bogus. All of you surely know what is going on, we are all being deceived. It's obvious! Only the rich are getting chosen. Do you mean just to overlook the poor? We are dying here, just like this. There is no way we can escape."[21]

At this point, announcements of who will get to evacuate have already reached the "seventh group." What distinguishes those who have evacuated long before from those who continue to wait for their numbers to be announced? While the government insists that people are chosen equitably, those never cleared to evacuate first feel, and then come to know, that the weight of their individual lives is being measured and ranked, that they are being placed into hierarchies. This is the anxiety that people in reality actually feel about the radiation damage. People worry that at the point of crisis they may find themselves abandoned. Here lies the latent anxiety: one wonders if they too may be one of those who have no worth and therefore are not chosen for evacuation. Sano-san had been married and had given birth to two sons, the youngest of whom died from neglect; she thinks this may be the reason that her evacuation number never comes up. Tanya assumes that her number never comes because she is a refugee.

Sano-san's lament "We've all become refugees, haven't we? It's like, even if we got evacuated, we'd likely be persecuted anyway, in those other countries" seems to come from the experiences of many of the people who actually evacuated from the radiation from Fukushima Daiichi. Individuals beg for their numbers so that they can evacuate, but, even if they are actually able to flee, an easy happiness will not necessarily follow. Thus, in those places to which they have evacuated, persecution will cause them still to live with bodies easily harmed (vulnerable). We see in this film, in the relationship between Tanya and her lover Satoshi, this exclusion and hate.

Satoshi used to live near Tanya, but after the accident, he returned to Shizuoka to live with his family. His house was extremely close to the nuclear power plant. Now that everyone has left it seems more like an abandoned ruin. Satoshi rides his bicycle through the town, which now resembles the "hard to return to" areas of present-day Fukushima, screaming "You bastards!" Satoshi's mother is Korean and his father was born in Japan to Korean parents, so that he is "resident Korean in Japan" (*zainichi kankokujin*).

Satoshi's nationality is therefore officially Korean. Once, during the time Satoshi was dating Tanya, his mother telephoned. She reported that his father, who suffers from dementia, says he wants to return to Korea and has been crying nonstop since the morning. In the past, whenever there was conversation about becoming naturalized, his family, who had been raised in Korea, were in favor, but his father objected. Satoshi's remark that "Given how things have turned out, it's a good thing we never took Japanese citizenship" thus probably means that since he does not possess Japanese citizenship he can cast off Japan at any time. When Tanya says to Satoshi that "I want us to get married," he blithely responds, "Good idea, we should do that, marry"; in fact, when they are able to evacuate, he and his family leave Japan—and Tanya—behind.

In this tale about refugees, given that the main characters are Tanya, a refugee who fled from South Africa, and Satoshi, a *zainichi* (Korean resident in Japan) in Japan, an evacuation from Japan is not necessarily the same as giving up the hometown of your ancestors. It is obvious that many non-Japanese are living in Japan, but this fact is often overlooked within Japan. This film is also able to weave in the multiple layers of those trying to live in Japan. Although Satoshi never explains why he left Tanya in Japan, the film suggests through the conversations between the two of them that discrimination was at the root of it. Tanya once explained that she is a refugee who needed to evacuate South Africa when whites were being killed by black people right after the abolition of apartheid. Tanya added that when her father got drunk, he would start spouting things like "White people too are discriminated against" and "Yes, the whites have done some terrible things but so have the blacks." At the moment he hears this Satoshi suddenly jumps up and leaves the room because, for *zainichi* Satoshi, talk of whites and blacks is the same as talk of the issues between Japanese and *zainichi* (Korean resident in Japan). The things that Tanya's father says are quite likely things Tanya believes as well. As far as Satoshi is concerned, we can easily imagine, this sounds as though he was being told, "The Japanese have done some terrible things, but in the end, so have the *zainichi*." When leaving, Satoshi asks Leona if the massacre of South African whites was a real thing. Asking the android means that he doesn't trust the grievances and memories of the people who were actually involved. So, whether in debates about *zainichi* or in those about massacres, such levels of personal experience mean people will always be talking past each other.

After Satoshi leaves, Tanya begins thinking about what just happened. She is made to see first that her memories of South Africa are entirely based on things her parents have said. She mumbles to herself, "What actually happened? Why did Papa, Mama, and I have to leave our home in South Africa and become refugees? Were we victims? Were we aggressors?" Leona answers the questions: "If it is a question of whether victims or not, I think you were victims. But as to whether you were aggressors or not, I'm sorry, but that I am unable to answer." By this point Satoshi has already departed and Sano-san commits suicide. When the Bon-odori festival of August dances is held at the evacuation center, Sano-san seems totally entranced by the fire burning brightly in the sacred wooden structure, and eventually jumps in and dies. Her ex-husband and eldest son have been cleared to evacuate to Indonesia, leaving her behind and most likely hopeless.

All Tanya's friends and acquaintances are now gone, she remains with Leona; both of them are left behind.[22] She has Leona read her poems; she has long conversations with Leona; she comes to think that it is just the two of them now living together. But, in fact, these conversations with Leona are limited to output comprised of information that was initially programmed into her as an android and from what she has accumulated and learned from Tanya. Left behind by lovers and friends, embracing the sickness that will take her to her death, Tanya feels extreme loneliness. For Leona's emotions merely mimic patterns learned from Tanya: she does not really understand Tanya's feelings. Tanya comes to realize that what she took to be sympathy from Leona is no more than information output. Tanya says, "I have been just nodding along to all of my own feelings. It's just dumb." It is not exactly a matter of talking to one's self, and yet to Leona this sense of talking to another personality follows from an android's never forgetting something once inserted into memory, whereas since humans forget there is a schism. Tanya is now not just left behind as a single individual: she comes to know that Leona is nothing more than a copy of herself. In *Precarious Japan*, Anne Allison cites Tsukino Kōji to show how *hikikomori* are "homeless inside home,"[23] and continues, "Home reduced to bare life; a dis-belonging that starts at home; a home that goes nowhere."[24] We see in Tanya an embodiment of bare life.

Near the end of the film the camera lingers on ears of pampas grass swaying in autumn on Suwa's Kirigamine highlands, in the mountains of central Japan in Nagano. It looks as desolate as the end of the world. Tanya goes daily with Leona to the bamboo grove her father liked; she stays until she has worn herself out. Her father had told her about bamboo flowers, and she goes in hopes of someday seeing them. Bamboo flowers are said to bloom all at once every few decades or once in hundreds of years. The odds of witnessing them in a single lifetime are exceedingly low.

Slightly before the scene of the walk to the bamboo forest we have a scene where the frame warps strangely. We see Tanya from behind pushing Leona's wheelchair on the road from their house. The two of them flicker out of view and then appear again slightly further down the road in a jump cut that makes them look like ghosts. With their light brown clothing they seem to melt into the dry grass around them. They suddenly disappear from the frame only to reappear soon after. From this ghostly (*bōrei*) shot an odd feeling remains with the viewer: it as though the two have now moved on to the next world, as though they now appear in a dream. Perhaps they have now melted into each other in a hauntological type of relationship; such a reading also seems possible. It is during this walk that Tanya tells Leona about the bamboo flowers. Tanya relates how once, when her father was a boy and was able to see the flowers on a trip, he found it "so beautiful I thought I would cry." Leona asks, "Cry because it is beautiful?" The idea of being moved to the point of tears is something else she learned from Tanya. For an android, it is only through such study that they can come to their own opinions or feelings. Thus she gives no thought to being left behind alone. She will in all likelihood be able to see these flowers that exceed the lifespan of a single human being. That long period before the flowers bloom again—"tens of years, hundreds of years"—represents a period exceeding a single human life, but it also of course here correlates to the unknown period that is the half-life of radioactive materials. Ultimately we are shown how, after death, Tanya's body rots, turns to bleached bones, and fully disappears, all to show the long process of time. We're led to suppose that Leona will continue to go every day to this grove, even after Tanya has died, and one day will witness the brilliance of these flowers blooming all at once. It is clear that even should her wheelchair catch on something and throw her to the ground, she will start crawling toward the bamboo. This scene of Leona focused on getting to the bamboo grove, this resolution to do whatever it takes to see the flowers: I think it a mistake to see in this scene a representation of Tanya's strong desire to see the flowers. At the very least, in the last scene of Leona gazing at the flowers, viewers will understand the strong desire of an android and see in her expression the uncanny: an android acting in ways for which she was not programmed.

Now if the expression of feeling on Leona's face is nothing other than a copy of Tanya's, then the Leona whom we see gazing at flowers is, in a way, actually the Tanya programmed into Leona. That is, Leona as android is one who is completed by this haunting of Tanya; we can say that Tanya's soul (*tamashii*) continues to live on in Leona, and that Leona, given this composition, is also Tanya's ghost (*bōrei*). If *Jimen to Yuka* can be said to exhibit the potential for *hikikomori* to preserve the Japanese language, then *Sayonara* expresses the phenomenon of an android, on the ground of a Japan where no one remains, that is able to preserve both the Japanese language and the Japanese people.[25]

Following Tanya's death Leona's clothing falls into tatters, her hair becomes a tangled mess; she decays step by step. Androids have strong resistance to radiation. Thus, even should the world be contaminated by radiation, there is no need for her to evacuate and she is left behind, alone. Humans are extinguished by death, but Leona is not. The image of an undying Leona can also be profitably read overlapping with works such as those of Tawada Yōko, who writes of an irradiated world where the old are unable to die. With radiation, the issue is not whether one may die or not; the issue is in the fear that our easily wounded (vulnerable) and proceeding toward death (mortal) bodies will be assigned different values and be sorted and classified. Not only is Tanya never assigned an evacuation number, she is prevented from getting treatment at hospital and cast off by her lover. Beyond this, Tanya comes to realize that even Leona, whom she lives with, is no more than an echoing spirit (*kodama*) of her words, that in this land where no one remains she has been cut off from her body as it functions in society, that the body that can act (agency) has been forfeited/lost, and has become Giorgio Agamben's "bare life." The only path left to her is the body moving toward death (mortal). This is the same path to be trod by the immortal Leona. We very likely read in the image of Leona gazing on the bamboo grove in full flower the dejection of an android left behind. In the same manner that Tanya lived a life that was merely allowed to go on living, Leona will also, until she completely dissolves, live only (bare life), nothing more. In this way the question of what "bare life" might mean for an immortal android is asked. While an android may not be an actual lifeform, in this film what is expressed as the "bare life" of a body isolated from society is actually found in the android, the one that continues living and is unable to die. The tale of radiation *Sayonara* presents is one that suggests the fear of the collapse toward a "bare life" where one is simply living and nothing more.

NOTES

1. Of these dialogues, scholar Miyamoto Dōjin has written: "Given that it falls in the space between utilitarian writing (*jitsuyōbun*) and literature, this is a fictional draft proposal. Literature is here being used in the political sphere, but, if anything, this also means that literature has extended its reach and taken this opportunity to use politics." He projects the possibilities of literature being used by politics. As a further example, Miyamoto draws from the words of Wakasugi Retsu in *Genpatsu howaitoauto* (Nuclear whiteout), which was written with an eye to preventing future events that have every possibility of occurring: Genkaiken editorial collective. *Higashi Nihon Daishinsai-go bungakuron* (Tokyo: Nan'undō, 2017), 340.

2. *Tokyo Shimbun*, February 20, 2016.

3. *Tokyo Shimbun*, February 20, 2016.

4. The Japanese rendering of this phrase, which Kimura relies on, is *mukidashi no sei*, which is not just "[laid] bare" but "peeled back and raw."—Trans.

The reference is to Giorgio Agamben, *Homo Sakeru: Shuken kenryoku to mukidashi no sei*, translated by Takakuwa Kazumi (Tokyo: Ibunsha, 2007).

5. The morning edition of the *Asahi Shimbun* newspaper of July 24, 2011, in an article titled "Dying alone, aging society, depopulation: With the East Japan disasters, societal contradictions exposed," began by reporting that "The East Japan disasters laid bare the weaknesses of postwar Japan. Our society was already directly facing the advanced aging of society, the change to a society of households of one lone person; a stratified society has come to feel the weight of natural disaster even more heavily on our shoulders," before taking up the issues of "lonely death." Further, "according to an internet survey of 10,000 people conducted in June by the AXA life insurance group, eighty percent responded that they 'had come to feel anxiety about the future of the country,' with just under seventy percent responding that they 'had come to feel the importance of the connections between individual people'."

6. Furuichi Noritoshi, *Zetsubō no kuni no kōfuku na wakamonotachi* (Tokyo: Kodansha, 2011), 335. Translated by Raj Mahtani as *The Happy Youth of a Desperate Country: The Disconnect between Japan's Malaise and Its Millennials* (Tokyo: Japan Publishing Industry Foundation for Culture, 2017).

7. Judith Butler, *Precarious Life: The Powers of Mourning and Violence* (London: Verso, 2004), 26. Kimura quotes from the Japanese translation by Motohashi Tetsuya (Tokyo: Ibunsha, 2007).

8. I take Kimura's use of the phrase *kanashini tsuitō sarerubeki sei*, "mourn and feel sad," to conform to Butler's term "Grievable."—Trans.

9. Butler, *Precarious Life*, 20, italics original.

10. Shōno Yoriko, *Hyōsube no kuni: Shokumin hitokui jōyaku* (Tokyo: Kawade Shobō Shinsha, 2016).

11. Shōno Yuriko, *Saa, bungakude sensō wo tomeyō: Neko kicchin kōjin* (Tokyo: Kodansha, 2017), 273–74.

12. Kimura tells me that this is a usage unique to Shōno. It is intended to incorporate Butler's "grievable life" together with her idea about a hierarchy of grief.—Trans.

13. Toshiki Okada, "Jimen to yuka," *Shinchō* 111, no. 1 (2014): 50.

14. Okada, "Jimen to yuka," 46.

15. Okada, "Jimen to yuka," 46.

16. Okada, "Jimen to yuka," 49.

17. Okada, "Jimen to yuka," 55.

18. The entire play is available online at https://www.youtube.com/watch?v=fIZ5i27XXCY.

19. Hirata Oriza, "Human Android Theater-Sayonara," The Japan Foundation, YouTube video, 24:16.

20. Onda Riku, in *Sabita taiyō* (Rusted sun) (Tokyo: Asahi Shimbun Shuppan, 2017) describes a near future in which, after a series of multiple nuclear accidents, at a point somewhere in the mid-twenty-first century, there occurs a massive meltdown that becomes referred to as "the final accident" in which nearly 20 percent of the land of Japan is deemed "restricted access only." The novel is set within the "Northern Kantō restricted access zone." The premise is that humanoid robots will be employed to undertake the nuclear clean-up. At the height of opposition between the humans and the humanoid robots, unfeeling and never-dying zombies are introduced to the story. At the time of the nuclear explosion nearly thirty thousand people died and

were all cremated *en masse* in an area next to the perimeter of the restricted entry zone. It is suggested that as a result of the radiation they were transformed into the zombies now active in the Zone. They have hardly any memories of their previous lives: "We understand [only] that we were part of a terrible accident. All we remember is being irrationally, mercilessly, destroyed. Therefore, we now move with no other impulse other than to exact revenge on the humans, on the country of Japan" (316). By bringing these ghosts (*bōrei*) onto the stage, we get a proxy for criticizing nuclear energy and further, a way of ending the reckless government policies where humanoids are programmed by humans and have no means of taking on a critical stance. Instead, this scenario, where it is the dead who can "embody" that critique, comes to resemble a faith in vengeful returning spirits, the *onryō* spirits found in the rituals of folk religion.

21. *Sayōnara*, directed by Kōji Fukada (n.p.: Hatsubaimoto Fantomu Firumu, 2016).

22. To be precise, it is not that there is absolutely no one, as one shot suggests that homeless people continue to live in the area. It would seem appropriate to consider that people may remain who never received an evacuation number.

23. Tsukino Kōji, *Ie no naka no homuresu* (Homeless in their own homes) (Niigata: Niigata Nippō jigyūsha, 2004).

24. Anne Allison, *Precarious Japan* (Durham: Duke University Press, 2013), 85. Allison references Agamben, *Homo Sacer: Sovereign Power and Bare Life*, trans. Daniel Heller-Roazen (Stanford, CA: Stanford University Press, 1998).

25. This idea of preserving within the memory of a single being a language, here Japanese, that has died out, resembles the premise of Ray Bradbury's *Fahrenheit 451*, where every single book in the world is forbidden and disappeared, and individual people then commit to memorizing the entire contents of a single book in order to pass it on to the next generation; this parallelism was pointed out to me by a graduate student from Toulouse University. The theme at the 2014 Yokohama Triennale, "The art of *Fahrenheit 451*: In the middle of the Earth is an ocean of forgetting," directed by artist Morimura Yasumasa, also resonates with this.

Epilogue

I wrote my previous book, *Shinsaigobungakuron* (A Theory of Postdisaster Literature), in what now seems one fell swoop of feverish activity. Once I finished writing I felt as though I had been possessed by something; I didn't know what, but it seems to me now that I was, in fact, possessed by something. I began to think on just what it was that had possessed me so. Whether or not I was actually possessed, it is clear to me now that what had gotten its hooks into me was the same as the things haunting Japanese society following the disasters. All of the fiction, film, and art that were published after the disasters reflected that society. Thus all the things that haunted us, the situation by which we are haunted, via the wide variety of art productions—that is what I began to think on. I anticipate that these are things I will be wrestling with for some time to come, in the same way that postwar society is unable to escape the memories of war, in the same ways that Hiroshima and Nagasaki must continue to shoulder the memories of nuclear radiation; in ways that the postwar recovery is said to have pushed the wartime past away and moved on, even though we clearly have not, we may again have to plod along that well-worn road. One may think the exorcism was successful, yet those invisible things remain submerged somewhere. That is what I was considering in this book by using the concept of "hauntology."

I have come to call it postdisaster literature (*shinsaigobungaku*), but the works I take up are much broader than fiction. Film, theater, fine arts all came within my purview, and I have read widely in these texts.

Over time I have come to have connections with France and for one year, from April 2017, I was able to be associated with INALCO, the Institut national des langues et civilisations orientales in Paris. This helps explain why I consider so many French works in this book. In Europe, rather than the postdisaster periods being referred to as post 3.11, it is more likely to be referred to as post-Fukushima, because among the three disasters of earthquake, tsunami, and nuclear meltdown, it is the latter, the radiation, that garners the most attention there. The reason is that radiation is not an event that stops at a single country or region but is a danger to the human race, a huge issue shared across the globe. For example, following the accident that occurred at Fukushima Daiichi Nuclear power plant, many countries decided to cease nuclear activity; even so, there remains the issue of how to dispose of the spent radioactive fuel. In that sense the mountains of plastic bags filled with contaminated earth and piled high across an expanse of Eastern Japan's rice fields are representative of the difficult issues confounding decision-makers across the globe.

Within overseas research on Japan, research on postdisaster Japan is already well-established. For example, in Spring of 2017, the European Association of Japan Studies was convened at Lisbon university. Not just literature but many fields were represented, including sociology, anthropology, and media studies. There were any number of presentations with "post Fukushima" or "post 3.11" in their titles. There was also coordination with a number of conferences scattered throughout Europe. Within Japanese literary research the genre of "postdisaster literature" is completely established, with a variety of works being analyzed. Consistently central to research conducted on the literature of Japan, right up to the immediate present, has been coverage of literature from early premodern to contemporary. It has become the role of public intellectuals in the style of Karatani Kōjin or Etō Jun to analyze the newest Japanese fiction. Even so, the research on Japan that is undertaken in the various countries across the globe must of course account for the needs of students and, perhaps even more, shoulder the burden of translating and introducing new fiction, such that lectures on contemporary fiction are not unusual; many professors teach widely, from the earliest fiction to contemporary works. These are further reasons that, particularly with literary research, we see that among overseas researchers engagement with new works has followed the disasters, they having come to this more quickly than scholars in Japan. Therefore, research on postdisaster fiction has taken place in the context of collaborations with overseas researchers.

I have thought deeply within myself about this matter of working together with scholars from other countries: what to write about and how to go about it. Research overseas takes place as research on Japan, meaning that the methods of comparative research are not necessarily the same, but for me, to the degree possible, I wanted to look at the issues following the disasters not just from Japan but within activities across the globe. I say "world," but because the languages available to me are English and French I am limited to specific corners of the world. Nonetheless, no matter the language there are works that interact with the disasters, so I was thinking that I would like to position postdisaster literary theory within the framework of world literature. Having said all of that, what to theorize about was entirely dependent on the works themselves. I consider the text to be a subject and I operate by reading and analyzing what the text itself expresses, following the path wherever it leads. Obviously, the reading of a text changes with the reader and with the reading, whether the first or third time through—all of that is a given. I do not consider the readings I am hinting at here to be the sole readings available for those works. Multiple readings are possible; the more one reads the richer the readings become, and it seems to me that coming up against those numerous readings allows us to revitalize the work in the space of research. There are times when I find it frustrating to be limited to talking about single works without space for my own opinions, but no matter how one proceeds the words with which one thinks are learned from the text itself, thus to read and then contemplate as the method of literary analysis does not seem to be a mistake.

In my last book I grumbled about how students were likely to complain, "There she goes again" whenever I started to lecture on postdisaster literature, but in the brief span of the last six years the disasters have become ancient history to these students. There are, of course, those in the class from the Tohoku region whose experiences remain raw, but now the majority of students respond, "I knew nothing about this, I am so glad we are studying it." Students are also likely to express how important it is that such works have been written so that the details can be passed down to them, which itself seems to give the lie to the earlier charge that writing about the disasters is somehow inappropriate. When those from the disaster areas begin to tell of their experiences, other students tear up and shake with emotion. It is true that some students from the region have suffered little and therefore feel they have no qualifications to speak of the disasters. And yet, when we read Svetlana Aleksievich's *The Unwomanly Face of War* in Miura Midori's translation, they come to realize that even the most trivial of experiences is part of history. They then go on to tell of their childhood excitement when playing video games in the car, or washing their hair with cold water in the public park, only now coming to realize that they were in the midst of such exceptional times.

I recently had an opportunity to lead a seminar session over the internet with graduate students from Canada's University of British Columbia along with undergraduates and graduate students from my own Tsuda University. We read and exchanged opinions from the poems in the postdisaster collection *Kawaranai sora: Nakinagara, warainagara* (The Sky Unchanged: Tears and Smiles) collected by fifty-five people who survived the triple disasters and in dual translation. Among the most interesting differences was that on the Japanese side, students tended to read and take in an unfiltered, if sentimental, reality of being affected by disasters, while on the Canadian side they tended to read with a consideration of how these poems fit in the traditions of waka poetry. As time passed there was less emotion and we were able to engage in more theoretical discussion. This was not simply a matter of the disasters already being forgotten but an issue of distance in time. For young students the disasters are already history. But this also means that there are many possibilities for an expansion of postdisaster literature in the future. I still feel sharply the many works I couldn't discuss, the many works I couldn't include. I would like to take them up in a later project.

I am deeply indebted to the researchers and friends who made opportunities for me to discuss and lecture on this, who were willing to read and comment on drafts, and who encouraged me by telling me how important this work is. I feel very grateful for the many editors who gave me opportunities to write book reviews and columns which were opportunities for me to think about this research. Finally, I express my gratitude for the courage of my editor Hishinuma Tatsuya, who made the publication of my work a reality not once but twice.

December 25, 2017

Bibliography

Abe Auestad, Reiko. "Ibuse Masuji's *Kuroi Ame* (1965) and Imamura Shōhei's Film Adaptation (1989)." *Bunron: Journal of Japanese Literary Studies*, no. 4 (2017): 106–24.

Abraham, Nicolas, and Maria Torok. *The Wolf Man's Magic Word: A Cryptonymy*. Translated by Nicholas Rand. Minneapolis: University of Minnesota Press, 1986.

Adorno, Theodor W. "Cultural Criticism and Society." In *Prisms*, translated by Samuel Weber and Sherry Weber, 17–34. Cambridge, MA: MIT Press, 1983.

———. *Negative Dialectics*. Translated by E. B. Ashton. New York: Seabury Press, 1973.

Agamben, Giorgio. *Homo Sacer: Sovereign Power and Bare Life*. Translated into English by Daniel Heller-Roazen. Stanford, CA: Stanford University Press, 1998. Translated into Japanese by Takakuwa Kazumi as *Homo Sakeru: Shuken kenryoku to mukidashi no sei*. Tokyo: Ibunsha, 2003.

Alexievich, Svetlana. *Charnobyl'skaia malitva: Khronika pryshlastsi*. Minsk: Rėspublikanskae hramadskae ab'iā̆dnanne "Litaraturna-mastatski fond 'Hronka'," 1999. Translated into English by Keith Gessen as *Voices from Chernobyl*. Normal, IL: Dalkey Archive Press, 2005. Translated into Japanese by Matsumoto Taeko as *Chiyerunobuiri no inori*. Tokyo: Iwanami Shoten, 2011.

———. *U voǣiny--ne zhenskoe lieĭiso*. Minsk: Mastat͡s͡kai͡a͡lit-ra, 1985. Translated into English by Richard Pevear as *The Unwomanly Face of War: An Oral History of Women in World War II*. New York: Random House, 2017. Translated into Japanese by Miura Midori and Sawachi Hisae as *Sensō wa onna no kao o shite inai*. Tokyo: Iwanami Shoten, 2016.

Allison, Anne. *Precarious Japan*. Durham, NC: Duke University Press, 2013.

Apelfeld, Aharon. *The Immortal Bartfuss*. Translated by Yaacov Jeffrey Green. New York: Weidenfeld & Nicolson, 1988.

Asada, Akira, and Azuma Hiroki. "'Fukushima' wa shisōteki kadai ni nariuru ka." *Shinchō* 111, no. 6 (June 2014): 417–47.

Asada, Jirō. "Asada jirō intabyū '*Sensō* to iu fuhen wo kaku'." *Seishun to dokusho* 51, no. 7 (July 2016): 2–9.

———. *Kikyō*. Tokyo: Shūeisha, 2016.
Assmann, Aleida. *Cultural Memory and Western Civilization: Functions, Media, Archives*. New York: Cambridge University Press, 2011.
Ayase, Maru. *Yagate umi e to todoku*. Tokyo: Kodansha, 2016.
Bailly, Jean-Christophe. *The Animal Side*. Translated by Catherine Perter. New York: Fordham University Press, 2011.
Bataille, Georges. "A propos des récits des habitants d'Hiroshima (1947)." In *Oeuvres Complètes*, Vol. 11, 172–87. Paris: Gallimard, 1991. Translated into Japanese by Takeshi Sakai as *Hiroshima no hitobito no monogatari*. Tokyo: Keibunkanshoten, 2015. Translated into English by Alan Keenan as "Concerning the Accounts Given by the Residents of Hiroshima," *American Imago* 48, no. 4 (1991): 497–514. http://www.jstor.org/stable/26303925.
Bayard-Sakai, Cecile. "Writing by Circumventing the Unrepresentable: The Case of Post March 11 Literature." Paper presented at "Japanese Studies After 3.11," 24th Nichibunken International Symposium, Leipzig University, Germany, November 9–11, 2017.
Boltanski, Christian, and Catherine Grenier. *La vie possible de Christian Boltanski*. Paris: Seuil, 2007.
Borrmann, Mechtild. *Die andere Hälfte der Hoffnung: Roman*. München Droemer, 2014. Translated by Akasaka Momoko as *Kibō no kataware*. Tokyo: Kawade shobo, 2015.
Butler, Judith. *Precarious Life: The Powers of Mourning and Violence*. London: Verso, 2004. Translated by Motohashi Tetsuya as *Sei no ayausa: Aitō to bōryoku no seijigaku*. Tokyo: Ibunsha, 2007.
[*Cahiers d'Art?*]. Hiroshi Sugimoto. *Cahiers d'Art Revue*, no. 1 (2014) *Revue*, no. 1 (2014).
Camus, Albert. *Camus at Combat: Writing 1944–1947*. Edited and Annotated by Jacqueline Levi-Valensi. Translated by Arthur Goldhammer. Princeton, NJ: Princeton University Press, 2006.
Caruth, Cathy. *Unclaimed Experience: Trauma, Narrative, and History*. Baltimore and London: Johns Hopkins University Press, 1996.
Current 93 (David Tibet, Maja Elliott, Petr Vastl, Michael Cashmore, Steven Stapleton, and Andria Tibet). *Soft Black Stars*. Audio Recording. London: Durtro, 2005.
Deguy, Michel. *À ce qui n'en finit pas: threne*. Paris: Éditions du Seuil, 1995. Translated by Robert Harvey as *To That Which Ends Not: Threnody*. New York: Spuyten Duyvil, 2018.
Derrida, Jacques. "Fors: The Anglish Words of Nicolas Abraham and Maria Torok." In *The Wolf Man's Magic Word: A Cryptonymy*, edited by Nicolas Abraham and Maria Torok and translated by Nicholas Rand, xi–l. Minneapolis: University of Minnesota Press, 1986.
———. *Specters of Marx: The State of the Debt, the Work of Mourning and the New International*. Translated by Peggy Kamuf. New York: Routledge, 1994.
———. *The Animal That Therefore I Am*. Translated by David Wills. New York: Fordham University Press, 2008.

Duras, Marguerite. *Hiroshima Mon Amour*. Translated by Richard Seaver. New York: Grove Press, 1961.
Ferrier, Michaël. *Fukushima: Récit d'un désastre*. Paris: Gallimard, 2012. Translated by Yoshie Makiko as *Fukushima noto: Wasurenai saika no monogatari*. Tokyo: Shinhyoron, 2013.
Fisher, Mark. *Ghosts of My Life: Writings on Depression, Hauntology and Lost Futures*. Winchester, UK: Zero Books, 2014.
Fujita, Naoya. "'Sei' yori mo warui unmei." In *Higashi Nihon Daishinsai-go bungakuron*, edited by Iida Ichishi and Yutaka Ebihara, 419–66. Tokyo: Nan'undō, 2017.
Fukada, Kōji, dir. *Sayōnara*. [Japan], Hatsubaimoto Fantomu Firumu, 2016.
Fukazawa, Shichiro. "Furyu mutan." *Chūō Kōron* 75, no. 13 (December 1960): 328–40.
Furuichi Noritoshi. *Zetsubō no kuni no kōfukuna wakamono tachi*. Tokyo: Kodansha, 2011. Translated by Raj Mahtani as *The Happy Youth of a Desperate Country: The Disconnect Between Japan's Malaise and Its Millennials*. Tokyo: Japan Publishing Industry Foundation for Culture, 2017.
Furukawa, Hideo. *Shōsetsu no dēmontachi*. Tokyo: Suicchi puburisshingu, 2013.
———. *Tōmin suru kuma ni soineshite goran*. Tokyo: Shinchōsha 2014.
———. "Zusetsu tōhō kyōfu tan." *Bijutsu techō* 63, no. 950 (April, 2011): 99–115.
Gamzou, Assaf. "La mémoire visualisée: discours de la Shoah et bande dessinée." In *Shoah et Bande Dessinée: L'image au service de la memorie*, exposition, Paris, Mémorial de la Shoah, January–October 2017, edited by Didier Pasamonik and Joël Kotek, 6–7. Paris: Denoel & Mémorial de la Shoah, 2017.
Genkaiken (Iida Ichishi, Sugita Shunsuke, Fujii Yoshinobu, Fujita Naoya, Ebihara Yutaka, Tsuruba Nobuhiro, Tomizuka Ryōhei, et al.). *Higashi Nihon Daishinsai-go bungakuron*. Tokyo: Nan'undō, 2017.
Gen'yū Sōkyū. "Amenbo." In *Hikari no Yama*. Tokyo: Shinchō bunkō, 2016.
Georget, Anne, dir. *Festins imaginaires*. [Paris]: Montparnasse, 2015.
Guenin, Hélène, ed. *Sublime: Les tremblements du monde*. Exhibition Catalog. Metz: Centre Pompidou-Metz, 2016.
Hara, Tamiki. "Natsu no hana." In *Natsu no hana: Shōsetsushū*, 7–32. Tokyo: Iwanami bunkō, 1988.
Hatakeyama, Naoya. *Kesengawa*. Translated by Corinne Quentin and Marc Feustel. Paris: La Madeleine, Editions Light Motiv, 2013.
Hayashi, Kyoko. "Futatabi Rui e." *Gunzō* (April 2013): 8–27. Reprinted as Hayashi Kyoko, *Tanima: Futatabi rui e*. Tokyo: Kodansha, 2016. Translated by Margaret Mitsutani as "To Rui, Once Again." *Asia Pacific Journal/Japan Focus* 15, no. 3 (April 1, 2017): n.p. https://apjjf.org/2017/07/Hayashi.html.
Heller-Roazen, Daniel. *Echolalias: On the Forgetting of Language*. New York: Zone Books, 2005. Translated into French by Justine Landau, edited by Agathe Sultan, as *Écholalies: Essai sur l'oubli des langues*. Paris: Éditions du Seuil, 2007.
Hersey, John. *Hiroshima*. Expanded Edition. New York: Knopf, 1985.
Higaki, Tatsuya. "Shizen wa ranbō de aru ni kimatte iru." In *Shishō to shite no 3.11*, edited by Atari Sasaki, Shunsuke Tsurumi, Takako Yoshimoto, Hisao Nakai,

Gen Kida, Tetsuo Yamaori, Norihiro Kato, Masaki Tajima, Ichiro Mori, Shinya Tateiwa, Yoshiyuki Koizumi, Tatsuya Higaki, Yuichi Ikeda, Tsutome Tomotsune, Takako Egawa, Iwasaburo Koso, Jun Hirose, 131–40. Tokyo: Kawade shobo, 2011.

Hirata Oriza. "Human Android Theater-Sayonara." The Japan Foundation. YouTube video, 24:16. https://www.youtube.com/watch?v=fIZ5i27XXCY.

Hōjō, Yūko. *Utsukushii Kao*. Tokyo: Kodansha, 2019.

Hosomi, Kazuyuki. *Furankufuroto gakuha: Horukuhaimā, Adoruno kara 21 seiki no 'hihan riron' he*. Tokyo: Chuokoronshinsha, 2014.

Hotta, Yoshie. *Jikan*. Tokyo: Iwanami Shoten, 2015.

Ibuse, Masuji. *Kuroi ame*. Tokyo: Shinchōsha, 1970. Translated by John Bester as *Black Rain*. Tokyo: Kodansha, 1969.

Iizawa, Kōtarō, and Hishida Yūsuke. *Afutāmasu: Shinsaigo no shashin=Aftermath*. Tokyo: NTT Shuppan, 2011.

Imamura, Shōhei, dir. *Kuroi Ame (Black Rain)*. New York: Fox Lorber Home Video, 1999.

Itō, Seikō. *Donburako*. Tokyo: Kawade Shobō Shinsha, 2017.

———. *Fukushima monolōgu*. Tokyo: Kawade Shobo, 2021.

———. "Gaza, Nishikichishiku, Anman" (Gaza, West Bank, Amman) *"Kokkyō naki ishidan" wo mi ni iku*. Kodansha bunkō i-65-5. Tokyo: Kodansha, 2020.

———. *"Kokkyō naki ishidan" wo mi ni iku* (Report of *Médecins Sans Frontières*). Tokyo: Kodansha, 2017.

———. *"Kokkyō naki ishidan" ni narō* (Let's Become *Médecins Sans Frontières*). Tokyo: Kodansha, 2019.

———. *Nihon bungaku wo 3.11 go no shiza de yomu—Sakka Itō Seikō to tomo ni*. Presentation, *3.11go bungaku wo konnichiteki ni kangaeru*. Paris: INALCO, 2 February, 2019.

———. "Sōzō rajio." *Bungei* 52, no. 2 (Spring 2013): 17–94. Reprinted as *Sōzō rajio*. Tokyo: Kawade bunkō, 2015.

Iversen, Margaret. *Photography, Trace, and Trauma*. Chicago, IL: University of Chicago, 2017.

Iwama Sen. *"Tabisuru chō" no yō ni: Aru genpatsu risan kazoku no monogatari*. Tokyo: Riberuta Shuppan, 2017.

Iwata-Weickgennant, Kristina. "'Gendering Fukushima': Resistance, Self-Responsibility, and Female Hysteria in Sono Shion's *Land of Hope*." In *Fukushima and the Arts: Negotiating Nuclear Disaster*, edited by Barbara Geilhorn and Kristina Iwata-Weickgenannt, 110–26. New York: Routledge, 2017.

Jelinek, Elfriede. *Kein Licht*. Frankfurt am Main: Rowohlt Theater Verlag, 2011. Translated by Hayashi Tatsuki as *Hikari no nai (No Light)*. Tokyo: Hakusuisha, 2012.

Kahoku, Shinpōsha, ed. *Banka no atesaki: Inori to shinsai*. Tokyo: Kōjin no Tomosha, 2016.

Kakiya, Miu. *Hinanjo*. Tokyo: Shinchōsha 2014. Reprinted as *Onnatachi no hinanjo*. Tokyo: Shinchōsha, 2017.

Kanehara, Hitomi. *Mazāzu=Mothers*. Tokyo: Shinchōsha, 2011. Reprinted as *Mazāzu*. Tokyo: Shinchōsha, 2014.

———. "Motazaru mono." *Subaru* 37, no. 1 (January 2015): 82–189, 201–32. Reprinted as *Motazaru mono*. Tokyo: Shūesha, 2015.

Kanō, Mikiyo. *"Hiroshima" to "Fukushima" no aida: Jendā no shiten kara.* Tokyo: Inpakuto shuppankai, 2013.
Kariya, Tetsu. *Oishinbo 110: Fukushima no shinjitsu* (1). Tokyo: Shogakkan, 2013.
———. *Oishinbo 111: Fukushima no shinjitsu* (2). Tokyo: Shogakkan, 2014.
Karube, Tadashi, Fujino Kaori, and Inaba Mayumi. "Sōsaku gappyō." *Gunzō* (March 2014): 324–36.
Katagiri, Atsunobu. *Sacrifice: Mirai ni sasagu saisei no ikebana.* Kyōto-shi: Seigensha, 2015.
Kawakami, Hiromi. *Kamisama 2011.* Tokyo: Kōdansha, 2011.
———. *Ōkina tori ni sarawarenai yō.* Tokyo: Kodansha, 2016.
Kimura, Saeko. "Kotoba no yurikago in yurarete: Jakka Dofunī *Umi no kioku no monogatari* wo yomu." In *Tsushima Yūko no sekai = The World of Yuko Tsushima*, edited by Inoue Takashi, 74–99. Tokyo: Suiseisha, 2017.
———. *Shinsaigobungakuron: Atarashii Nihon bungaku no tame ni.* Tokyo: Seidosha, 2013.
———. "Shinsaigo bungakuron 2021—atarashii bungaku no hō he." *Subaru* 43, no. 4 (April, 2021): 153–167.
Kirino, Natsuo. *Baraka.* Tokyo: Shūesha, 2016.
Kobayashi, Erika. *Hikari no kodomo.* Tokyo: Ritoru Moa, 2013.
———. *Madamu Kyurī to chōshoku wo.* Tokyo: Shūeisha, 2014.
———. *Toriniti, Toriniti, Toriniti—Trinity, Trinity,* Trinity. Tokyo: Shueisha, 2019. Translated by Brian Bergstrom as *Trinity, Trinity, Trinity: A Novel.* New York: Astra House, 2022.
Kobayashi, Masahiro, dir. *Nihon no higeki.* Tokyo: Tōei Bideo Kabushiki Kaisha, 2012.
Kōno, Fumiyo. *Kono sekai no katasumi ni.* Tokyo: Akushon Komikkusu (Futabasha), 2008.
Kotobuki, Shiriagari. *Gerogero pūsuka.* Tokyo: Entāburein, 2007.
Kudō, Rein. *Tsurara no koe.* Tokyo: Kodansha, 2021.
Kudo, Yuka. "Shishatachiga kayou machi—takushii doraibaano yūrei genshō." In *Yobisamasareru reisei no shinsaigaku*, edited by Kanebira Kiyoshi. Tokyo: Shinyosha, 2016.
Kurabayashi, Yasushi. *Shinsai no āto: Ano toki, geijutsu ni nani ga dekita no ka.* Tokyo: Bukkendo, 2013.
Kuroki, Kazuo, dir. *Chichi to kuraseba.* [Japan]: Bandai Bijuaru, 2004.
Kyō, Machiko. *COCOON.* Akita: Akita Shoten, 2010.
———. *Paraiso.* Akita: Akita Shoten, 2015.
Léon, Christophe. *Mon père n'est pas un héros: Fukushima.* Paris: Oskar, 2013.
Luke, Elmer, and David James Karashima. *March Was Made of Yarn: Reflections on the Japanese Earthquake, Tsunami, and Nuclear Meltdown.* New York: Vintage Books, 2012.
Medoruma, Shun. "Denreihei." In *Sensō shōsetsu tampen meisakusen.* Tokyo: Kōdansha bungei bunko, 2015.
Michimata, Tsutomu, ed. *Ano hi kara: Higashi Nihon Daishinsai chinkon Iwate-ken shusshin sakka tanpenshū.* Morioka: Iwate Nippōsha, 2015.
Miki, Akiko. "The Exhibition is a Machine for Stopping Time." *Cahiers d'Art Revue*, no. 1 (2014): 172–73.

Minear, Richard H. *Hiroshima: Three Witnesses*. Princeton, NJ: Princeton University Press, 1990.

Miyauchi, Yūsuke. *Kabūru no sono*. Tokyo: Bungei Shunju, 2017.

Miyazawa, Kenji. "Nametokoyama no kuma." In *Kōhon Miyazawa Kenji Zenshū*, Vol. 9. Tokyo: Chikuma Shobō, 1973. Translated by John Bestor as "The Bears of Nametoko." In *The Oxford Book of Japanese Short Stories*, edited by Theodore W. Goossen, 103–111. Oxford: Oxford University Press, 1997.

Nagashima, Yū. "Toi no nai kotae." *Bungakkai* 66, no. 10 (October 2012): 58–77. Reprinted as *Toi no nai kotae*. Tokyo: *Bungei Shunjū*, 2013.

Nakagami, Kenji, Tsushima Yuko, Mita Masahiro, Takahashi Michitsuna, Taki Shūzō. "Zadankai: Warera no bungaku no tachiba—sedairon wo koete." *Bungakkai* 32, no. 10 (October 1978): 98–117.

Nancy, Jean-Luc. *Équivalence des catastrophes (après Fukushima)*. Paris: Éditions Galilée, 2012. Translated by Charlotte Mandell as *After Fukushima: The Equivalence of Catastrophes*. New York: Fordham University Press, 2015.

Numata, Shinsuke. "Eiri." *Bungakukai* 71, no. 5 (May 2017): 9–37. Reprinted as *Eiri*. Tokyo: Bungei Shunju, 2017.

Okada, Toshiki. "Chimen to yuka." *Shinchō* 111, no. 1 (January 2014): 43–59.

Okuno, Shūji. *Tamashii demo iikara, soba ni ite: 3.11.go no reitaiken wo kiku*. Tokyo: Shinchosha, 2017.

Ono, Kazuko. *Aityakute Kikitakute tabinideru*. Sendai: Pumpquakes, 2019.

Ōoka, Shōhei. *Nobi*. Tokyo: Sōgensha, 1952. Translated by Ivan Morris as *Fires on the Plain*. New York: Knopf, 1957.

Orr, James Joseph. *The Victim as Hero: Ideologies of Peace and National Identity in Postwar Japan*. Honolulu: University of Hawaii Press, 2001.

Osada, Arata. *Genbaku no ko: Hiroshima no shōnen shōjo no uttae*. Tokyo: Iwanami Shoten, 1990. Translated by Jean Clark Dan and Ruth Sieben-Morgen as *Children of the A-Bomb: The Testament of the Boys and Girls of Hiroshima*. New York: Putnam, 1963.

Otsuka, Julie. *The Buddha in the Attic*. New York: Knopf, 2011. Translated by Iwamoto Masae and Kotake Yumiko as *Yaneura no hotokesama*. Tokyo: Shinchosha, 2016.

Ozeki, Ruth. *A Tale for the Time Being*. New York: Viking, 2013.

Parry, Richard Lloyd. *Ghosts of the Tsunami: Death and Life in Japan's Disaster Zone*. London: Jonathan Cape, 2017.

Quentin, Corinne, and Cécile Sakai, eds. *L'archipel des séismes: Écrits du Japon après le 11 Mars 2011*. Arles: P. Picquier, 2012.

Raynal, Gérard. *Fukushima, mon amour!: [roman]*. Pollestres: TDO éd, 2011.

Rilke, Rainier Maria, *Duino Elegies: A Bilingual Edition*. Translated by Stephen Cohn. Evanston, IL: Northwestern University Press, 1998.

Rimer, Thomas. "*Taema* a Noh Play Attributed to Zeami." *Monumenta Nipponica* 25, no. 3/4 (1970): 431–45.

Rossiter, Marie, Carole Langer, and Tim Cappello. *Radium City*. New York: Carole Langer Productions, 1986.

Roulet, Daniel de, Anne Waldman, Silvia Federici, Constantine George Caffentzis, and Sabu Kohso. *Fukushima Mon Amour*. New York: Autonomedia, 2011.

Sato, Yoshiyuki, and Taguchi Takumi. *Datsu genpatsu no tetsugaku*. Tokyo: Jinbun shoin, 2016.

Sekigawa, Hideo, dir. *Hiroshima*. Tokyo: Shin Nippon Eigasha, 1953.

Sekiguchi, Ryōko. *Ce n'est pas un hasard: Chronique Japonaise*. Paris: POL, 2011. Japanese Publication as *Katasutorofu zen'ya: Pari de san ichichi o keiken suru koto*. Tokyo: Akashishoten, 2020.

———. *La Voix sombre*. Paris: P.O.L, 2015. In Japanese as "Koe wa arawareru." *Bungakukai* 71, no. 3 (March 2017): 140–98. Included in *Katasutorofu zen'ya: Pari de san ichichi o keiken suru koto*. Tokyo: Akashishoten, 2020.

———. *L'astringent*. Paris: Argol éditions, 2012.

———. "Le Goût de Fukushima." In *L'archipel des séismes: Écrits du Japon après le 11 Mars 2011*, edited by Corinne Quentin and Cécile Sakai, 274–85. Arles: P. Picquier, 2012.

———. *Manger fantôme: Manuel pratique de l'alimentation vaporeuse*. Paris: Les ateliers d'Argol, 2012.

Sekiguchi, Ryōko, and Felipe Ribon. *Dîner Fantasma*. Paris: Manuella éditions, 2016.

Seo, Natsumi. *Awaiyukukoro: Rikuzentakada, shinsaigo wo ikiru*. Tokyo: Shobunsha, 2019.

———. *Nijū no machi/Kōtaichi no uta*. Tokyo: Shoshikankanbō, 2021.

Seo, Natsumi and Komori Haruka, dir. *Nijū no machi/Kōtaichi no uta wo amu*. Tokyo: Unknown, 2019.

Serai, Yūichi. "Kanashimi to mu no aida." *Bungakkai* 68, no. 7 (July 2014): 10–55. Reprinted as *Kanashimi to mu no aida*. Tokyo: Bungei Shūnjū, 2015.

———. "Koyubi ga moeru." *Bungakkai* 71, no. 1 (January 2017): 58–130.

———. "Koyubi wa omokute." *Bungakkai* 64, no. 11 (November 2010): 62–89.

Shimazaki, Chifumi, ed. and trans. *The Noh: In Parallel Translations, With a General Introduction and Running Commentaries*, Vol. 2. Tokyo: Hinoki Shoten, 1987.

Shōno, Yoriko. *Sā bungakude sensō wo tomeyō: Neko kicchin kōjin*. Tokyo: Kodansha, 2017.

Sion, Sono, dir. *Kibō no kuni*. Tokyo: Third Window Films, 2012.

Shimada, Masahiko. "Shō wa kekkyoku unjidai." *Bungei shunjū* 95, no. 9 (September 2017): 388.

Shiriagari, Kotobuki. *Gerogero pūsuka*. Tokyo: Entāburein, 2007.

Smethurst, Mae, trans. "Sanemori." In *Like Clouds or Mists: Studies and Translations of Nō Plays of the Genpei War*, edited by Elizabeth Oyler and Michael Watson, 147–62. Ithaca, NY: Cornell East Asia Series, 2013.

Sugimoto, Hiroshi. *Āto no kigen*. Tokyo: Shinchōsha, 2012.

———. "Kyō sekaiwa shinda moshikasuruto asu kamosirenai." *Shinchō* 111, no. 2 (February 2014): 256–73.

Takagi, Makoto. "Bōrei no toki/ bōrei no uta, arui wa intātekusuchuaritii no naka no *Gikeiki*: mirai no 'kioku'/mirai kara raihō suru 'bōrei'." In *Nihon bungaku kara no hihyō riron: Bōrei, sōki, kioku*, edited by Takagi Makoto, Kimura Saeko, and Andō Tadao, 305–28. Tokyo: Kasama shoin, 2014.

Takahashi, Gen'ichirō. *Koisuru genpatsu*. Tokyo: Kōdansha, 2011.

———. *Sayonara Kurisutofā Robin* = Goodbye, Christopher Robin. Tokyo: Shinchōsha, 2012.
Takahashi, Hiroki. "Yubi no hone." *Shinchō* 11 (November 2014): 7–55. Reprinted as *Yubi no hone*. Tokyo: Shinchōsha, 2017.
Takahashi, Nobuko. "Utsukushikumo ozomashii." *Bungei Shunjū* 95, no. 9 (September 2017): 378–88.
Taki, Kōji. *Sensōron*. Tokyo: Iwanami shoten, 1999.
Tanaka, Masako. *Kurisuchan Borutansukī: Animitasu sazameku bōreitachi*. Tokyo: Pai International, 2016,
Tawada, Yōko. "Higan." In *Kentōshi*, 7–164. Tokyo: Kōdansha, 2017. Translated by Jeffrey Angles as "The Far Shore." In *Words Without Borders* (March 2015). https://www.wordswithoutborders.org/article/the-far-shore.
———. "Idaten." In *Kentōshi*, 165–88. Tokyo: Kōdansha, 2017.
———. "Kentōshi." *Gunzō* (August 2014). Reprinted in *Kentōshi*. Tokyo: Kōdansha, 2017. Translated by Margaret Mitsutani as *The Emissary*. New York: New Directions, 2018.
———. *Kumo wo tsukamu hanashi*. Tokyo: Kōdansha, 2012.
Tendō, Arata. *Mūn naito daibā* = Moonnight diver. Tokyo: Bungei Shunjū, 2016.
Treat, John Whittier. *Writing Ground Zero: Japanese Literature and the Atomic Bomb*. Chicago, IL: University of Chicago Press, 1995.
Tsujimoto Isao, ed. *Kawaranai sora—Nakinagara, warainagara* = The sky unchanged, tears and smiles. Tokyo: Kodansha, 2014.
Tsukino, Kōji. *Ie no naka no homuresu: Kamisama boku o hikikomori ni shite kureta koto o kansha shimasu*. Niigata: Niigata nippō jigyūsha, 2004.
Tsushima, Yūko. *Ashibune tonda*. Tokyo: Mainichishinbunsha, 2011.
———. *Hangenki o iwatte*. Tokyo: Kodansha, 2016.
———. *Hi no yama: Yamazaruki*. Tokyo: Kodansha, 1998.
———. *Jakka Dofunī: Umi no kioku no monogatari*. Tokyo: Shūesha 2016.
———. *Kari no jidai*. Tokyo: Bungeishunju, 2016.
———. "Nyū yōku, Nyū yōku." *Gunzō* 69, no. 2 (February 2014): 134–44.
———. "Ōtobai, arui wa yume no tezawari." *Gunzō* 71, no. 2 (February 2016): 87–100.
———. "Yamaneko dōmu." *Gunzō* 68, no. 1 (January, 2013): 7–167. Reprinted as *Yamaneko dōmu* = Yamaneco dome. Tokyo: Kodansha bungei bunko, 2017.
———. *Yume no uta kara*. Tokyo: Insukuriputo, 2016.
Tsutomu, Michimata, ed. *Ano hi kara: Higashi Nihon Daishinsai chinkon Iwate-ken shusshin sakka tanpenshū*. Morioka: Iwate Nippōsha, 2015.
Tyler, Royall. *Japanese Nō Dramas*. London: Penguin Books, 1992.
Uchida, Nobuteru, dir. *Odayaka na nichijō*. Tokyo: Kabushiki Kaisha Esudīpī, 2012.
Wagō, Ryōichi. *Shi no tsubute*. Tokyo: Tokuma Shoten, 2011.
Weibel, Peter. "Repression and Representation: The RAF in German Postwar Art." In *Art of Two Germanys: Cold War Cultures*, edited by Stephanie Barron, Sabine Eckmann, and Eckhart Gillen, 256–59. New York: Abrams & Los Angeles: In Association With the Los Angeles County Museum of Art, 2009.
Yamada, Yōji, dir. *Haha to kuraseba*. Tokyo: Shōchiku, 2015.
Yoshimura, Man'ichi. "Borādobyō." *Bungakkai* 68, no. 1 (January 2014): 10–79. Reprinted as *Borādobyō*. Tokyo: Bengeishunjū, 2014.

Index

2Chan, xxvii-xxviii, xlvin8
3.11. *See* Earthquake, Great Eastern Japan
4Chan xlvin8
9/11, xi, xxxviii, 129-30

Abe Shinichiro prime minister, xlviii, 17, 64n9
Adorno, Theodor, 25–26, 40nn10–11
Agamben Giorgio, 127, 140
Akasegawa Genpei, 35
Akihabara, xxvii; Akihabara massacre of 2008, xxviii
Aleksievich, Svetlana, xxii, 46–47
Allison Anne, 123n15, 128–29, 138, 142n24
Ameya Norimizu, 45
Amuro Namie, xxviii
Anno Hideaki, 113
Appelfeld Aaron, xxxvi
Asada Akira, 25
Asada Jirō, 71
Asia-Pacific War, xxv, xxxv-xxxvii, xlv, 17, 31–32, 40n2, 45–46, 49, 51–55, 63, 67–74, 78, 101-3, 119
Assmann, Aleida, 116
Atomic Bomb, xxx-xxxi, xlv, 40n2, 47–48, 50–55, 57–60, 62, 72–79, 82, 101-2, 109, 113, 115

Atomic bomb literature, xlvi, 53, 72, 94
Atomic Bomb museum, 55, 76
Atomic bomb victim. *See hibakusha*
Atomic energy, xxxv
Atomic Energy Commission, Japan, 126
Auestad Reiko Abe, 73
Auschwitz, 17, 25–26, 39, 52, 84n32, 116
Ayase Maru, 94
Azuma Hiroki, 25

Bailly, Jean-Christophe, 60–62
Bataille, Georges, 51–52, 57–58
Bayard-Sakai, Anne, 19
Berenbaum Michael, 39
Boltanski, Christian, 79–82
Borrmann, Mechtild, 46–47
boshi hinan. See mother and child evacuation
Bradbury, Ray, 142n25
Burke, Edmund, 111
Butler, Judith, 45, 118, 128, 130

Camus Albert xlviiin39, 16, 57–58
Cannibalism, 31, 70–72
Caruth Cathy, 59
Celan, Paul, 26
Chelfitsch, 85

155

Index

Chernobyl, xxii, xlii, 25, 27, 30, 37, 45–47, 58
cherry blossoms, 43n30, 60, 103
China, 11, 31, 44n34, 92
concentric circles, 28, 30, 109, 111
cows, 60
Crypt, 87, 98
Current 93, 77; *Larkspur and Lazarus*, 77

"damaging rumors" (*fuhyō higai*), xxvi, 35, 113
Dazai Osamu Prize, 67
"decontamination" (*josen*), xxvi, 34–35, 42n18113
Deguy Michel, 87–88
Derrida, Jacques, 78, 86–87, 89, 94
Diet Building. *See* National Diet Building
divorce, 6, 9–10
dogs, xxxiii-xxxv, 32, 34–35
Dörrie, Doris, 120–21
Duras, Marguerite, 55, 58–59, 63

earthquake, xxxii, xxxix, 5–6, 8, 16, 30, 102; Great Eastern Japan, xxv, xl, 17, 27, 36, 45, 49, 51–52, 67, 80, 82, 102, 126; Great Kantō, 17; Hokkaido, xv; Kobe-Awaji/Hanshin xlixn54, 45; Kumamoto, xv; Lisbon, 107
Edo period, 16, 30, 32, 43
evacuation/evacuation orders/centers, xviii, xxvi, xxix, xl-xli, 4–10, 12, 20, 24–30, 43n3052, 113, 119, 123n8, 125–27, 129, 132–33, 135–39
extinction, 21, 31, 117

Ferrier, Michaël, xxv
Fisher, Mark, 86–87
France, 10, 29, 33, 37, 56, 63, 65n27, 75–76, 79, 120
Freud, 87
fuhyō higai. *See* "damaging rumors" (*fuhyō higai*)
Fujino Kaori, xli
fukkyō (reconstruction) xviii, xxiii, xxivn7, xxvi

Fukuda Kōji, 9
Fukushima Daiichi Nuclear Power Plant, xxvi, xliii, xlvi, 9, 17, 24–25, 27–28, 30, 36, 40n2, 41nn15–20, 43n20, 45–48, 100, 102, 108–10, 113, 115, 119–22, 125–26, 134–36
Furuichi Noritoshi's *Zetsubō no kuni no fukō na wakamono tachi* (*The Happy Youth of a Desperate Country*), 129
Furukawa Hideo, xxxi–xxxii, xxxv–xxxvi
Futabamachi, 29, 134

gaichi, 17
Gebhardt, Lisette xxxvi, xlviiin38
Geiger counter, 24, 65n21, 110
Germany, 29–30, 41, 81, 116, 119
ghosts, xliii, xlv, 30, 37, 76–79, 82, 86–87, 89–93, 99, 101–3, 104n23, 112, 116, 121–22, 132, 138–39, 141n20
Godzilla, 54, 60, 112–16
Gojira. *See Godzilla*

Hara Tamiki, 50–51, 75
Hasegawa, Kazuhiko, 54
Hatakeyama Naoya, xliii
haunt/Haunting, 29, 77–79, 82, 86–89, 118, 122, 139
hauntology, 78–79, 86–90, 94, 100, 102–3, 107, 112, 118–19, 122, 139
Hawker, Lindsay Ann, xxviii
Hayashi Fumiko Literary Prize, 67
Hayashi Kyōko, xxxi, 30, 54, 62, 72
Hayashi Tatsuki, 25
Heller-Roazen, Daniel, 78
Hersey, John, 51, 55, 58
hibakusha, xxxi, 18, 47–51, 55, 58, 62, 65n21, 72–75; defined xlviin19
Higaki Tatsuya, 26
Hikikomori, 133, 138–39
Hino Keizō, xxi
Hirata Oriza, 123n8, 125, 129, 134–35
Hi-Red Center, 34–35
Hiroshima x, xii, xxiiin3, xxix, xlv, xlviin12, 26–27, 40n2, 40n14, 45–63, 73–79, 109, 113, 115, 120, 124
Hitler Youth, 18

Index

Hōjō Yūko, xvii
holocaust, xxxvi, 14, 27, 39, 40n14, 73, 81–82, 84nn29–30
Hotta Yoshie, 64

Ibuse Masuji, 73
Iizawa Kōtarō xlii, xlixn54
Imamura Shōhei, 50, 73
Inaba Mayumi, xli
Indonesia, 67, 138
Introjection, 87, 94, 102–3
Ishihara Shintarō xlviin18, 30
Ishimure Michiko, xxii
Ishinomaki, xxix, 93, 100
Ishiuchi Miyako, 62
Itō Seikō, xx-xxi, 85, 89–90, 93, 116, 118–19, 124n21
Iversen Margaret, 81–82
Iwata-Weickgennant, Kristina, 65n21

Japanese Colonies. *See gaichi*
Jelinek, Elfriede, 23–26
josen. *See* "decontamination" (*josen*)
Journalism, xviii, xxi. *See also* media

Kaikō Takeshi, xxi
Kakiya Miu's, 4–5
Kamaishi, 3, 120–22
Kamikaze, 41, 103, 124
Kanehara Hitomi, 8–9
Kan Naoto, 125–26
Kanō Mikiyo, 47, 54, 65n21
Kant, Immanuel, 111
Kariya Tetsu, 36
Karube Tadashi, xli
Katabuchi Sunao, 74
Katagiri Atsunobu, 111
Kawakami Hiromi, xliii-xliv
Kawamata Tadashi, 107
Kirino Natsuo, 113, 126
Kisennuma, xxii
Kitahara Hakushū, 18
Kizuna, xxvi, xlv, 6–7, 13
Kobayashi Erika, xxivn10, 23, 40n2, 108
Kobayashi Masahiro, 123n15, 128
Komori Haruka, xviii, xix

Kōno Fumiyo, 74
Korea/Koreans, xxi, 17, 49, 120, 124n18, 136–37
Kudō Rein, xxii
Kurabayashi Yasushi, 25
Kuroki Kazuo, 101
Kyō Machiko, 74

Lucky Dragon Incident, 56–57, 113

Mallarmé, 26
Manchuria, xxi, 17
Manzanar, 74
Media, ix, xviii, xx–xxi, xxv, xxxvi, xlviiin38, 3, 5, 42n18, 82, 46, 52, 55, 107, 109, 114–15, 120, 144
mediums, 93, 104n23
Medoruma Shun, 103
Melancholy/melancholia, 86–88, 94, 100, 111–12
meltdown. *See* Fukushima Daiichi Nuclear Power Plant
Minamata, xxii, 14, 27
Minato Chihiro, 109–12
Miyamoto Dōjin, 140n1
Miyauchi Yūsuke, 74
Miyazawa Kenji, xxxiii-xxxiv
Mourning, 80, 86–90, 92, 94, 100, 103, 129–30

Nagasaki, xxiii, xxix-xxxi, xlv, xlviin12, xlviin19, 27, 40n14, 45–47, 50–59, 62–63, 72, 74, 101–2, 113, 115
Nagashima Yū, xxvi
Nakagami Kenji, xxxi, xxxvi
Nakanishi Natsuyuki, 35
Nancy, Jean-Luc, 40n14, 58, 108
Nanjing Massacre, 64
Narita airport, 32, 135
National Diet Building, 32, 126
Natsume Sōseki, xxi
New Guinea, 68, 71
Ninagawa Yukio, xxxiii
Noda Hideki, 103
Noh Drama, 89–93, 99–100, 121, 132
Numata Shinsuke, 1

Okada Eiji, 55
Okada Toshiki, 85, 89–90, 131–34
Okinawa, 17, 42, 45–46, 74, 103
Olympics xv, xxivn10, 17, 35, 127
Onda Riku, 141n20
Ono Kazuko xix-xx, xxivn10
Ōoka Shōhei, 70–71, 103
Orr, James, 73
Ostriches, 60
Otsuka, Julie, 73
Ozeki Ruth, 40n13

Périot, Jean-Gabriel, 77, 79
Pompidou Centre, 107, 111
Precariat, 128, 130
Precarious/Precarity, 45, 62, 118–19, 123n15, 125, 128–29, 138

radioactivity (*hōshanō*), xvi, 27–30, 62, 116
Radium, 40n2, 108, 123n3
reconstruction. See *fukkyō* (reconstruction)
Resnais, Alain, 55, 75, 120, 124n19
Rikuzentakada, xviii, xix
Rilke, Rainer Maria, 60–61

Sakoku. See Edo period
Sawaragi Noi, 35, 45
Sea wall, xxiii
Seirai Yūichi, xxx–xxxi, xxxv–xxxvi, 71
Sekigawa Hideo, 48
Sekiguchi Ryōko, 33–39, 78, 88
Seo Natsumi, xviii-xix
sex, xxxiv-xxxv, 21
Shimada Masahiko, 19n6
Shinchō New Writer's Prize, 68
Shiriagari Kotobuki, xlii
Shoah. See Holocaust
Shōno Yoriko, 130
Sono Sion, 27, 52, 65n21
South Africa, 135, 137
Specter, 68, 78, 86, 89
sublime, 107–13

Sugimoto Hiroshi, xxxvii-xxxviii
suicide, 46, 57, 71, 90, 98, 117, 122, 138
Syria, 34, 38

Taiwan, 120
Takagi, Makoto, 90
Takagi Nobuko, 19
Takahashi Gen'ichirō, xliii, 43–44
Takahashi Hiroki, 67, 71
Takamatsu Jirō, 35
Takayama Haneko, 65
Taki Kōji, 26
Tawada Yōko, xvi, xxxix, xli, xliv, 9, 29–31, 42, 43n30, 53, 140
taxi drivers, 4, 93, 100
Tendō Arata, 100
Tokyo Electric Power Company (TEPCO), xxvi, 42nn18–20, 126
von Trier, Lars, 111
Trump, Donald J. xxiiin2, 8, 20n19
Tsukamoto Shinya, 103
Tsunami. See Earthquake, Great Eastern Japan
Tsushima Yūko, 15–18, 21n46
Tuna (contaminated), 56–57
twitter, xx, xxvii-xxx

Uchida Nobuteru, 27

victim (*hisaisha*), xxx, 25, 30
Vietnam, xxi
volcano, 8
vulnerability, 48, 60–62, 129, 135–36, 140

Wago Ryoichi, xxvii
Weibel Peter, 81
World War II. See Asia-Pacific War

Yamada Yōji, 101
Yamakawa Fuyuki, 45
Yoshimura Man'ichi, 12
Yozuri Jūroku, 67
Yu Miri, xvii

About the Author and Translators

AUTHOR

Saeko Kimura is professor in the Department of International and Cultural Studies at Tsuda College, Tokyo, Japan. She received her PhD from Tokyo University. She was trained as literary scholar of the Heian period—for example, *Homosexuality and Love Tales: Court Society and Authority* (Tokyo: Seidosha, 2008) and *Breasts for Whom?: Sexuality and Authority in Japanese Medieval Tales* (Tokyo: Shin'yôsha, 2009). The latter volume was awarded the Japanese Women's History Studies Prize in 2009. She is also the author of *A Theory of Postdisaster Literature* (Tokyo: Seidosha, 2013) and *After a Theory of Postdisaster Literature* (Tokyo: Seidosha, 2018) the volume translated here. She is also the author of many important articles on artistic production following the triple disasters of 2011.

TRANSLATORS

Rachel DiNitto is professor of Japanese literature in the Department of East Asian Languages and Literatures at the University of Oregon. Her current research focuses on post-2011 cultural production. In addition to her monograph *Fukushima Fiction: The Literary Landscape of Japan's Triple Disaster* (Hawaii UP, 2019), she has published on the films and manga of this disaster and postwar Japan. See her work in *Religions*, *The Asia-Pacific Journal*, and *Japan Forum*, and in the edited volumes *The Representation of Japanese Politics in Manga* (2020), *The Japanese Cinema Book* (2020), and *Negotiating Disaster: "Fukushima" and the Arts* (2017).

Doug Slaymaker is professor of Japanese at the University of Kentucky in the United States. His research focuses on literature and art of the twentieth century, with particular interest in the literature of post-3.11 Japan, and of animals and the environment. Other research projects examine Japanese writers and artists traveling to France. He is the translator of Kimura Yūsuke's *Sacred Cesium Ground* and *Isa's Deluge* and Furukawa Hideo's *Horses, Horses, in the End the Light Remains Pure* (Columbia University Press). He is currently working on a translation of Tawada Yoko's *Yōgisha no yakō ressha*.

www.ingramcontent.com/pod-product-compliance
Lightning Source LLC
Chambersburg PA
CBHW020120010526
44115CB00008B/901